# FAIRBANK REMEMBERED

[redacted]

# FAIRBANK REMEMBERED

*Compiled by*

Paul A. Cohen and Merle Goldman

Published by the John K. Fairbank Center for East Asian Research, Harvard University and distributed by the Harvard University Press, Cambridge (Massachusetts) and London 1992

The John K. Fairbank Center for East Asian Research at Harvard University encourages and sponsors research projects designed to further scholarly understanding of East Asia.

Library of Congress Catalog Card Number: 92-72445

ISBN# 0-674-29153-0

# *Preface*

John King Fairbank (1907-1991) was best known to the public as the dean of Chinese studies in the United States. Although the tributes, memoirs, and recollections assembled in this volume amply document this as well as other aspects of Fairbank's public career, their purpose—and justification—lies elsewhere.* The contributors, many of them Fairbank's students (and students of his students), but also including relatives, old friends, professional colleagues in the United States and abroad, and acquaintances from the various arenas of public life in which Fairbank was active, were asked to search their memories for details of personal interactions with Fairbank that they found particularly meaningful and/or revealing. The resulting pieces are alternately incisive, affectionate, personal, deeply affecting, and hilariously funny. Cumulatively, they form a book that is unusually intimate and honest, not only in what its authors have to say about John Fairbank, but also in what they have to say about themselves and the importance Fairbank had in their lives.

Since the contributors were given free rein to say what they wanted, certain themes—and incidents—crop up again and again. Also, since people's memories did not always tally, the same events are occasionally recounted in different, even contradictory ways, as are aspects of John Fairbank's personality and behavior (although here, of course, we are dealing not just with memory but also with

*Readers interested in learning more about Fairbank's academic career and public life are referred to John King Fairbank, *Chinabound: A Fifty-Year Memoir* (New York: Harper & Row, 1982) and Paul M. Evans, *John Fairbank and the American Understanding of Modern China* (New York: Basil Blackwell, 1988).

variant individual perceptions). In general we have confined ourselves as editors to correcting inaccuracies of an easily verifiable empirical nature (dates, book titles, place names, spellings of people's names, and so on), but have not tampered with divergent qualitative recollections.

In our editorial procedures, we have made a strenuous effort to preserve each writer's individual "voice." We have not sought to impose a single scheme of romanization on all of the contributions; we have, however, sought consistency (Wade-Giles or *pinyin*) within each piece. Where writers preferred the use of an acronym (such as OSS) to the full name of an organization or institution (Office of Strategic Services), we have honored that preference; a list of abbreviations is included to assist the reader. Since the way in which a given author chose to address the subject of this book—Professor Fairbank, JKF, Fairbank, John, or whatever—often was directly related to how that individual felt about Fairbank or what kind of a relationship they had, we have been meticulous in preserving the original form of address. The main interventions we have made, as editors, have been in two areas: prolixity and stylistic obscurity. In the case of all major changes, unless given carte blanche in advance to cut and edit at will, we have sought the individual author's approval.

Creating a coherent book out of 127 pieces that fit together only in the roughest and most approximate way has been no small challenge. We have tried, in our arrangement, to strike a balance between chronology and thematic content. But since many of the individual memoirs cover long time spans and embrace disparate themes, we have often had to be quite arbitrary in deciding what piece ought to be placed where. We think of this book as a mosaic of many interchangeable parts. We beg the reader's indulgence if some of our choices with respect to placement seem obscure or differ from ones that he or she would have made.

The idea for this collection of memoirs was broached by Roderick MacFarquhar, who also supplied continuous encouragement and every kind of practical assistance from the outset. Alison Groppe typed the manuscript and performed many of the other tasks on which the book's completion depended. Daniel McCarron designed and supervised production of the book. Wilma Fairbank checked the manuscript for factual accuracy. Eriberto Lozada made available his expert knowledge of computers. Brett Rubel provided administrative support. Anne Denna kept a tight rein on the financial aspects of the production process. Peter Amirault and Thomas Pixton handled all technical aspects of the process with patience and skill. Gwendolyn Stewart provided valuable assistance on the cover photograph. Katherine Keenum gave expert advice on matters of composition. Nancy Hearst scrutinized the final proofs with care. To all of these individuals, we are much indebted.

P.A.C.
M.G.

# *Chronology*

| | |
|---|---|
| 1907 | Born May 24 in Huron, South Dakota |
| 1911 | Family moves to Sioux Falls, South Dakota |
| 1923 | Enrolls at Phillips Exeter Academy, Exeter, New Hampshire |
| 1925 | Enrolls at University of Wisconsin |
| 1927 | Transfers to Harvard College |
| 1929-31 | At Balliol College, Oxford, as Rhodes Scholar |
| 1932 | Begins work on Oxford D. Phil. in China in February; weds Wilma Denio Cannon in Peking in early summer |
| 1933-34 | Lecturer at Tsinghua University, Peking |
| 1935 | Departs China on Christmas Day |
| 1936 | Begins teaching at Harvard in fall as instructor |
| 1941 | Starts working in Far Eastern section of Research and Analysis branch of Office of the Coordinator of Information (COI) in Washington, D. C. in August |
| 1942 | Sent by COI— in June 1942 renamed Office of Strategic Services (OSS) — to Chungking; arrives late summer |
| 1943 | Returns to Washington late in year; transferred from OSS to Far Eastern section of Office of War Information (OWI) |
| 1945 | Returns to China in September, working for United States Information Service (USIS) |
| 1946 | Resumes teaching at Harvard in fall |
| 1948 | Publication of first edition of *The United States and China* (Harvard University Press) |
| 1952 | Testifies on March 10-11 before McCarran Committee (Senate Internal Security Subcommittee) after being accused of being security risk |

1952-53 In Japan as Guggenheim Fellow

1953 Publication of *Trade and Diplomacy on the China Coast: The Opening of the Treaty Ports, 1842-54* (Harvard University Press)

1956 Assumes directorship of newly established Center for East Asian Studies (Harvard), renamed East Asian Research Center in 1961, then Fairbank Center for East Asian Research in 1977

1958 Elected president of Association for Asian Studies

1960 First trip to USSR, to attend International Congress of Orientalists

1960 Publication of *East Asia: The Great Tradition* (Houghton Mifflin), coauthored with Edwin O. Reischauer

1965 Publication of *East Asia: The Modern Transformation* (Houghton Mifflin), coauthored with Edwin O. Reischauer and Albert M. Craig

1966 Planning begins for *The Cambridge History of China*, a multivolume work under the general coeditorship of Fairbank and Denis Twitchett

1966 Testifies on China policy before Senate Foreign Relations Committee (March 10)

1967 Sixtieth birthday celebration in Cambridge; presented with festschrift, *Approaches to Modern Chinese History*, edited by Albert Feuerwerker, Rhoads Murphey, and Mary Wright (University of California Press)

1968 Elected president of American Historical Association

1972 Six-week visit to China with Wilma in summer

1973 Steps down from directorship of East Asian Research Center in March; assumes chairmanship of newly formed Harvard Council on East Asian Studies

1977 Last lecture as Harvard faculty member in May

1979 Suffers near-fatal heart attack on Thanksgiving Day

1982 Publication of *Chinabound: A Fifty-Year Memoir* (Harper & Row)

1991 Completes manuscript of *China: A New History* (Harvard University Press)

1991 Dies in Cambridge on September 14

# *Contents*

# *List of Abbreviations*

| | |
|---|---|
| AAS | Association for Asian Studies |
| ACLS | American Council of Learned Societies |
| AHA | American Historical Association |
| *AHR* | *American Historical Review* |
| CCAS | Committee of Concerned Asian Scholars |
| CCP | Chinese Communist Party |
| *CHOC* | *Cambridge History of China* |
| EALS | East Asian Legal Studies (Harvard Law School) |
| EARC | East Asian Research Center (Harvard University) |
| FAS | Faculty of Arts and Sciences (Harvard University) |
| *HJAS* | *Harvard Journal of Asiatic Studies* |
| IPR | Institute of Pacific Relations |
| *JAS* | *Journal of Asian Studies* |
| NDEA | National Defense Education Act |
| NSC | National Security Council |
| OSS | Office of Strategic Services |
| OWI | Office of War Information |
| SOAS | School of Oriental and African Studies (University of London) |
| SSRC | Social Science Research Council |
| USIS | United States Information Service |

# *Beginnings*

JOANNA DOWNS LEE
*San Antonio, Texas*

Growing up in Sioux Falls, South Dakota, my early memories of John are all tied up with memories of his mother, Lorena Fairbank, "Aunt Loey" to me. She was a charming gracious woman who had a great talent for attracting young people. Always with praise and appreciation she made us long to succeed in whatever talents we possessed and also made us feel nothing was impossible, that success would be ours! John, in *Chinabound*, wrote, "She found kindred spirits everywhere, especially among young people, and shared her interests generously throughout her life" (p. 7).

She was adored and protected by her handsome, down-to-earth husband. Mr. Fairbank, a successful lawyer, liked to fish and hunt, was an enthusiastic Shriner, and had a wonderful sense of humor. Though he might not have understood all the "arty" people coming to the house, he was always there, passing out cigars and drinks, and being polite and convivial.

The Fairbank house, "The Cedars," was situated on the outskirts of town. On either side of its long expanse of lawn there were cedar trees. This was a perfect place for drama! There were times when "Aunt Loey" would direct scenes from Shakespeare under the trees, no reading from the text, please—we had to memorize! The last time we acted scenes from Shakespeare, John was home. He was on his way to China and had brought his fiancée, Wilma Cannon, with him. We were all charmed with her, a perfect match for John, we said.

My first clear memory of John is when we were in our early teens. He and his cousin, Jack Roe, drove from New York to Sioux Falls in an old weatherbeaten red roadster. Jack was a year older than John and always thought of himself as a sophisticated man of experience. He looked on John and me as innocent babes. We had a merry time that summer. What we did I can't remember, except walking between the two of them; Jack, Joanna, John, we rather liked that sound. If I would mistakenly call John, Jack, or vice versa, I had to forfeit a kiss.

When John went to Exeter, I went to Dana Hall. On one of our school vacations, I met the Fairbanks in New York, and I remember having dinner with Jack and John in an elegant restaurant, then going on to a musical. Jack always did all the talking—John was usually very quiet and silent around Jack.

When John graduated from Exeter, the Fairbanks took me to his Senior Prom. John was a celebrity, had taken top honors and prizes in his class, and one prize was a trip to Europe! He was a tall, handsome boy, self-confident, already being and looking serious, and had that dry sense of humor which later became a trademark. And how he could dance!

We danced a lot during the summer vacations, usually at the Sioux Falls Country Club. We especially liked to waltz. Sometimes we would go to the Club when no one was there, and to a phonograph record would see how long we could turn without getting dizzy! During these summers, I would spend many hours at "The Cedars." I remember a time when John, his mother and I spent the night on cots under the cedars. We talked, we looked at the stars, and we listened to the sounds of night until the birds awakened us at dawn.

One summer—I think it was the summer he came home exhausted from his heavy work with the Canadian Railways—John would lie on the couch while his mother read to us, mostly poetry. She also taught us how to read, and how to use our voices properly. She loved Browning, and I will never forget her reading his "My Last Duchess."

Sometimes John was at my house and we would listen to records, mostly the current popular songs, or I would play the piano. He liked all kinds of music, but always preferred piano to any other instrument. John's idea of a romantic evening at that time was to sit outside in the dark, while he explained all the stars—their formations, names, etc.

It was all so long ago that the memories get vague. When John went to Oxford, we each followed different paths; his was a straight goal-oriented one, mine had many variations. I would hear about him when I visited his mother in Sioux Falls and in Georgetown. She would never mention any sadness at his years of absence. I know it must have been difficult to give him up to his world, but she had encouraged him every step of the way and gloried in it.

I have her book of Sara Teasdale's poems, and there is one she marked "September 1929."

I have no heart for any other joy,
 The drenched September day turns to depart,
And I have said good-bye to what I love;
 With my own will I vanquished my own heart.

On the long wind I hear the winter coming,
 The window panes are cold and blind with rain;
With my own will I turned the summer from me
 And summer will not come to me again.*

In fall of 1929, John left for Oxford.

DUDLEY W. ORR
*Concord, New Hampshire*

The friendship with John Fairbank, which dates from 1923 when we began two years in the same class at Exeter, influenced all the subsequent, happy sixty-eight years of my life. By precept and example, he opened my mind to learning. After Exeter, our paths diverged, but we frequently met. In 1930, for example, John came to Paris with a pack of Chinese vocabulary cards and a jug of cod liver oil. It was then I met Wilma for the first time. The cod liver oil was to make up for the lack of sunshine at Oxford in the winter.

Over the years, I sought his opinion about academic and political matters. We rejoiced in his scholarly and professional achievements

* This poem, entitled "An End," is reprinted from *The Collected Poems of Sara Teasdale* (New York: The Macmillan Co., 1937), pp. 261-262.

and his service to our country, but our meetings were mostly to feel the warmth of an old friendship. Only last fall it was a joy simply to share with him the sunshine as we looked westward from his porch in Franklin, New Hampshire, across the Pemigewasset Valley.

When I think of John Fairbank, I recall the words of Henry Adams about a friend of his: "He was always generous and kind, easy, patient and loyal."

## William S. Youngman
*Vero Beach, Florida*

John Fairbank was the best organized man I ever knew. He stayed that way from his arrival at Harvard College from the University of Wisconsin until he finished his last book hours before his death. His energy was incredible.

John planned his time carefully, including his recreation. I recall that as an undergraduate he located two canoes on a remote section of the Concord River for a spring day's outing for the two of us and two young ladies, one of whom was Wilma Cannon. Unfortunately we did not anticipate the swarm of mosquitoes that shortened our trip.

John went to great lengths to help his friends. For example, when we were taking Professor Gay's advanced course in the history of economics, I had failed to attend any lectures or do any reading because of extracurricular activity as football manager. The night before the final examination, I had attended a club dinner and was in poor shape to study. I visited John's room where he made me sit down, shone a bright lamp in my eyes to keep me awake, and read me his notes for about three hours. The next day I wrote all that I remembered that he told me on the examination. The paper was graded "A."

In 1930 when he was a Rhodes scholar at Oxford, I visited him there, where he put me on a regime of tennis, swimming, hot tubs, and good conversation. Shortly thereafter we stayed together in a room in London that had no bath, so we went daily a long distance by bus to the YMCA to take a shower. En route John studied Chinese with small cards with Chinese characters on one side and English on the other.

John as a friend took continuous interest in my welfare. From Peking in the mid-thirties, where Wilma and he had one or two young ladies boarding with them, he wrote me a note saying he had found just the girl for me, Elsie Perkins, one of their boarders. He enclosed a magazine picture of the young lady playing polo. Later in 1936 at one of the renowned Fairbank teas at 41 Winthrop Street, I met her for the first time. Soon thereafter we were married.

Through visits, conversations, and his books, John did much to educate his friends about China. He liked to emphasize the importance of Chinese sources of fact rather than foreign writings.

By chance in 1941 I became during World War II chief American adviser of T. V. Soong, who later became Chinese Foreign Minister and Prime Minister. While I sensed occasional differences of opinion with John, his views were always thoughtful, patient, and often persuasive.

I was happy to testify in John's favor in the 1950s when he came under fire in the McCarthy era, from which he emerged with flying colors.

When John wrote his autobiography *Chinabound*, he told me that a difficulty was having too much material since he wrote a letter almost every day to his mother who lived to be a hundred and five.

A superb teacher and leader has departed, one who set his mark on Chinese history, Harvard, and his friends. We shall always remember him with deep gratitude and affection.

## Anthony Lambert
*Foreign Office, London*

John Fairbank was a scholar who would have shed luster on any college or university he belonged to, and I am glad to claim him as a Balliol man, and to acknowledge a debt of gratitude to Cecil

Rhodes, whose institution of the scholarships that bear his name brought JKF to the College in my year.

I see a tall, well-built man, blond, dressed in the normal undergraduate style of the day, but unmistakably American. He strides purposefully across the quad, swinging his arms rhythmically. If addressed his face lights up with a shy half-smile. He spends long hours in his rooms, memorizing Chinese characters inscribed on cards, in the intervals of his reading. He is careful of his health, appears to support life on a diet of yoghurt and baked beans. Behind the rather elusive demeanor and the slightly freakish sense of humor, there lurks a warm and generous spirit and a priceless capacity for friendship. This is no ordinary undergraduate, but a man already mature, and dedicated to the pursuit of the highest aims that scholarship can offer. A man eminently worth cultivating; one in a million in fact. We become friends, play tennis with Harold Li and Kenneth Chang from Hong Kong, I am introduced to his remarkable and beloved mother when she pays a visit to Oxford —and who will always remember the friends her son has made. In the years that follow our paths diverge and we do not see each other often, but with our marriages a quartet has grown up, and there is no interruption of a correspondence that is to last for more than sixty years.

As these years unfolded the early promise was amply fulfilled. JKF's increasing eminence in scholarship, his monumental industry, his wisdom in politics, his courage in adversity and the depth and breadth of his vision placed him in a position of exceptional authority. So did his command of English. In his cultivation of a style suited to the message he had to convey he was as judicious as Gibbon—and as successful, for his is a prose that we read, mark, learn, and inwardly digest. Above all, what set him apart was his utter integrity. Here was a man, one felt, whom nothing could deflect from proclaiming the truth as he saw it in the light of his profound knowledge and judgment—and since he was one of the greatest scholars and wisest heads of his generation, he could not be set aside. He stood out from the generality of men like the Rock of Gibraltar. In my eyes he was one of the few, the very few, wholly admirable people I have met in the course of a long life.

Knight Biggerstaff
*Cornell University*

During the 1930s Peking was an exciting center for study and research by an energetic group of young Western scholars, including John Fairbank, who provided much of the leadership in the remarkable growth of Chinese studies in the United States during the 1940s and 1950s. There they studied the Chinese language, acquainted themselves with Chinese life, and pursued research on the special topics each had chosen. Prior to the 1930s there was very little scholarly writing or teaching about China in the United States. What there was was provided by a few scholarly ex-missionaries, for example Kenneth Scott Latourette and Arthur W. Hummel; by several specialists like George Blakeslee and Stanley K. Hornbeck, who did not know the Chinese language and so did not have access to Chinese documents; and by two or three Chinese like N. Wing Ma. Among the young Western scholars working in Peking during the early 1930s, besides John and Wilma Fairbank, were Woodbridge Bingham, Derk Bodde, Herrlee Creel, Owen Lattimore, Cyrus Peake, Laurence Sickman, Harold Shadick, George Taylor, and Martin Wilbur.

It was a stimulating time to be in Peking. Of great importance was the rapidly growing body of modern trained Chinese scholars such as Hu Shih, T. F. Tsiang, William Hung, and V. K. Ting, who were very helpful to serious foreign scholars. Air and railway lines and coastal and river steamers made it relatively easy to get around the country. A variety of financial resources had become available such as Harvard-Yenching, the Rockefeller Foundation, ACLS, SSRC, and some local teaching positions. These new conditions, together with the growth of American interest in China after World War I, stimulated the remarkable movement of scholars to Peking in the 1930s.

My first contact with the Fairbanks occurred during the spring of 1932 while I was a graduate student at Harvard. Wilma Cannon called on Camilla and me at the suggestion of a mutual friend saying that John, then in Peking on a Rhodes scholarship, wanted her to join him there but some friends wondered whether it would be safe for her to go. Since we had returned from Peking the previous summer after three safe and exciting years there, we reassured her and urged her to go, which she did. When we went back to Peking in June 1934 the Fairbanks were away in Shansi for the summer but they soon returned to their home at 10 Ta Yang Yi Pin Hutung, which was near where we were living on Tung Piao Pei Hutung. Thereafter we saw them and most of the other Western scholars often, much more often, in fact, than we saw them later in the United States. Here a number of lifelong friendships were made as we shared information about teachers, archives, interesting places to visit, and servants. We even met informally once a month at the Hotel du Nord to hear and discuss reports on our research. It was a wonderful time to be in Peking. We consulted helpful Chinese scholars, familiarized ourselves with reference works and documentary collections, practiced the colloquial Chinese that most of us had started in the very good North China Union Language School, visited imperial palaces, temples, bookstores, and markets, walked on the city wall, hiked in the Western Hills, and took occasional trips to other parts of China.

The Fairbanks were more active than most of the rest of us. They explored Peking thoroughly, visited the ancient Buddhist temples at Yun-kang and Lung-men, climbed T'ai-shan, examined the remnants of ancient buildings in Shansi province, and during the winter of 1934-35 collected material for John's Oxford D. Phil. dissertation at British Consulates and Chinese Customs Offices along the Southeast China coast. Although most of the Western scholars working in China at this time took some interest in Chinese political and social developments, John paid more attention than most. Wilma, a talented artist, though concentrating on Chinese painting and architecture, shared John's interest in broader cultural matters.

The Fairbanks left China at the end of 1935 and spent some time in England, where John completed his research on the Chinese Imperial Maritime Customs in the Public Record Office and passed his examination for the D. Phil. degree. Returning to Cambridge in January 1936, he was appointed to the faculty of the Harvard Department of History. From his positions there and later in the Harvard East Asian Research Center, which he helped to create, he became the most influential leader of Chinese studies in the United States, always helpful not only to Harvard students, but to anyone else who appealed to him for assistance.

Derk Bodde
*University of Pennsylvania*

About John's ideas and activities during the past forty odd years, others can say much more than I, because after 1945 our paths crossed only occasionally. Earlier, during the war years, I had seen him much more often, at first when we were both at OSS and later at OWI. However, my most vivid memories go back to the golden years in the 1930s when he and I formed part of that handful of young Americans who were all students together in old Peking. One incident from those years appears in a letter that I wrote to John in 1967 at the time of his sixtieth birthday:

April 24, 1967

Dear John,

Hearty congratulations on your achievement of a cycle of Cathay! I wonder if you remember, when you had reached less than half a cycle—I think it was around 1934—the luncheon given in Peking for a number of young American students by H. E. Nelson T. Johnson, then American Ambassador to China. The guests, besides ourselves, included, I think, Knight Biggerstaff, Herrlee Creel, George Kates, perhaps Larry Sickman, and probably others. The Depression was then at its height, and in most American universities China was still an almost unknown quantity. After the lunch was over, somebody asked the ambassador whether he thought many of us had a fair chance, on returning to the United States, to teach or otherwise make use of what we had been studying in China. His reply was jocular but at the same time serious. "Not a chance in the world, boys," he said. "Your best bet will be to become butter-oozing swamis, preferably in Los Angeles."

> The force of history, coupled with the work of many individuals, has fortunately prevented this dire prediction from becoming true. Among these individuals, I know of none who has done more than you—through teaching, writing, personal example, promotional activity, and encouragement to others—to make China a solid and respected field of study. Today, as a result, the field far transcends a narrow circle of specialists. Increasingly, it has come to be taken for granted by the world of scholarship at large, and even by the lay public, including an occasional politician! May China, which was and is the first love of many of us, continue to absorb your best energies during many decades of your second cycle!
>
> Ever yours,
>
> Derk

The validity of the words in the second paragraph is even more evident today than it was in 1967. John's handwritten reply is brief and typically Fairbankian:

> May 24, '67
>
> Dear Derk,
>
> I appreciate your letter of Apl. 24 very much indeed. We must arrange a reunion sometime for a reminiscence about our time in Peking. I have such a vivid recollection, for example, of the courtesy and military bearing of Col. Speshneff when we went riding one time. As time passes we represent an era and probably should try to record it—as you did in your Peking Diary—but for the 1930s.
>
> Our love to you and Galia.
>
> John

That reunion, alas, has never taken place. Col. Speshneff was a gifted Russian who, since coming to Peking with his family from eastern Siberia in 1925, had variously taught not only horseback riding but also French, German, Russian, English, Japanese and mathematics to numerous individuals and in several institutions.

His daughter Galia is the woman I married in Peking more than fifty years ago.

One of John's most admirable traits has been his lifelong readiness to do good things for other people. A recent example is the blurb he wrote for a book of mine which he read only in manuscript because its publication did not occur until a few weeks after his death. I treasure these several sentences not only for what they say but also because they probably belong among his very last printed utterances.

C. Martin Wilbur
*Columbia University*

Professor John K. Fairbank
The Elysian Fields

Dear John:

I have read that guiltless persons reside in the Elysian Fields where they follow the chosen pursuits of their former lives in a land of spring, sunlight, happiness and song. This you deserve. Surely you are writing another book on China, encouraging a group of students on their way to becoming teachers of Chinese history, while prodding some foundation executive to make a large grant to enhance the field.

We met in Peking nearly 60 years ago, both of us studying Chinese and soaking up the wonderful sights and sounds about us—street sellers with their haunting cries, plodding camels bringing the city its coal, shrieking pigs being lugged to slaughter, the bustling Great Eastern Market, and the glorious Forbidden City. There we became acquainted with a crop of future China scholars—Woody Bingham, Herrlee Creel, Owen Lattimore, Derk Bodde, Larry Sickman, George Kates, John DeFrancis, George Taylor, Cyrus Peake, and several junior Foreign Service Officers such as Edmund Clubb, John Paton Davies, and John Service. Carl Whiting Bishop of the Freer Gallery became the mentor for some of us, and there were honored Chinese faculty members of Shih-ta, Tsinghua, and Yenching, whom some of us got to know. You, I remember, had the privilege of studying documents of the Tsungli Yamen with Professor T. F. Tsiang. For relief from our daily toil with the language, we and our wives sometimes tripped to the Western Hills or the Great Wall, danced at the Peking Hotel, or occasionally had a beer with steak and eggs at the German Hotel, though I seem to remember that even then you did not imbibe.

One by one we returned to America to complete our doctorates or take on first teaching jobs, curatorships, or consular posts. Your start was in teaching at Harvard, where you created a course on modern Chinese history, later to become famous as "Rice Paddies." We pro-China types all were terribly concerned with Japanese aggression in China, which had started in Manchuria in 1931, and periodically expanded southward and westward till it became full-scale war. Inevitably the United States became involved, and Washington seemed to need our help.

You were called to the newly-created Office of Strategic Services, and then moved to the Office of War Information. This took you to Chungking, and you and Wilma, who became Cultural Officer in the Embassy, made many Chinese friends in government and in the Communist liaison office, headed by Chou En-lai. There you knew the American war correspondents and the Foreign Service Officers whom McCarthy attacked after the war, even as he, or other scoundrels, also attacked you.

After the war was over, we China scholars went back to our teaching jobs and created a remarkable boom in China studies in American universities and colleges. You largely steered this, at least in the modern sector. How? By the production, with Eddie Reischauer, of really modern textbooks on Eastern Asia; by producing such seminal early works as *China's Response to the West*, *A Documentary History of Chinese Communism*, and the Harvard *Papers on China*, which issued early examples of what your better students were to do at the doctoral level; and by your several editions of *The United States and China*, which explained to the American public what modern China was really like.

You, along with a few others among us, encouraged the Ford Foundation to pick up where the Rockefeller Foundation had left off and pour money into the development of Foreign Area Studies, especially the study of modern China. Your later advocacy of recognition of the PRC made you for a time persona non grata in Taiwan, but that didn't prevent you from promoting a most fruitful committee to develop American scholarly cooperation with scholars in Taiwan, many of them friends from your Peking and Chungking days.

We were both involved in the academic "China Boom," but you were the most effective among us in getting public and foundation attention. You astounded colleagues by writing book after book, while also supervising a stream of pathbreaking dissertations. Your students are devoted to your memory.

Now in the Elysian fields, you may be supervising from afar the production of your new book, after which there surely will be other projects to advance the study of China. May you enjoy it all.

Affectionately,

Martin Wilbur

RICHARD W. LEOPOLD
*Northwestern University*

I first met John on May 13, 1937, at a Harvard Faculty Club luncheon when the history tutors received their assignments for 1937-38. He was finishing his first year as a full-time member of the Department; I would begin mine in September. That autumn we saw each other at least three times a week at the fistball game in the Sargent gymnasium, described accurately but too modestly in *Chinabound*. John was among the best players. Then in May 1938 we participated in Theodore H. White's ludicrous examination for the degree of summa cum laude in History.

The examining board of James R. Ware, Assistant Professor of Far Eastern Languages, and Instructors Fairbank and Leopold was unusual. Two departmental examiners normally handled all summa orals, while John should have been excluded as the candidate's tutor. My presence resulted from a decision a month earlier to entrust me the next year with a lecture course and a graduate seminar in American diplomatic history, a field in which I had no previous training or interest. For that reason I was also one of three readers of White's honor thesis dealing with Japan's Twenty-One Demands on China. William L. Langer gave it a "magna plus, no bar to a summa minus," Albert E. Hindmarsh, Lecturer in Government, a "summa," and I a "magna," typically the lowest grade from the youngest and, perhaps, most ignorant reader. During the examination in the Adams House Upper Common Room John and I said very little, though for different reasons. That left the floor to Ware whose pedantic and inappropriate questions are described with restraint in *Chinabound* and ignored with reason in *In Search of History*. As I wrote John in 1982: "I recall being amazed and outraged by the questions that James Ware asked. Your customary impassive face betrayed your own anguish."

The next few years are rich in memories. There were teas in the yellow cottage at 41 Winthrop Street and debates over the publications of American Defense: Harvard Group. At weekly departmental luncheons John, still the beginner but always the missionary, tactfully promoted the cause of East Asian studies. Fistball continued with another beginner, Eddie Reischauer. Summers saw tennis on the courts by Andover Hall; John's serve had a high bounce. In December 1938, while I was struggling to keep one lecture ahead of my first History 64 class, John gave me a forty-eight-hour breathing space with a dazzling digest of Sino-American relations to 1898, a subject about which I knew next to nothing. Most typical of his scholarly dedication was a scene I recalled in a letter in 1979 which read: "It will be thirty-nine years ago this coming December 31 that we traveled back to Boston by train from New York, with you on one side of the aisle studying your vocabulary cards and with Wilma, on the other side, telling me that I must get married at once. I fear there was more success on one side of the aisle than on the other."

These almost daily contacts ended when John, with Bill Langer and Don McKay, joined the predecessor of the OSS in August 1941. Although I followed him to Washington fifteen months later, we saw little of each other, for he was frequently overseas. Even when we both returned to Cambridge in 1946, the pressure of large classes, the advent of new area studies, and the demise of fistball ended the old intimacy. What I remember best from that period was the rapidity with which John produced by dictation his seminal *United States and China*, published in 1948, the year in which I moved to Northwestern. By then he was a beginner no longer, having become an Associate Professor in 1943 and a Professor in 1948.

My subsequent relations with John were not unique. I watched him demolish William Yandell Elliott in a debate before the Associated Harvard Clubs in Chicago in May 1951 right after Truman had removed MacArthur. I aided in forming his Committee on American-East Asian Relations in 1967. I saw him struggle with Howard Zinn for the microphone at a tumultuous business session of the American Historical Association in 1969. We shared the platform as members of a visiting committee at Exeter in 1973, where he was still the missionary. And I played a part in Northwestern's awarding him an honorary degree in 1978. But these episodes are worth mentioning only because they and others elicited letters that revealed John's wisdom, industry, loyalty, self-deprecating manner, and puckish sense of humor.

Responding to my inquiry about enlisting in the intelligence service of the navy, he wrote on April 20, 1942: "I have discovered by devious means that if you have a rating of 20/20 in one eye and 20/30 in the other eye correctable by glasses, you can do intelligence work, if you are intelligent." Commenting on July 13, 1967 on the cultural differences between Americans and Chinese, he admitted: "It is a devil of a problem to see how to deal with it in research form rather than by merely giving sermons and writing essays." Thanking me on January 27, 1972 for some very critical comments on the manuscript of a young scholar, he declared that I had demonstrated "how the good may be made the best" and that I had done "a great service for him, for scholarship, for me, for Harvard, and for humankind, as we now call it." In acknowledging on August 2, 1977 a reminiscent letter I wrote upon his retirement, he called such epistles "one of the boons of extreme age." In accepting Northwestern's offer of an honorary degree, he asked on March 2, 1978 whether I could arrange a talk at some ladies' club "for a paltry $400 or $500," saying that "I try to make it a rule never to go anywhere without making a speech." As an afterthought he added: "I might remark that the major motive in this enterprise would be to get together with you and historicize old times. The value of extreme age lies in its perspectives and we must obviously get in practice." Finally, after reading my appraisal of *Chinabound* in the Exeter alumni magazine, he wrote on August 18, 1982: "Wilma and I are both much gratified by your very deft review (we felt honored by it) and I am also indebted for your catching howlers or errors that had escaped the author, his professional publishers, and all other reviewers. Obviously a good historian has skills that should be more widespread if we are to keep our society on the rails as it rushes toward its unknown and fortunately unknowable future. While I grant that all dogs must have their day, I still feel that our leaders of the moment are being overly canine. Let us try to get together." We did only once more.

*Ave atque vale*. Hail and farewell.

# *In Friendship*

VIOLA R. ISAACS
*Lexington, Massachusetts*

As I sat in the chapel listening to the moving tributes to John Fairbank, in my mind I was far away and long ago.

The time was 1934-35. The place was Ta Yang Yi Pin Hutung, just inside the East Wall of old Peking. John and Wilma lived in Number Ten and Harold and I were in Number One, modest old buildings and courtyards that had once been attached to an official's palace, possibly the servants' quarters now sectioned off and modernized with electricity and running water for the convenience of foreigners. Two young couples in our early twenties, newly married, we shared much of the magic that was Peking.

No matter what we did or where we went, John always carried with him his box full of Chinese character cards, and no matter what was going on, no matter what the conversation, it seemed that John was always shuffling the cards and studying them intently. This is the picture of John that I have always carried in my mind—tall, blond, handsome, intense, attached to his box.

Those years in Peking profoundly influenced the four of us. Wilma painted the world around her. I taught English in a middle school for boys and studied *ou-shou*, Chinese theater dancing. Harold worked intently on the book that became *The Tragedy of the Chinese Revolution*. John perfected his Chinese and worked on his thesis.

John and Harold had a running friendly argument. Harold, deeply and passionately involved in the politics of the time, particularly the Kuomintang terror, could not understand how John could immerse himself in the past. John strongly argued for the historical approach. As it worked out, they were both right. John later became much involved in the current scene and Harold wrote history. They remained respectful friends. We will miss them both.

John Paton Davies
*Asheville, North Carolina*

John King Fairbank was, among other things, a man of various lives. Although I never studied or worked with him, from intermittent, brief contacts in a variety of places over almost sixty years I came to think of him as a close friend.

When first I encountered John, in the mellow Peking of the mid-1930s, he was a graduate student contemplating the creation and development of the Chinese Imperial Maritime Customs. And I was a callow attaché for Chinese language studies at the American Legation.

With the essential Wilma, his bright, buoyant wife, John lived in a spare small house enlivened by her paintings of the North China countryside. In this felicitous setting he pursued with diligence and poise his life as a novitiate Sinologue.

Next, at Chungking early in World War II, John's life was that of an agent of Wild Bill Donovan's OSS, predecessor of the CIA. His role here did not commit him to cloaks, daggers and bloodletting. Rather, his mission was impeccable: to organize the collection of Chinese publications for those in Washington presumably seeking intelligence therefrom. My memory of John in Chungking (a singularly inelegant city) was of his slithering with characteristic aplomb over slimy streets in his bookish quest.

Appropriately, John soon moved to Washington, to a life as an official of the Office of War Information. This introduced him to bureaucratic wheeling and dealing on a large scale, necessary to the functioning of government—and big institutions from industrial to academic. John had an aptitude for this mode of getting things done. It served him well in later worthy causes.

Then it was back to academe and to the little yellow house on Winthrop Street. In this life as sage and promoter of Chinese studies he reached the peak of his profession. His influence was nationwide—and international. Through it all he kept his lively dry humor.

It was in the late 1960s that I saw John living the life of filial son. He regularly came from Cambridge to Washington to visit his mother who lived self-sufficiently alone in Georgetown. She was in her nineties.

Mrs. Fairbank confessed to my wife that she was frustrated in her desire to enjoy contemporary Russian poetry in the original because she did not then feel quite up to learning Russian. On more familiar ground, Mrs. Fairbank conducted Twelfth Night rites for my youngest daughters to whom she issued invitations inscribed by her in mirror writing.

As she approached one hundred John finally persuaded her to engage someone to lend a hand around the house. Mrs. Fairbank chose a lass in her eighties whom she dressed in Mary Petty attire.

It should be small wonder whence came John King Fairbank's inquiring mind, independent ways and whimsy.

ARTHUR SCHLESINGER, JR.
*City University of New York*

My first encounter with John Fairbank was in Peking in 1933. My father, on sabbatical leave from Harvard and scheduled to give the Commonwealth lectures at London University, decided to go to England by the long route, taking his whole family around the world. We reached Peking in time for my 16th birthday. John was still working for his Oxford D. Phil., but my father probably knew him because of his Harvard *summa* in 1929; at any rate, John and Wilma came to the Peking Hotel one day and told us, in an exceedingly well-informed and thoroughly engaging way, about the state of things in China.

We were all much impressed by John's scholarship, so easily worn, by his acute political concerns and by his wry humor. When he returned to Cambridge in 1936, I was then in my junior year at Harvard. Though I never took any of his courses, I became a frequent caller at 41 Winthrop Street and something of a regular at the Thursday afternoon teas. Another regular, my classmate Theodore H. White, was John's devoted student. When I set off for Cambridge University on a Henry fellowship in September 1938, John gave me wise counsel about English universities and their peculiar folkways. He also repeated to me Wellington's advice to the new recruit—advice that it might not be seemly to reproduce here.

My diligent attendance at 41 Winthrop Street, it must be confessed, was in pursuit less of lore about China than of Wilma's younger sister Marian, whom I eventually married in 1940. The status John and I shared as sons-in-law of the great physiologist Walter B. Cannon solidified a lifelong friendship. During the war, each of us followed his historical bent, John going west to the eastern front while I went east to the western front. When I was demobilized at the end of 1945, John's mother kindly turned her charming house in Georgetown over to Marian and me for a fortnight's decompression.

I joined the Harvard History Department in 1946, and thereafter John and I found ourselves allies on a multitude of issues and appointments. The 1950s brought Joe McCarthy and vicious attacks on old China hands, scholars as well as diplomats, who had made honest (and prescient) reports about Kuomintang corruption and the probabilities of Communist success. Even John Kennedy, then a young congressman, sideswiped John on one occasion; years later he separately told Teddy White and me how much he regretted what he had said. John's rueful composure in face of bitterly unfair attacks was impressive, especially when they came in one or two cases from scholars he had befriended, like Karl Wittfogel. Perhaps long acquaintance with the cycles of Cathay reassured him that this too would pass.

Instead of returning to Harvard after the Kennedy years, I moved on to the City University of New York. Forty years in Cambridge,

Massachusetts, were enough; and I concluded, like Thoreau after Walden, that I had more lives to live and could spare no more time for that one. Happily John and Wilma came often to the wicked city. In 1972 I moved to a house on East 64th Street across the way from Teddy White. The Fairbanks stayed sometimes with the Whites, sometimes with us, and always brought great cheer and delight.

Also John once saved our house from burning down. The stove caught fire while my wife was cooking breakfast; water flung by me only heightened the flames. John meanwhile sat composedly by, carefully reading instructions in small print on a fire extinguisher; then, having mastered the theory, he arose, worked the complicated spray and put out the fire in thirty seconds.

I always thought that John would live nearly as long as his mother did. That would have given him—and us—another quarter century or so. He had a good long run nevertheless, and he died, as he would have wished (as we all wish), after completing one more book. But what was particularly impressive about John was that he not only produced that series of elegant and powerful books but that he gave so generously of time and energy to several generations of students and thereby created a new field of historical inquiry.

I lack the standing to appraise his contributions to the historiography of China; but I can point out that he marvelously succeeded in writing witty history—all too uncommon in our distinguished but too often ponderous profession. When I think of John, I think not only of his generous spirit, his erudite scholarship, his political and moral courage, but of what great fun it always was to be in his company.

MILTON KATZ
*Harvard University*

Aristotle in his *Poetics* belittled the historian in comparison with the poet:

"Poetry, therefore, is a more philosophical and a higher thing than history: for poetry tends to express the universal, history the particular. By the universal I mean how a person of a certain type will on occasion speak or act, according to the law of probability or necessity. . ." (trans. Butcher).

Lion Feuchtwanger translated the same passage with greater freedom in an epigraph on the flyleaf of his novel, *Proud Destiny*:

"The artistic representation of history is a more scientific and serious pursuit than the exact writing of history. For the art of letters goes to the heart of things, whereas the factual report merely collates details."

John Fairbank as a historian confounded Aristotle. Let there be no mistake. I do not pretend to intimate familiarity with John's writings. But from time to time he did bring his learning within the reach of lay readers. I have in mind such books as *The United States and China* (1948), *East Asia: The Great Tradition* (with E.O. Reischauer) (1960), *East Asia: The Modern Transformation* (1965), and most recently, *The Great Chinese Revolution: 1800-1985* (1986). In these writings, John went "to the heart of things" and expressed "the universal" in the Chinese historical experience.

I write as a longtime personal friend of John and Wilma. Our careers, largely disparate, first intersected early in World War II when John and I found ourselves within the then newly established Office of Strategic Services. After the war, our continued association was fostered when we both returned to Harvard University, John to the Faculty of Arts and Sciences and I to the Law School.

When John suffered a heart attack on Thanksgiving Day, 1979, he notified his friends in a communication that was quintessentially John in style and spirit. In an effort to reply in a manner that might match his own and help to sustain his mood, I sent him a copy of a letter written by President Lyndon Johnson to Justice Felix Frankfurter on December 6, 1958, shortly after Justice Frankfurter had suffered a coronary thrombosis. The President wrote in part:

"I have been sitting down here on my ranch watching the Pedernales River flowing past my door, and cleaning my guns for the quail and deer hunting season. I have been thinking about you lying in that hospital and staring at the ceiling and remembering that I did quite a lot of it more than three years ago."

The President then went on to offer the Justice three bits of advice:

"The third, and only really important bit of advice is something you already know: the only important thing is work, and good work."

"So the important thing is to keep yourself in shape at the moment so you can get back to that work. . . ."

Like the President and the Justice, John Fairbank did get back to his work, and good work, for eleven productive years which gave us, among other books, *Chinabound* (1982), *Entering China's Service* (1987), and a series of contributions to the *Cambridge History of China*, of which he served as editor.

In February 1987, I wrote John a note expressing my appreciation for a copy of *The Great Chinese Revolution: 1800-1985* which he had sent me. His reply was vintage Fairbank:

"You do me too much honor. But I like it."

## Nancy B. Hector
*Coconut Grove, Florida*

I write today in part for Theodore White because he is not here to do it, and partly for myself. I met John and Wilma when Teddy and I were married in 1947 and, from that time on, they were two cherished friends.

For Teddy they were much more. He has written about it and I vowed not to look at his texts while writing this. So my memory of what they meant to him was, first, a primary source of learning. Later John and Wilma would become mentors to a young man, poor of means, but not of intellect nor energy, who fought his way into the world of letters where he wanted to be and to which he ultimately did belong.

At that time in the 1930s as a scholarship student, Teddy had to make straight A's to maintain the scholarship and to graduate. There were two obstacles to that: a professor who taught graduate students into whose class Teddy had been admitted as the only undergraduate; and he couldn't swim (then a requirement for graduating). When all was at the finish line, the professor of Chinese could not deny him his A; and the swimming instructor held out a pole and enticed him to the end of the pool. Recalling this, I am reminded of words from another student whom his daughter Holly quoted at the memorial service for John: "I had the feeling, wherever I was, whatever I was doing, that he was interested and gave his support." I believe John was that extra support that pushed Teddy then and stayed with him always.

To me, the astonishing sequel of all this was that John and Teddy moved so easily from the teacher/student relationship into full partnership and friendship. John was always a bellwether for Teddy's thinking; and the friendship dwelt in a special place.

My memories are many—ranging from early celebrations, trips taken together, families shared, and on down to the last time I ever spoke quietly to John, upstairs in his sitting room. He sat with a throw over his knees, rocking his chair. I don't remember exactly what we discussed, but I remember it was a time of trouble in my life, and that I left with a feeling of serenity and belief, somehow, in my own worth.

Just before he died, I wrote to a young scholar who asked about interviewing him: "He is one of the most remarkable men I have ever known, not just for his erudition, but for his quiet search for truth and a way of talking straight with nuances that few human beings manage."

To that fact I add his special smile. Some people thought it enigmatic, but I always thought it mirrored accurately a razor-sharp mind, an antic sense of humor and a heart at peace with itself and the world.

## Yen-Tsai Feng
*Chestnut Hill, Massachusetts*

Not being a Sinologist, I could claim neither the honor of being his colleague nor the privilege of being his student. I met John and Wilma in 1955, through my good friend Sally who was then John's assistant. Wilma's incomparable hospitality soon made me practically a member of the family, and in addition to, or perhaps instead of, their legendary Thursday afternoon teas, there were the impromptu suppers in Cambridge and the quiet weekends in Franklin, when Wilma and I would indulge in desultory reminiscences of people and places we both knew, perhaps even a little delicious academic gossip, while John worked in the studio on his latest book or article. Being forewarned by his awe-stricken students that the master frowned upon any wasting of time on nonessential matters, I would never think of engaging in small talk with John King Fairbank! Occasionally, not too often, I might venture to argue with John on some matters Chinese, and when I sensed that my arguments were losing ground, which was often, I would always resort to my "trump card" and declare that being a Sinologist did not make him a Chinese and that being Chinese enabled me to feel in my bones how it really was, or ought to be. Thereupon John smiled, inscrutably of course. And I never confessed to him that my ignorance of Sinology was such that before I met him I thought Fei Cheng-ch'ing* was Chinese.

As all who knew John quickly learned, he liked to call attention to his South Dakota roots. I think indeed he bragged more than a little about his pioneer ancestry. He was so fond and proud of the "roughing it" state of their Franklin cottage which until the later years was without running water and practically no heat. I think John relished the challenge, and his enthusiasm for it was indeed quite contagious, so much that I, a cowardly city person, would never want to miss the opportunity whenever offered. Summer in Franklin was always a great delight: the New Hampshire hills at sunset were serenity itself and the canoe ride on the sparkling water was pure joy.

* Fei Cheng-ch'ing was Fairbank's Chinese name.

But winter was very special. I particularly recall one weekend in January when I joined Wilma and John for an overnight in the cottage. With the courtly solicitousness of the lord of the manor and the no-nonsense know-how of the frontiersman, John taught and helped me to put newspapers under and above the mattress to ward off the cold. The temperature dropped to below zero that night, but the *Boston Globe* and the *New York Times* did their work. I was duly impressed by his practical knowledge, and grateful. He was smugly pleased and proud of his nonacademic achievement.

John seldom volunteered comments on people, even and perhaps especially those who were close and dear to him. But one day shortly after Wilma had her article on Chinese bronze published, John stopped by my office in Widener and announced with great pride that finally Wilma had had time to work on *her* research. And he added, somewhat wistfully, that for so long she had spent all her time helping him.

It is not quite accurate to say that John was incapable of small talk. I used to be enormously intrigued when he would pick up the telephone after supper and chat quietly and happily with the person on the other end about matters of no great moment. Consumed with curiosity, I nevertheless knew it would be bad manners to inquire with whom he was talking so regularly, and in so un-Fairbank a way. One day by chance I learned that it was his mother, Lorena King Fairbank, who lived in Washington, D.C. I learned also that it was John's unbroken habit to call his mother every evening, just to have a chat.

I soon met Mrs. Fairbank, and saw her on many occasions in Cambridge and in Franklin, where she used to spend the month of August every year. To be impressed by her was only to be expected: gentle and firm, gracious and warm, she was truly an exemplary lady, as much at home in her Georgetown town house as I could well imagine she had been in Sioux Falls, South Dakota many, many decades earlier. One spring day, when I was in Washington, I stopped by her house to say hello. It was a fascinating house, full of memorabilia of a century-rich life. I noted a handsome bust on the mantelpiece—a wavy-haired young man who looked vaguely familiar. She caught my glance and said: "That was John when he had his hair! He hasn't changed much otherwise." And she patted the head and smiled. Suddenly she looked familiar to me—she reminded me of my own grandmother when she had smiled at the sight of her favorite son. And it dawned upon me that perhaps John King Fairbank was indeed Chinese, a good Chinese son. John did not preach filial piety, he lived it. I should have told him that.

## Haru M. Reischauer
*La Jolla, California*

It was with great trepidation that I arrived in Cambridge from Tokyo in the summer of 1956, as the bride whom Ed Reischauer (John called him Eddie) acquired on his sabbatical leave following the death of his wife Adrienne. Not only was I to start a new life in America with Ed and his three young children, but even more formidable, I was to enter an unfamiliar and awesome world of erudite academics at Harvard. They were hardly the familiar foreign and Japanese press correspondents with whom I had been working since the beginning of the Occupation of Japan.

I was introduced to Harvard when Ed took me through the friendly doors of 41 Winthrop Street, the home of John and Wilma. It took me only moments to realize the close bonds Ed had with them, for they welcomed me as already a member of the family. As time passed I appreciated the fact that John and Ed were not only the closest of colleagues but also lifelong best friends. Wilma and I were the beneficiaries of this warm relationship. Thus Harvard has always meant the Fairbanks to me.

Since John and Ed always seemed to talk only business whenever the four of us got together, it was at social functions when they were required to participate with others that I really got to know John as a person. During the early years before East Asian studies became as large as it is today, the faculty and staff were fewer in number and those in the Japanese, Chinese, and Korean field were a close, clubby group. We had many social functions together and invariably at these John was the organizer and leader. It was at these relaxed times I began to know John best, not as the tall, awesome professor he was to his students, but as a smiling, cheerful person, always with a twinkle in his eyes who loved making jokes with a straight face.

I remember well when John was at his best, showing his talents as the prime organizer and entertainer at the celebration of Ed's sixtieth birthday in 1970. As the cake was brought in, there was a lusty singing of "Happy Birthday" by the assembled group. The song then was repeated in three-part harmony by a choir composed of Iris Pian, Teruko Craig, Bunny Hightower, Aki Hibbett, Namhi Wagner, Glen Baxter and Hack Bishop in English, Japanese, Chinese and Korean.

A review of the various incarnations of Ed's life was then enacted. John wore a Tokyo University undergraduate cap and spoke of Ed's days as a student. This was followed by the singing of many verses about Ed's life. The solo part was sung by John who had composed all the lyrics and the chorus was sung by the choir to the tune of the Battle Hymn of the Republic.

Shortly after Ed passed on last September [1990] I had a long visit with John at his home at 41 Winthrop Street. I treasure the time I had with him for he comforted me more than I can ever say. And as Ed's best friend, he gave me the encouragement I needed to stand on my own and carry on. This meeting with John was my last with him. Just one year and three days after Ed's memorial service at the Memorial Chapel, I was sitting with Wilma and her family at John's. John was a real friend to me, and his memory will always be accompanied with gratitude to him for enriching my life at Harvard.

## Liang Congjie
*Beijing, China*

Sitting in the familiar house at the corner of Winthrop Street in Cambridge, in his usual quiet voice he gave me a clear and methodical account of the basic ideas in his new book on Chinese history. It was as if he were doing a summation of a lifetime's study of China. Although he looked weak, his thought was as clear as ever.

Before parting, I took some pictures together with him and Wilma and said: "I hope I can come to see you again next year." Smiling, he said "Good-bye." This was on July 4th [1991]. In early September I returned to China. Only ten days later Emily [MacFarquhar] called long distance and, sobbing, said: "He's gone. A few hours ago." For a long time I held the phone, unable to speak. I don't know what I finally said.

I must have called them Fei Bobo and Fei Yi (Uncle Fei and Aunt Fei) from the time I learned to speak. That was in the 1930s. When I was a child, my sister and I used that form of address only for our parents' closest friends. John and Wilma were the first Americans I had ever seen. Throughout my childhood, they represented America and Americans in my mind. In the collective memory of my family, they were so familiar and close that I never felt any difference between them and my other—Chinese—uncles and aunts.

John and Wilma had many close friends in China. But my parents were the closest. In those years, their common love of Chinese culture and the concern they shared for China's fate created a bond of intimacy between them and my parents that transcended any national or ideological barriers. After John and Wilma left China in the mid-thirties, my parents corresponded with them often, pouring out the joys and sorrows of their lives, as good friends are wont to do. During the war, they returned to China, and both came to see us in the remote countryside in the Southwest where at the time our family and my father's research institute were both domiciled in an old rundown farmhouse. I can still remember, when John visited us, he had to stay in my father's "office" on a rickety canvas army cot, which was too short for him to sleep on and had to be supplemented at one end by two stools for his feet. As it was very cold and we had no heating, he had to cover himself with a lot of blankets at night. In those days no one felt embarrassed at having to let a "foreign guest" like him see the difficult circumstances under which we lived.

After 1949 all contact between my parents and the Fairbanks was cut off. My mother died in the 1950s, my father in the early 1970s; neither was able to communicate with them again. I believe that my parents all along cherished deep affection for John and

Wilma in those years, although they couldn't show it openly. This was, I have no doubt, very painful for them. Therefore, when John and Wilma again visited Beijing in 1979 and I had a chance to see them, paying no heed to the potential "risks," I burst into the hotel they were staying at and embraced them tightly. The truth is, this was more for my parents' sake than for my own. I knew they had longed for this day for years. At the time I was already almost fifty myself, a little older than the age of my parents when they last saw John and Wilma. In 1972, during their first return visit to China (post-1949)—I was still laboring in the countryside at the time and had no chance to see them—John had said that for Wilma and him my parents, Liang Sicheng and Lin Huiyin, represented China, and that coming back and being unable to see these dear old friends was like losing half of China! I knew that in their eyes I was still a child and could never take the place my parents held in their hearts. There was no consolation for the sorrow they felt over the loss of these lifelong friends.

My dear Fei Bobo: You have left us. By all rights the persons in China who ought properly to mourn you are your dear old friends. But, once again, it is I who am called upon to pay you this last tribute. This makes me feel all the sadder. Nevertheless, I firmly believe that in this quarter of the earth with which your whole life has been so indissolubly linked you will always be remembered.

May you rest in peace.

Jonathan A. Wright
*Florence, Massachusetts*

The moment we arrived in Franklin, John bounded out of the house and raised the tailgate of the old green Rambler, revealing a tightly packed array of large glass water jugs. In a tone usually reserved for visiting dignitaries or for announcing massive archeological discoveries, and with typical sparsity of words, Fairbank presented his "technology." We shortly set out for the local spring, repeating, Franklin style, a scene from all over the world.

Fairbank's passionate delight in this simple practical solution was typical of him. He reassured the assembled company that the bottles rattling dangerously in the back were, in fact, close enough together that there was no danger of breakage; this was announced as though it reflected on the nature of human communities in which a judicious combination of noise, intimacy, and water assured survival.

Filling these jugs at the spring, still clear but now far heavier, somehow also reflects on the life of an extraordinary mentor, who believed in the essential value of colleagueship. Students, fellow scholars, friends, statesmen, children, and, in my case, godsons, were all vessels at this spring. It runs today, always available to the needy or the curious.

John reported on his grandmother's recollection of the invention of the friction match, and was also fully alive in the age of fiber optics; this history of technology was his intimate experience, and carried real fascination for him.

Water in Franklin was the subject of many technologies, as it is on most rocky mountaintops; only much later did the artesian well supplant the kitchen hand pump and the in-house outhouse. Rebuilding the leathers on the hand pump one spring, John worked with a watchmaker's precision and a lumberjack's energy, fairing and greasing the gaskets, assembling the anonymous parts from a rusty tray. This pump had to be primed with water from the glass bottles, in a carefully orchestrated rhythm of splashes, spits, gurgles and gushes.

Fairbank technology also included items of sharpness and great precision, ranging from the axe to the battery-powered electric shaver; he played the role of pioneer with both. Any who saw him wield the axe, or split with sledge upon wedge knew the power of this technology. Planning his cutting from a chair on the deck, he felled the interlopers in his long view with a perfunctory whip of his index finger, as if the trees were only ordinary bureaucrats or minor State Department officials. He then completed his field work with perseverance, measured tactical efforts, brute force and practice. It is not surprising that they burned the wood or cleared land; there was just a sense that the "effort" was simultaneously very modest and very grand. In the moan of a rising autumn wind we heard the gongs of distant temples. Here, in Franklin, with the buzz of the black flies and the hum of the electric shaver, the mundane and the metaphysical were unusual partners.

Fairbank's long fascination with the battery was not limited to shaving; his lifetime of flashlight purchases could, I suspect, detail 60 years of technology for a Smithsonian exhibition. He would reach for what appeared to be a pen in his suit jacket and quickly flash a small focused beam, accompanied by the shortest and most efficient one-syllable laugh. I never asked him his view on the advent of the rechargeable battery, but I suspect he was quite excited. Batteries carry power and illumination, characterizing preparedness, safety, and investigation. These were Fairbank hallmarks.

We can remember him for the enthusiasm and humor with which he engaged the world of simple and complex technology. We should also remember the energy and urgency he expressed for progress in human activities, which technology should serve. A few years back I asked him if he had plans to go to China again. He answered: "I don't think so. If I go, I have to go to dinners, and I don't go to dinners. They take a lot of time. We don't have much time." Those sky clear eyes, moistened, told of an urgent personal mission. But he spoke of "we," as our scout at the outer reaches of life, warning us all of the vast promises and vast perils of our lives here. He had moved through scholarship and institution-building, on to the edge of a new dimension of knowledge: scholarly, earthly, and synthetic. He had extracted this peace from the clamor and bureaucracy of life; well-primed, the hand, the pump and the well know what to do, and now, how to continue.

•

Sol M. Linowitz
*Washington, D. C.*

I first came to know John Fairbank when he became a member of the International Advisory Board of Pan Am World Airways. I was Chairman of the Board and for a period of several years had an opportunity to know John as a friend and colleague. He and Wilma and my wife and I traveled together to meetings of the International Advisory Board—including one memorable one in China several years ago.

As you might suspect, traveling with John King Fairbank in China was like touring the Vatican with the Pope. In official and unofficial circles, people on every side wanted to meet Professor Fairbank, yet he was often hard to find. Very simply, he wandered off on his own and talked to the people in the street, had a real interest in what was going on in human terms. As we learned on this and other trips with him, John was a listener as well as an articulate expounder. His sense of wit was delightful, and my wife and I always enjoyed spending time with John and Wilma.

From time to time I would talk to John about universities or China or what was going on in the world elsewhere. I always found him responsive, interested and perceptive in his comments. Although we saw him and Wilma too infrequently during the years of our association, my wife and I will never forget the impact he made both here and abroad, and how much we treasured the hours we could spend with both of them.

# *Scholarly Contribution*

BENJAMIN I. SCHWARTZ*
*Harvard University*

As one of those whose lives have been decisively shaped by my contacts with John Fairbank and as one who has been his close colleague for some forty years, I find it difficult to sum up my thoughts in a brief compass. John was a complex man of many facets. Despite his deep seriousness one was continually confronted with his impish and sardonic humor. At a rather late point I was surprised to discover his love of Beethoven quartets. I could go on in this vein, yet at the cost of appearing impersonal, I shall concentrate my attention on what seems to me to be at the core of his life—what I shall call his life mission and also his life project.

Having come to the study of China at an early point in life and having experienced life in China, he early became convinced that it would be crucial for us as Americans and Westerners to establish meaningful relations with a vast society and ancient civilization which would inevitably play a crucial role in the future history of mankind. As a scholar, he also became convinced that it was only through achieving an understanding of China that it would be possible to communicate with her. Without understanding, there could be no meaningful communication and without meaningful communication, there could be no understanding. I add the phrase "life project," because I have never met anyone as capable as John of marshalling such a vast array of practical talents and resources toward the end of implementing his mission on both the national and academic scenes. Adjectives which come to mind are single-minded, dedicated, resourceful, persistent and relentless.

* This memoir, in slightly different form, was delivered at the memorial service for Fairbank, held at Harvard University on October 21, 1991.

As one of the first group of graduate students (most of us war veterans) who met John at Harvard when he had returned from a China in turmoil, we were immediately struck by his overwhelming sense of urgency. Having witnessed the tragic demoralization and disarray of the late war years in China, having been in close touch with the despair of leading Chinese intellectuals, and witnessing the growing disconnection between the U.S.A. and the new revolutionary regime, he was desperately anxious to reverse the total rupture of communications which seemed to be taking place. He was, of course, determined that we as a group should achieve as much understanding as we could acquire in our relatively short M. A. area studies program. He insisted on the intense study of language and on a deep immersion in the study of the modern experience of China in all its disciplinary dimensions. With his usual resourcefulness he exposed us to the wisdom of some of the leading luminaries of the time: Talcott Parsons, Clyde Kluckhohn, Carl Friedrich, Karl August Wittfogel and others. At the time, he seemed to have high hopes that they would provide us with total illumination. Later both he and I realized that total illumination remained elusive and that we would have to continue to think for ourselves.

Despite this strenuous yet rather short immersion in the effort to understand China, our group felt that what John envisioned for us most immediately in his sense of urgency was a turn to the world of government and public affairs in order to engage in a desperate effort to reverse the tragic breach in Sino-American communications which had taken place. Yet when John concluded that the rupture would not soon be healed, he resolutely turned all his formidable energies to the long-term enterprise of achieving the understanding of China within an academic setting. He had, after all, become a China scholar grounded in all the canons of historical scholarship and equipped with all the paraphernalia of Sinology long before turning his attention to current affairs and he now applied his superb skills as editor, bibliographer, and academic adviser to the promotion of scholarship. He was bent on raising scholars and on establishing Chinese and East Asian studies as a legitimate, respected and non-exotic part of the intellectual life of the university. By the term "non-exotic" I do not mean to suggest that he meant to prove that "the

Chinese are just like us." On the contrary, I soon came to realize that he had a much more emphatic sense of China's difference than I did. What we came to share, I feel, was a faith that these differences did not reflect the totally inaccessible and incommensurable otherness of China and that it was possible to grasp these differences in a language of our own, however hazardous the enterprise. Nor was his non-exoticism applicable only to the study of contemporary China. His own conception of "modern Chinese history" was firmly based on the conviction that we could never understand contemporary China without thoroughly immersing ourselves in the world of late traditional China and his famous seminar on Ch'ing documents was a pioneer effort in using documents written in abstruse classical Chinese not for philological analysis but as sources for understanding political systems, political thought and political behavior. He thus emboldened some of us to believe—perhaps presumptuously—that it might even be possible to understand Chinese culture of the past in terms of shared universal human concerns despite the implicit cultural baggage which we all bring to our studies.

But while John Fairbank definitely had his own ideas on China, he never attempted to force any of his students to follow him all the way or to share his perceptions of what was important and what was unimportant. When it became clear to him that some were moving off in other directions, he simply insisted that they pursue their own explorations assiduously and relentlessly. To the very end he exposed all his own ideas to the criticism and scrutiny of others and also read all the monographs. To the end he continued to regard the search for an understanding of China as a collective enterprise.

In sum, when one views John Fairbank's mission in its broadest dimensions, one finds that it was based on his keen and early perception that we are now entering a global society in which we are all inextricably involved with each other. This statement, which is now commonplace, is often made in inspirational tones to imply that the harmonious reconciliation of mankind is at hand. Whatever may have been his ultimate hopes, John's insights for the immediate future were far more sober. We may not care a fig for the differences between Shiites and Sunnis. Yet we can no longer afford to ignore these differences. When John spoke of understanding a foreign culture, he did not mean that we would necessarily like what we understand any more than the Latin saying "I find nothing human alien to me" means that we will therefore learn to like everything human. Not only must we learn to understand others; we must also learn to contemplate and scrutinize ourselves and our own limitations. This was another one of John's messages. John Fairbank's mission was a noble and indispensable mission.

PHILIP A. KUHN*
*Harvard University*

John encouraged his students to bring to Chinese history the insights of social science. He was of course too modest to admit that he himself had made some distinguished contributions to social-science theory. For example, in some notes dating from the late 1940s, we find him grappling with the problem of how to relate the anthropologist Clyde Kluckhohn's work on the cultural effects of toilet training to the sociologist Karl August Wittfogel's search for the origins of Oriental despotism in the central control of large-scale waterworks. John creatively integrated Kluckhohn and Wittfogel into a higher synthesis, which he aptly called "The Kluckfogel model." "The human body is an irrigated economy. Because it is an economy of abundance, overconsumption leads to overproduction, sometimes expressed as 'one drink leads to another.' Therefore it can be seen that a hydraulic society has a fluid matrix," the establishment of despotic control over the alimentary canal.

JKF's special brand of dead-pan wit throve upon absurdity and incongruity. As a scholar operating between cultures, he found plenty of both. In one bit of vintage Fairbank inscrutabilia, he describes Emperor Tao-kuang, who ruled China during the Opium War: "[He] came to the throne at age thirty-eight, and everything we know about his private life (which is next to nothing) suggests he

* This memoir, in slightly different form, was delivered at the memorial service for Fairbank, held at Harvard University on October 21, 1991.

was devoted, in the fashion of his time, to his empress, and on family matters (allowing for cultural differences) would have been at one with Queen Victoria."

When did John become aware of his role as a man of the cultural frontier? When he began studying China in 1929, it was as a problem of diplomatic history. At the outset, he seems to have shared the general concern of the profession to uncover the hidden background of the Great War. The secret Chinese foreign relations documents just published in Peking would be the basis for bringing China in. As a Rhodes Scholar at Oxford, John began to train himself in the Chinese language, while at the same time exploring the "peculiar Anglo-Chinese institution," China's Imperial Maritime Customs, at the Public Record Office. But his memoirs of these Oxford days reveal no awareness of the immensity of the cultural frontier he was soon to explore.

Exposure to China, where he began his fieldwork in 1932, made him aware of it quickly. John's fascination with Chinese life and values, aided by Wilma's sensitivity as an artist and social observer, put him right in line with what Westerners had experienced for a century: one came to China to *do* something, but soon found oneself involved in the larger quest to make sense of the incongruity between Chinese culture and one's own.

The Chinese documents that John studied were themselves a theater of incongruity. Chinese and Western actors in the Opium War period spoke their lines from two different cultural scripts. The disparities between China as the center of the civilized world, and her total inability to cope with barbarians who thought otherwise, were inscribed in the brushstrokes on every page. Soon John was able to discern a thin stratum of men—some Chinese and some Western—who made the job of bridging this gulf their lives' work.

The first generation of Chinese who dealt with "barbarian affairs" pursued their work as (in John's words) "a disagreeable but necessary job, like sewer-inspecting." The Western China hands, equally sure of their own superiority, went about building institutions to make the Sino-Western frontier actually work, to the profit (as they saw it) of both sides.

John quickly sensed his kinship with these frontier personalities. The Ulsterman Sir Robert Hart, Inspector-General of China's Imperial Maritime Customs, was the dominant figure. But John felt closer to the American, H. B. Morse, Harvard 1874, who, after a career as a Customs official, founded the Western study of China's foreign relations and became John's direct historiographical predecessor. John's work on four volumes of Hart's letters and journals, and his biography of Morse (still incomplete when he died) were labors of love. On the Chinese side, John cherished friends such as Ch'ien Tuan-sheng, Chiang T'ing-fu [T. F. Tsiang], Liang Ssu-ch'eng and Kuo T'ing-i, Western-educated scholars who shared John's life on the frontier.

And it was a gloriously strenuous life. I remember a sign that used to hang above John's desk: it displayed the Chinese characters "*i-lao yung-i*" ("after hard labor, eternal ease"), an entirely reasonable view—that rest is earned by work. Watching John's work schedule, I could never figure out where the hard labor might end, and the eternal ease begin. Now we know.

THOMAS A. METZGER
*Hoover Institution on War, Revolution and Peace*

JKF's passing was a great shock. Because I had heard that his family had a tradition of longevity, I had developed a comfortable feeling that he would be around for another ten years at least. His passing made me still more aware that, to a large extent, when writing about China, my purpose was to influence him. What he thought mattered so much to me and to so many others. The reason for this is, above all, that he was truly perspicacious and intellectually honest, besides having a wonderful sense for the possibilities of the English language. There was indeed nothing accidental about his fame, which in no way exceeded the extent of his accomplishments. He just happened to be an extraordinarily gifted, likable, and hardworking person, who deeply impressed a huge number of people, scholars and other readers of the *New York Times* alike.

Many of us loved to write letters to him, knowing he would catch every nuance, believing he would accept the truth felt by the writer at that moment, knowing that he was constantly rethinking his approach to the major issues of Chinese history, and hoping to influence him. Needless to add, JKF loved the battle of ideas, keeping up contact with people who disagreed with him. This is an uncommon trait in the case of eminent scholars, so far as I know. So calling him a "great academic entrepreneur" is quite misleading. He was that beyond a doubt, but he was far, far more—intellectual perspicacity, not organizational talent, was his claim to fame. He not only turned modern Chinese history into one of the world's most interesting historiographical fields but also did more than anyone else to develop an interdisciplinary approach to this field.

Besides perspicacity, modesty was perhaps his most salient trait, so far as my experience goes. Some degree of modesty is not rare, but JKF had completely replaced the need to feel important with quiet self-assurance. I suggest that this highly unusual achievement was the basis of his charisma, his ability to put others in awe of him, his immense likeability.

Nor should we overlook why his way of discussing Chinese history will constitute a major viewpoint for the foreseeable future. He did not just weave facts together in an elegant, interdisciplinary, witty, thoughtful way. Instead, his point of departure, I believe, was the reform agenda that Chinese and Westerners have been arguing about since the Opium War. His commitment to this general Chinese cause of reform, together with his convictions about how reform could most effectively proceed, underlay his more political views about China, with a good number of which I disagreed. His writing will continue to be important because, I believe, it consistently and so seriously speaks to this cause of reform.

Suffering over the loss of this person, I am struck by the usefulness of monuments. They do indeed console to some extent. The fact that Harvard's East Asian Research Center has been named after JKF will help to nourish the pleasant illusion that he is still in our midst, and this illusion may inspire at least some people to build on the scholarly ideals he did so much to advance.

JEAN MAYER
*Tufts University*

I knew John Fairbank for a very long time because his father-in-law, the great American physiologist, Walter B. Cannon, was a very good friend of my father and had collaborated with him during World War I. After I grew up, I became more and more aware of the fact that John Fairbank was a promising young scholar. As I in turn became a Harvard professor, I came to realize he was one of our very great colleagues, whose work enriched not only the academy but also all of mankind. He had the attributes that we like to see in a great scholar: a profound sense of history, total respect for facts, a lucid style, and great philosophical courage in defending his convictions.

IMMANUEL C. Y. HSU
*University of California, Santa Barbara*

As a graduate student in John's seminar on modern Chinese history and later as a postdoctoral research fellow, I had ample opportunity to learn his teaching and research methods as well as to observe him administer a large and growing research center. To this day, I remain impressed with his prodigious, seemingly inexhaustible energy. His working schedule reminded me of that of Ch'ing Emperor Yung-cheng and Inspector-General Robert Hart. He spent his mornings in classes or in his spacious study in Widener Library. At midday he would come over to the research center for lunch with friends, visitors, and staff members. After a short rest in the afternoon—à la Li Hung-chang's famous daily nap—he dictated memos and replies to the everflowing mail, received researchers and visiting scholars, or presided over meetings, seminars, and conferences. Rarely did he leave before six o'clock.

In his seminars and in the research center John was an eloquent proponent of the multi-archival, multilingual, interdisciplinary approach to the study of Chinese history. I was very much drawn to this methodology because of my study of several European languages and also my earlier exposure to the writings of T. F. Tsiang. The similar approach was also impressed upon me by Professors Sidney B. Fay and William L. Langer in their seminars in European history. As one whose schooling had suffered during the Japanese occupation, imagine my delight at being able to sit at the feet of Fairbank, Fay and Langer. What a privilege for a struggling student from Soochow.

John's dedication to the application of the multi-archival, multilingual, social science methodology to the study of China led to the formation of what might be called a "New Sinology," distinguished from the linguistically and culturally oriented traditional Sinology. His investigations broke new ground and marked a giant step forward from earlier works by H. B. Morse, Henri Cordier, and Tyler Dennett which relied exclusively on the national records of Britain, France, and the United States. This dependence on Western sources reflected a self-righteous attitude that held Western scholarship to be sufficient and superior. Chinese sources were considered unreliable and Chinese perspective unnecessary, even though multi-archival research was already quite evident in studies of European diplomatic history. These pioneer works of the 1910s and 1920s in fact could only be regarded today as studies of British, French, and American diplomacy toward China and not studies of Chinese diplomatic history.

The 1930s saw the origin of a new direction in the study of China, as many Ch'ing documents were just becoming available for scholarly research. Under the aegis of Professor T. F. Tsiang of Tsinghua University in Peking, a new generation of scholars, including John, experimented with multi-archival and multilingual research into Chinese foreign relations. Returning to Harvard, John initiated the celebrated seminar in Ch'ing documents. In an effort to discover the Chinese perspective in all diplomatic, commercial, and religious transactions, John immersed his students, myself included, in the official terminology and bureaucratic practice of the Ch'ing court. For John himself, his mastery of the Ch'ing institutions and his felicity with the English language enabled him to state perceptively that the Ch'ing *monarchy* really consisted of a Manchu-Chinese *dyarchy*, followed by a Manchu-Chinese-Western *synarchy* by the second half of the nineteenth century. I know of no one else who could distill such complex political phenomena into such succinct concepts.

It must also be noted that while John expounded the multi-archival approach to subjects concerning trade, diplomacy and "China's response to the West," he was only too cognizant of the limitations of this approach to the purely Chinese subjects that eluded Western influence. Beginning in the late 1950s, he promoted research which delved deeply into Chinese sources to investigate problems of population, social mobility, intellectual trends, cultural history, economic institutions, taxation, the examination system, Communist ideology, etc. He must be credited as the founding father of a new school of Sinology.

We honor the memory of this grand historian, wise teacher, prolific scholar, and remarkable academic entrepreneur. Three generations of scholars of modern China in this country remain in his debt.

## WINSTON LORD
*New York, New York*

No scholar contributed more to the study and understanding of China than John Fairbank.

His research and writings illuminated the Chinese landscape. His stimulation, training, and encouragement of countless others illuminated the American landscape. Whatever one's link to China or Sino-American relations—policy maker, scholar, teacher, journalist, businessperson—reading and absorbing the rich trove of Fairbank work has been an absolute requirement.

John Fairbank will be missed not only by family and friends but by all who seek to know about China and shape our long march with that nation. He leaves a permanent legacy of writings and disciples that will help guide our journey well into the future.

# *Teacher and Mentor*

PETER DUUS
*Stanford University*

Boylston Hall was a mysterious place to most Harvard undergraduates in the early 1950s. Except for the Chinese stone lions guarding it, the dark stone facade looked for all the world like the Charles Addams mansion, and the furtive-looking characters who passed through its front doors—perfectly ordinary graduate students, I later realized—all seemed bent on arcane missions in its lower depths.

Every Monday, Wednesday and Friday afternoon of my junior spring at Harvard I climbed to the second floor of this mysterious building for my class on modern Chinese history. In these (to me) unusual surroundings, the professor, who sat at a small table, his neatly typed notes spread in front of him, was palpably normal. He lectured casually in a dry midwestern accent, and he talked about the decline and fall of the Ch'ing empire as matter-of-factly as if it had been reported in yesterday's *New York Times*. And when he turned toward more recent events, the defeat of the Nationalist government at the hands of the Chinese Communists, history became mingled with his personal reminiscences. If anyone in the class had been looking for the "mysterious East," this was not it. This was the real world, and it was exciting.

The professor, of course, was John King Fairbank. I had already taken the famous "Rice Paddies" course with him, and that had gotten me hooked. Until then my knowledge of East Asia had been an odd mixture of information gleaned from children's picture books, *Life* magazine, World War II propaganda, the March of Time newsreels, and back issues of the *National Geographic*. What I learned from John Fairbank in "Rice Paddies" was that Asia was a critically important part of the world that Americans would ignore at their peril. This was a refreshing point of view as everyone else in Harvard Yard at the time seemed obsessed with the Soviet Union.

What also impressed me was Professor Fairbank's insistence that Americans ought to understand the Chinese, or any other non-Western people, for that matter, in their own terms rather than in ours. I still remember the two or three introductory lectures in which he pointed out quite concretely why it would not be reasonable to expect the Chinese to behave like American liberals. And indeed, it was his ability to make the unfamiliar seem not only plausible but even rational and sensible that ultimately lured me into the study of East Asian history. Had I been confronted instead with mysterious cultural essences I might be in a different line of work today.

Toward the end of my junior spring, I decided to write my History senior honors thesis on China. But what to write about? I did not know Chinese—or much else I now realize. When I approached Professor Fairbank one day after class, he said, "Why don't you come over to my house for tea on Thursday, and we can discuss it." Tea? At a professor's house? I was nonplused. The closest I had ever gotten to the real habitat of a Harvard professor was awkward dinners at the House Master's residence.

The following Thursday, throttled by a tightly knotted tie and mildly awed by the gravity of the occasion, I appeared at the little house on Winthrop Street. The details of the encounter I do not remember, except that I had pink lemonade rather than tea. Professor Fairbank was as solicitous and attentive of this lone undergraduate as he was of the other guests, most of them the furtive characters I had seen going in and out of Boylston Hall. In the course of our conversation Professor Fairbank suggested that I do something on missionaries in China, and that modest suggestion, which led to an honors thesis on W. A. P. Martin, launched me on a life of scholarship.

If that were all that John Fairbank had done for me I would be grateful. In fact, he did a great deal more. He provided a model of what a teacher and scholar of history should be. For years, I tried to follow his classroom style. Although it was difficult to capture his dry ironic humor, let alone his authority and assurance on the lecture platform, I discovered that slides at the end of the lecture always seemed to work. And when I sat down to write history, particularly for nonspecialists, *The United States and China* was always there as a model of how to do it. Recently an anonymous reader commented that something I had written was "Fairbankian." I could not think of a nicer compliment.

His passing would be a sadder occasion for me if he were not still quite alive in my memory. I still recall the wry look on his face when he asked the only question I remember from my Ph. D. oral examination: "Into how many pieces did the Korean court cut Kim Ok-kiun's body when it came back from Shanghai?" I still ask that question of my own students, and I hope they have the wit to answer, "At least two." That was the answer I gave, and I remember that it seemed to please Professor Fairbank. I still wonder if he knew the right answer. Very probably he did.

RHOADS MURPHEY
*University of Michigan*

It was said by one of his students of Carl Becker, the Europeanist, that Becker guided his charges with "gimlet eye and fatherly hand." I never knew Becker, but ever since I first read this encomium many years ago, I have felt that it fitted John Fairbank even better. For John, it was a commitment which sustained his students throughout their careers. His keeping tabs on us was sometimes a spur, as he intended, but invariably friendly and in the best fatherly manner. Equally important, and equally in the Chinese mode, his example was always there, and continually renewed; perhaps that was, appropriately, the most effective of all his many ways of shaping the careers of his students, as well as those of countless others. It was not easy to stand in his shadow—or his radiance?—but he was an enormous influence for good, one which will go on affecting us almost daily as long as we live. My school's motto was "Behold I have set before thee an open door." School did introduce me to the life of learning, but it was John who opened for me the door which I entered as an undergraduate, into the fascination with China he so excitingly communicated and which I never lost.

Chinese fathers were often formal and impersonal with their sons, and he was often both, especially in those early years; he had his own way, and the way of the field, to make. When I was doing my thesis, to which he had of course directed me, I needed to see him sometimes; he would often say "Come by the house at 7 (a.m.!), even then for most students the middle of the night, but he was always long up, sometimes with a text propped beside his shaving mirror, sometimes finishing breakfast with the same accompaniment. We would walk, almost at a trot, to his Littauer office while I breathlessly asked about Chapter 4 or whatever, and then in the midst of this "discourse" he would disappear behind his office door. I knew it was a hectic time for him (1949-50), on top of *Trade and Diplomacy* (which became my guide), but he never left me dangling for long. I remembered, too, Thursday afternoons at 41 which we all looked forward to, where Wilma greatly contributed to the welcome warmth. I understood that now I was supposed to be, like him, a serious professional, no time for chitchat or wasted minutes.

Perhaps more than most undergraduates, I was lonely and lost to begin with at Harvard, and I gratefully drank in the warm and friendly atmosphere of 41, for me a bright spot in an otherwise vast and impersonal world. With keen anticipation Joe Levenson and I walked over there every week after dinner for our tutorials in modern European history (John had to pay his way too), many of which I still remember. In time we realized where his main interest lay, and took his course, History 83b. Then and later, like many of his students, including Levenson, I left, for a time and to a degree, the path he had in mind for me, but John and China soon reclaimed me; it became clear that his was the model I found most compelling—or was it just that he so effectively kindled in me an abiding interest in virtually all of the things about China which he had opened up, leaving me (and most others) faint, but pursuing? Doubtless others will write of how he never stopped following their work and letting them know what he thought of it, correcting their mistakes and urging them on to do more. That was appreciated as much as his care of us *in statu pupillari*, though I suppose in his view we never ceased to be so. I rarely published anything on China to which he did not respond, and he sent me a copy of everything he published, not I think as a prod or as implying "Do it *this* way," but as exemplary teacher and friend.

I left Harvard for four years in China in 1942, in part because of what John had inspired in me, and one typically rainy muddy day in Chungking, to my immense surprise, I encountered him in the street, also picking his way around the puddles. I think both of us felt it was a disjointed encounter. For the time, I was no longer his student, and he no longer (it seemed) a scholar. Although we were following distantly related paths, our Chinese meeting did not seem really to fit. It was different in 1972, when I first returned to China and ran into John and Wilma on a Beijing street. Then it all seemed to fit; we were again fellow adventurers on the same path, where 41 Winthrop and Boylston Hall helped to give it sense.

As many will say, John was a complicated person, of whom I suppose I saw only parts. He did of course have a talented wit, of which I remember many samples from our Boylston classroom, but it shone too whenever there were special occasions, such as the celebratory dinner in Chinatown for our first "Regional Studies" class graduation. We had devised what we thought an amusing skit to thank him, but he stole the entire show, complete with false beard whipped from his pocket. Lest it be forgotten, he was I think as good a teacher as he was a published scholar, and at all levels, from Ch'ing documents and thesis direction to Rice Paddies. It gives me satisfaction that I still teach much the same course, Great Tradition and Modern Transformation, Old Uncle Tom Cobleigh and all, and I hope with the same enthusiasm he transmitted.

But for all of whatever mixture of many things John was, my strongest and most enduring image of him is the one with which I began this little memorial: the caring combination of gimlet eye and fatherly hand.

David T. Roy
*University of Chicago*

I owe John King Fairbank a debt of gratitude that mere words can never repay. For years he was, by no choice of his own, a surrogate father for me, as he was, I feel sure, to many of his other students. I dreamt about him as an authority figure and, in my waking hours, frequently found myself asking what he would think of something I had done, or, perhaps more often, not done. In fact, had he not descended upon me like a deus ex machina, first when I was an assistant professor at Princeton and later an associate professor at the University of Chicago, and literally wrested my unfinished manuscript from my grasp, my doctoral dissertation and my first book would never have seen the light of day. Thus, for better or for worse, I owe my admission to the ranks of professional China scholars not only to the inspiration and instruction of this pedagogical genius, but to this peremptory parental act.

It was on a trip to Cambridge in 1951, during my senior year in high school, that I was first introduced to John Fairbank by my father, Andrew T. Roy, a Presbyterian missionary, who had known him in China during the 1930s. Shortly after my arrival at Harvard as a freshman, later the same year, I received a written invitation to one of the famous Thursday afternoon teas at the Fairbank residence. When I summoned up the courage to attend I was both impressed and bewildered by the polyglot mixture of famous scholars, old China hands, present and former students, and visiting firemen, all struggling to eat their cucumber sandwiches and balance their teacups while constantly being thrown off balance by the sardonic and unpredictable conversational curveballs served up by their host.

Later in my undergraduate career, I audited the famous year-long Fairbank course on modern Chinese history and found it to be the most rigorous and demanding of the many classes I had taken in the History Department. It was then that I read his *Trade and Diplomacy on the China Coast* and was amazed to find that his notes were devoted to pointing out new avenues for further research rather than demonstrating the author's unparalleled erudition. During my junior year I took a course on American diplomatic history from Ernest May, for which I wrote a paper on the Treaty of Wang-hsia

(1844). Unaccountably, it was only after handing in the paper that I thought to see what Fairbank had said about the treaty and was chagrined to find that every significant point in my twenty-page paper had been made more effectively by him in the space of one or two perfectly crafted paragraphs. I have never read the work of another historian who could say more, so memorably, in so few well chosen words.

But the greatest thing about John Fairbank was the fact that he had the gift of making his students feel, not always comfortably, that he really cared about them both as scholars and individuals, and that he expected them to want to live up to the same high standards of scholarship and integrity that his own career so brilliantly exemplified. No one who had the privilege of sitting at his feet will ever forget him.

ORVILLE SCHELL
*San Francisco, California*

Lying on my desk beside me as I write this remembrance is a creased and somewhat yellowed letter that recently turned up in an old file. It was written on Harvard East Asian Institute letterhead, dated May 26, 1962, addressed to me at National Taiwan University, and was signed J. K. Fairbank, in that spidery scrawl of his own hand with which I since became more familiar. It was doubtless just one of many such letters he wrote that day to his graduate students and colleagues around the world, but for me, a Harvard undergraduate who had dropped out of college on an uncertain impulse to study Chinese language on my own in Taipei, it made me feel like a lesser member of the evangelical clergy upon receiving a missive from the Pope at the Holy See itself. I was just 21 years old, and had with some trepidation written John Fairbank seeking counsel about what I needed to do in order to return to Harvard for my senior year, and possibly to go on at mid-term into graduate school. Even now I still remember with perfect vividness the day Fairbank's letter arrived at the bleak dormitory room in which I lived at National Taiwan University with seven Chinese roommates. "I am glad to have your letter, and have collected the following information," he wrote about my queries in his characteristically formal but never off-putting manner. What touched me deeply about his letter then, and what still touches me as I now reread it thirty-five years later, is the way in which he took my hopes and still inchoate plans about going on in China studies with utter seriousness, even to the extent of plotting a whole potential plan of study for me as if I were to become some kind of a protégé. The truth was that in 1962 I had very little idea about what I was really going to do with my life, and it would have been all too easy to have dismissed my puerile inquiry with a few pro-forma lines. Instead, he wrote at some length and then ended his letter on a tone that suggested that far from wishing to get rid of me as a bureaucratic detail, he wished to stay in touch. "Let me know if this doesn't answer your questions and please keep me informed of your plans," he wrote.

I was in Taiwan that fall of 1958 after making a decision that at the time seemed of no more consequence than most of the others I was making as a sophomore at Harvard College. Because I wanted to take a course with my sister who was due to graduate from Radcliffe that spring, we signed up for Social Sciences 111, or "Rice Paddies" as this survey of China, Japan and Korea had been irreverently dubbed by students. From my uninitiated perspective, Soc. Sci. 111's main virtue was that its three weekly meetings synchronized both with my sister's and my own class schedule.

I remember that first lecture at 2 Divinity Avenue in 1958 as if it were yesterday. John Fairbank and Edwin Reischauer appeared on the small stage, and in their uniquely gracious and deferential way began to explain the long historical odyssey that they would take us on.

Every Monday, Wednesday and Friday I trooped faithfully off to lecture at 2 Divinity Avenue over the next eight months, and almost immediately I found myself more interested in China than Japan. For the China lectures Fairbank would appear before us, fold his lanky frame up like a jack-knife in the chair behind the table that always stood out on the stage. Then, looking indulgently out at us undergraduates, he would begin another of his discourses, herding us one more step on our long trek through four millennia of history from the Shang dynasty 1200 B. C. to the ascendancy of Mao's Communist dynasty, which was at that moment in the throes of the Great Leap Forward. It was not difficult as a fledgling historian to get lost beneath this dizzying succession of dynasties and emperors heaped up one on top of the other on the chart that we were all issued so that they looked like so many undifferentiated geological strata of sedimentary rock at a deep road cut. I quickly came to depend on Fairbank's lectures and theories about dynastic cycles to give some sense of coherence to their incessant and infuriating rising and falling.

But, what I remember most about Fairbank's lectures was his modesty, his wryness, and his utter lack of pomposity. There was something about his manner that was sovereign but never self-promoting or aggrandizing. Nowhere was there a suggestion of competitiveness with his colleagues, much less his students. I think it was this quality that allowed so many of us to feel challenged without feeling belittled in his presence.

I remember one lecture in particular. Edgar Snow, Wilma and John's old friend from prewar Peking, had arrived in Cambridge to show our class the 16 millimeter films he had shot of student demonstrations in the mid-thirties. It was with a sense of great excitement that we in the crowded lecture hall awaited these two renowned Sinophiles. But when they at last mounted the stage to give some background on the footage we were about to see, both were overcome with such deference for the other that they quickly became engaged in a five minute Alphonse and Gaston routine over who would speak first on the subject of what it had been like to live in Peking in the thirties. All of us were charmed to the point of laughter at their courtliness toward each other.

Sometimes Fairbank seemed as awed and mystified by China as I was. In fact, instead of pretending that he had the answers, he would often frustrate those of us who wished to make him an infallible oracle by parrying our questions with paradoxes, irony, and oblique responses, almost as if he had decided that when it came to China, no definite answer could be the right answer. One day when a particularly earnest but bright student with whom I shared a tutorial pressed him on a question about his views on the origins of the Chinese Communist revolution, like a Zen master delivering a koan, he replied,

"Just remember one thing, Mao Zedong didn't make the Chinese revolution for you!"

Whereas coming from someone else such a retort might easily have sounded hostile, the bemused, almost impish, look on Fairbank's face suggested otherwise. It was almost as if he wanted to warn us against trying to draw too many grandiose and simple conclusions about the Communist movement that we had just begun to study.

The relationship between a student in a lecture hall and a professor is surely one of the strangest experiences of learning human beings have. There are few relationships that are at once as intimate and remote. A student is deeply involved and distant at the same time. Over the course of this year in Soc. Sci. 111, Fairbank became my mentor without my quite realizing it, for, even as it was happening, I was hardly aware of how his ministrations were inoculating me with a fascination of a certain kind for China. But if I was unaware of how deeply affected I was becoming by all that I heard him say in lecture and read, he had even less idea of me. In fact, he did not know I existed. It was not until the next fall when it came time once again to select classes and I found myself choosing two more courses in Chinese history that I realized how irrevocably possessed by China I had actually become. And it was not until Fairbank's gracious letter to me in Taiwan that my name became known to him.

During those first two years I used to love to retreat at night into the windowless stacks of the Harvard-Yenching Institute Library to study. I was, of course, perennially distracted by all the Chinese language volumes on the shelves around me. But that was precisely why I liked being there. They made me feel closer to this subject that was incubating inside me and about which I still knew almost nothing. I think it was the enigma of these silently opaque volumes in their blue box-like bindings with bone clasps that finally made me decide to take a leave from Harvard and go to study language in Taiwan, where I received the letter now lying beside me on my desk.

When I finally did return to Cambridge, all that I could think of was to seek out Fairbank. My excuse was that I needed to choose an honors thesis topic, and wanted some advice. And, I had glorified notions of writing about the Institute of Pacific Relations imbroglio in which he himself had been involved. But when I announced my idea to him in his Dunster Street office, he nodded, pursed his lips together, put his hands in front of his face in an almost prayerlike gesture, and then diplomatically and decorously suggested that perhaps I would find researching an American missionary, for which he assured me there were abundant archives in Boston, a more fruitful avenue of inquiry.

I still laugh at the memory of this meeting. As a young and politically excitable student the unplumbed tragedy of how the McCarthy years had decimated the China field of so many of its finest specialists held real fascination for me. But for those who had lived through the harrowing ordeal of the anti-Communist witchhunt, the wounds were still far too fresh and the memory too painful to be offered as the stuff of historical research. Moreover, I am sure that the thought of a naive, young, and often overly righteous young undergraduate student rummaging through these sensitive issues was not what Fairbank had in mind even if the time had come to exhume this bitter experience.

Instead of writing about the IPR or an American missionary, I ended up doing my dissertation on Wang Jingwei. But Fairbank bore no grudges. In fact, shortly after our meeting in his office, I was stunned when one afternoon he invited me to tea in the creaky wood-frame colonial house on Winthrop Street in which he and Wilma lived, and which always impressed me as being absurdly undersized to embrace a man whose reach and influence had been so wide.

It is hard to describe how honored I felt at being noticed, remembered, and then invited to tea. After all, I had still not even graduated, and was filled with grave doubts about the worthiness of myself as a viable enterprise, never mind about my viability in the highly specialized field of China scholarship. Like receiving his letter in Taipei, there was something about sitting in that small unpretentious living room, drinking tea, and chatting with graduate students and professors as he presided like a benign deity with his signature Daoist aloofness, that was as inspiring as all his lectures, the Qing documents that he taught, and the monographs that he helped publish put together. Simply being there in his presence allowed a young student such as myself, and many others besides, to imagine that it was possible, after all, to become a part of the great but often elusive enterprise of China studies.

## Jay Mathews
*Washington Post*

He was an infinitely kind and peace-loving man, but at first he frightened me.

I met John King Fairbank when I was a sophomore at Harvard, newly transferred from a small California college because I had discovered I was in love with China. He was the dean of Chinese studies, tall, lean, bald, usually expressionless save for a slight smirk when listening to something he considered unusually funny or ridiculous.

How was I to relate to a man like that? He had come out of South Dakota in the 1920s like an intellectual tornado, taking a *summa* in history, winning a Rhodes, marrying the brilliant daughter of a famous Harvard Medical School professor, spending years of adventure in China, defying the McCarthyites and then polishing off the legend by creating the postwar China studies industry. His students were everywhere, at all the major universities and leading their fields in government and journalism.

It was intimidating to see him standing before the 100 or so of us crammed into Soc. Sci. 111 (East Asian history, usually called "Rice Paddies"), celebrating the sweep of the Chinese cultural sphere (in which he thoughtfully included Japan) and demanding thought and synthesis and meaning from a confusing montage of Asian faces and strange tri-syllable names.

One can grow tired of a teacher like that, particularly at a place like Harvard. In some cases the name and legend leave little room for the shy and the uncertain, but I learned that John Fairbank knew that from the start, and spent much of his time throwing down ropes to us small fry.

There was, for starters, his house, a shaky little yellow frame three-story model lost in a jungle of tall dorms and university offices at 41 Winthrop St. There was barely enough room inside to move around during his regular Thursday afternoon teas, a clue that Professor Fairbank was not a man to put on airs.

This impression was fortified by his habit of appearing at darkened theaters with a flashlight in his pocket, to make sure that his large and ungainly feet did not tread on any toes. He also liked to throw frisbees in his front yard, a practice I could not square with my image of the man writing all those pieces in the *New York Review of Books*.

Then there was Wilma, Mrs. Fairbank. She was the oldest of four sisters of the celebrated Cannon family, a *magna* graduate in fine arts whose husband envied her "creative capacity for spontaneous play, thought and action." This was fortunate, since the man she married was the sort who rhapsodized about Sundays locked in the stacks of Widener Library: "Free for the day—no people, no phones, a sandwich, and the quiet of a Trappist monastery."

When I tried to write my first major piece of journalism, a profile of this professor who terrified me, it was Wilma who pulled out the phony "reader's note" her husband had once written about one of his own books and sent his publisher: "One cannot envy an editor who undertakes to make a nonrepetitive sequence out of this mishmash. Mr. Fairbank has obviously been talking to students for years but never to the same ones and his capacity for restatement of well-worn themes would excite the envy even of a Richard Nixon."

The Fairbank genius, I gradually learned, was to mix rigor and sweat with a great deal of fun. It was not something I expected, with a westerner's view of Harvard as a very serious place, but it had an enormous appeal. In his autobiography, *Chinabound: A Fifty-Year Memoir*, Fairbank said his conquest of Exeter, Harvard and Oxford came through a similar formula. Spend the first year on the books, he said, then get to know the people.

His forbidding appearance and his ultra-dry academic specialty, Qing dynasty diplomatic papers, gave his jokes that much more punch. You did not expect to see him don a long Confucius-style beard at the faculty-student party, nor did you expect the well-drawn quips that fell into nearly everything he wrote:

On how to survive academic skirmishes: "I was already learning how to be a Sinologist when among historians and, with a slight shift of gears, a historian when among Sinologists—much like a Chinese bandit who is never caught because he stays on the border between provinces and when pursued from one side quietly fades across into the other jurisdiction."

On Shirley MacLaine, seated to his right at a White House dinner: "She had acquired China by leading a menagerie of American women, one of every known kind, on a culture-shock trip to the PRC that simply beat the pants off any other culture shock she had ever had."

On his 1979 coronary: "A nonfatal heart attack is, I am sure, much more interesting than the other kind."

The idea was to draw his audience, even the most timid of us, into the web, where we could taste the rarer, sweeter joys of scholarship.

Fairbank has been celebrated for his popular works, *The United States and China* foremost among them. Even at personal moments he loved to speculate on the broad sweep of history. One of his letters to me when I was a soldier in Vietnam wondered if Western civilization could really survive "with this much firepower." When I announced my wife and I had had a daughter, he had a thought about the male of the species rapidly becoming superfluous.

But his memoir speaks most glowingly of one of his most narrow projects, *Modern China: A Bibliographical Guide to Chinese Works 1898-1937*, a 608-page tome coauthored with K. C. Liu which few hardy souls have ever bothered to read through. "I still get excited reading this volume," Fairbank said. "As long as I had it at hand I could give my student the knowledge of Chinese sources that he ought to have and show him how to proceed. It was like having an extra section of brain one could carry around; and a lot more reliable."

He had a tough time during the McCarthy era. Close friends lost their jobs and his outrage at the blow to civil liberties and intellectual freedom was palpable. I sense he was also distressed because

McCarthy and company *were wasting his time*, and the time of a lot of other people.

He decided at age 16 that in the game of life, "we all started equal in having 24 hours a day." Whoever used them best won. Fairbank clipped his nails during tutorials and shaved while on the telephone. A seminar that degenerated into a bull session grated on him like fingernails on a blackboard. At each session a student paper had to be read *and criticized*; no straying from the point.

As East Asian studies developed in the 1950s and 1960s, and his students began to fan out around the country, Fairbank made sure they were not wasting their time either. He waged war against something he called "manuscript retention," a post-graduate's insecure resistance to offering his work for publication. When David Roy, now professor of Chinese literature at the University of Chicago, was a "tenacious young instructor" at Princeton, Fairbank said he asked to see Roy's manuscript, then "picked it up and got out the door with it. It made a good book and helped his career."

When promising historians occasionally veered away from academia, Fairbank could be heard to complain. He was still ragging Fox Butterfield for not finishing his doctoral thesis years after Butterfield had become a distinguished foreign correspondent for the *New York Times*. But those of us who strayed knew this was mostly a joke. We extended his empire to a mass audience.

The point, he made clear, was to communicate. Stay in touch with your students, your professors, your readers, your friends, just as he did all his life. He knew the truth would never emerge unless all of us, from the humblest undergraduate to the wisest academician, took a whack at it.

## Fox Butterfield
*New York Times*

It was September 1958, the beginning of my sophomore year at Harvard, time to choose classes. A few weeks before, Mao Zedong had ordered the bombardment of Quemoy and Matsu, two small island outposts garrisoned by troops of the Chinese Nationalists on Taiwan. The "offshore islands," as they came to be called, were far from Cambridge, with its leaves changing in the autumn air and thoughts about finding a date for the football game on Saturday. But there was fear in the country that the Eisenhower administration might be drawn into war with someplace we termed Red China because of the Mutual Security Treaty between Chiang Kai-shek and Washington. So when I noticed an ad for a lecture at Adams House about the crisis, it seemed like a good idea to attend. The speakers were two Harvard professors whom I knew about only dimly: Edwin 0. Reischauer and John K. Fairbank.

Fairbank, a tall, spare man with a dry, ironic turn of phrase, told the audience that China had 800 million people and an ancient history. It was therefore a country to be taken seriously. You don't go to war with China lightly, he said.

This may not have sounded very dramatic, but as Fairbank expounded it, I began to appreciate that here was the oldest nation on earth, with the largest number of people, and I knew nothing about it. I decided to sit in on Social Sciences 111, the introductory course on the history of China and Japan that Fairbank and Reischauer had pioneered. It turned out to be the beginning of a lifelong romance. I was infatuated with China.

In the spring semester, I took what seemed to me at the time a daring step. I enrolled in a second Fairbank class, his history of modern China. I was the only undergraduate in the class; China was not yet a trendy subject, and I was often intimidated, not only by the complex material and the unpronounceable names, but by the intellectual superiority of my older classmates. That May, when final exam time came, I enclosed a stamped, self-addressed postcard with my blue test booklet, in keeping with Harvard practice, to learn my grade. The card came back with a summons to report to Fairbank's office. What had I done wrong? I wondered as I walked to Widener Library at the appointed hour.

"You wrote a wonderful exam," Fairbank said, to my relief. "Have you considered Chinese studies as a career? You ought to begin studying Chinese."

I was flattered. I didn't yet know that Fairbank, the proselytizer, tried this routine out on almost anyone eccentric enough to show an interest in his field. And so that summer I did start studying Chinese. It was still such an obscure subject that the next fall when I asked for Chinese tapes at the Harvard language laboratory the matronly-looking woman behind the desk peered at me over the top of her glasses as if I had stumbled into the wrong church. "Chinese? Chinese?" she repeated. "Isn't Chinese a dead language?"

There were other obstacles to overcome. Harvard could be a large, impersonal institution for undergraduates, with its bias for research and scholarship instead of teaching. Most professors were remote and unapproachable. But Fairbank understood the benefits of kindly nurture. And so he invited me, a mere undergraduate, to attend the Thursday afternoon teas at his yellow clapboard house on Winthrop Street. It made me feel part of the world of Chinese studies, even if I often had no idea who many of the other guests were. Fairbank would greet me at the door, take me by the arm, and rush me over to some recently arrived visiting scholar from Japan. He would make a quick introduction, mumble something about the other guest doing an important study of the tax system in the Tang dynasty, and then would cleverly vanish, to minister to his other guests. Since I didn't speak Japanese, and the visitor didn't speak much English, we would be left in awkward silence, to ponder our brownies and cucumber sandwiches. Still, I gradually came to realize that Fairbank the missionary was spreading his faith, and he would use whatever tools were helpful. Today, in that vulgar expression, we would call it networking. Fairbank understood it intuitively.

As the years passed, I remained under his spell. After graduating from Harvard, I spent a year on Taiwan as a Fulbright student studying Chinese. But when I proposed to extend my stay for a second year, Fairbank responded with a brief note explaining that the time for fun was over and I should report back immediately to graduate school at Harvard. Never mind how long he had tarried in Peking to learn Chinese.

Unlike many professors, Fairbank was always accessible, though often in surprise ways. There were the phone calls from him, usually at 7 a.m., with a suggestion about a paper. If I wanted to talk with him, he would fix a meeting at his office, say at 3 p.m. When I arrived, he would be putting on his overcoat and heading for a class or appointment somewhere else on campus. The drill was to talk while we walked. That way he not only made use of those wasted minutes walking, he insured that his supplicants had only a limited amount of time to blabber. The emperor himself could not have devised a more ingenious method.

There were also the rare and coveted invitations to visit the Fairbanks' cabin in New Hampshire for the weekend during the summer. Guests were issued a rigorous schedule. Reveille at 7, then a brisk walk for 10 minutes, followed by breakfast, half an hour of chopping wood, then a swim of perhaps 20 minutes to cool off. At certain intervals, Fairbank would announce he was retreating to his small study to read the latest dissertation. "I'll be out in 17 minutes," I recall him saying once. It was the Confucian master at work. He was obliquely imparting a lesson about efficiency and management without resorting to the crude need to explain it.

But there was still something of the mischievous American boy in him. One Saturday night after dinner he had the sudden urge to go to the movies, a considerable drive down the highway in New Hampshire. A glance at the newspaper suggested we would be late. Not so, Fairbank said. We jumped in his car and with JKF himself driving, roared down the narrow, darkened road at 75 miles an hour. Of course, we made it on time.

At the end of those weekends, I always left relieved, but also reinvigorated, knowing that there was a higher standard to aspire to.

RODERIC H. DAVISON
*George Washington University*

Graduate students in the late 1930s found a good friend in John Fairbank. He was a faculty member who would talk with you, would come up with an occasional useful bibliographic reference, would invite you to his house. Though his field was in East Asia, those who came under his influence—protégés in a sense—were from many fields. My own studies had nothing to do with East Asia, and I do not remember how I first met John Fairbank, but from 1937 to 1940 he and Wilma helped to make graduate life for me and others more enjoyable than it might otherwise have been.

One result of the friendship was my auditing informally, along with others, History 83b in the spring of 1939. It was a broadening experience. The notes proved useful in surprising ways after my own teaching career began in 1940. That year must have been toward the start of John Fairbank's own teaching career, for he was quite tentative and diffident in some of his lecturing, asking for feedback and for comments about course improvement. John wanted us to think not only about the subject matter as he presented it, but about the presentation itself.

What so many of us remember, of course, is the pleasure of a civilized tea with Wilma and John at their house. And on occasion there were musical evenings. I tried, and usually failed, to keep up with recorder playing on several occasions. And if memory serves properly, after these more than fifty years, there was occasional square-dancing in the house as well. John was the well-rounded mentor. Together with Wilma he imparted a kind of enthusiasm to academic life that was catching.

Robert Scalapino
*University of California, Berkeley*

My first contact with John was in the fall of 1946 when I had returned to Harvard after wartime service. I had completed my graduate work except for the doctoral dissertation prior to entry into the U.S. Naval Japanese language program. Like many others at Boulder, I had had no special interest in Asia before that experience. When I came back to Harvard, however, I had determined to make my career in the Asian field.

At the time, John was setting up the Center for Chinese Studies, and he wanted contact with a young political scientist. He asked me to talk with him, and subsequently I became affiliated with the Center's activities.

The opening years of the Center were characterized by the excitement of eager students—only a few of whom had had actual experience in China—discovering a new world. John himself was among the explorers—not of China, but of social science. Having been trained as a historian, he was eager (some felt overly eager) to unlock new doors to an understanding of the Central Kingdom.

Thus, we would find ourselves suddenly immersed in Talcott Parsons and sociological theory. Then, Parsons would be set on the shelf with most of us not quite certain of his utility (but not discarding him completely). We would then move on to cultural anthropology and Clyde Kluckhohn. The economists with few exceptions provided us with an example of unrequited love. They were too busy spinning mathematical equations to interest themselves in such an esoteric and irrelevant subject as China. But we pursued them relentlessly. Political science was just beginning to advance theories about "modernization" in addition to the long-standing studies of nationalism, Marxism-Leninism and international relations.

Throughout this period, the aspect of John Fairbank that most impressed me was his quizzical tolerance, verging on bemusement. He made all of us want to help him in finding new answers to old problems.

As the 1940s moved to a close and we entered the 1950s, the China field became increasingly politicized. As a Rooseveltian Democrat (coming from Kansas, then Santa Barbara, that was sufficiently radical!), I found my views compatible with those who were critical of the Chiang Kai-shek regime but not sanguine about the Chinese Communists. I had had my own conflict with young Communists in California, and I had the gravest doubts about them, whether American or Chinese. I can honestly say that I never heard John make any "pro-Communist" remark. Like many of us, he was outspoken in criticizing the manner in which the Kuomintang had operated during and after the war. Moreover, he maintained a variety of contacts with those who felt likewise, including some who were to his "left," politically. My inner feeling—then and later—

was that John was not cut out to be a political analyst or, indeed, to be involved in contemporary politics, but the John Fairbank I knew was not an ideologue.

During the 1947-1948 period, I became closely acquainted with one of Fairbank's house guests, Ch'ien Tuan-sheng from Peking University. Ch'ien had come to Harvard to teach a course on Chinese politics. I served as his teaching assistant and because he had left his family in China, we spent many hours together. He was a "Third Force" man, anti-Chiang but at the same time, having serious reservations about the Chinese Communists, regarding them as likely to be servants to Soviet doctrines and policies. I had the feeling that his views were heard by John, and were possibly persuasive, being somewhat compatible.

In later years, after I went to Berkeley, I had fleeting contact with John on numerous occasions, and I always enjoyed his wry humor, his good nature and his firm dedication to his chosen field. In addition to being a fine scholar, John was the greatest entrepreneur on behalf of China studies that the United States has had. Moreover, he had all of the qualities of an outstanding teacher, leading students to their own discoveries, and always ready to assist them long after they had left his fold. It is not easy to reproduce such a figure.

David S. Nivison*
*Stanford University*

Nine years ago I had the honor of writing for *The New York Review of Books* an article on John Fairbank's autobiography *Chinabound.* John called the book a "memoir," and the following part of my review—the part that has my heart—is itself a memoir. In February 1946, I had gotten out of the army, after three years of translating Japanese near Washington with Ed Reischauer's group. I finished undergraduate work in June, staying on in the fall at

* Portions of this memoir first appeared in *The New York Review of Books*, May 13, 1982. (Reprinted with permission from *The New York Review of Books*. Copyright © 1982 Nyrev, Inc.)

Harvard (in 1946, where else?) as a graduate student. I was in Far Eastern Languages, not History; but John Fairbank was a man to meet, and I sought an appointment with him quickly.

I wrote that I found the accounts of wartime Washington and Chungking in his book "a revelation of what was behind the face I first encountered in his office in Kirkland house. . . .Shortly afterward, I enrolled in Fairbank's seminar on Ch'ing documents. I also took the 'rice paddies' course in Far Eastern civilization given by Fairbank and Edwin O. Reischauer, and I can still repeat specimens of Fairbank's insightful wit in those lectures.

"The seminar was built around Fairbank's matchless knowledge of nineteenth-century Chinese government archives dealing with China's problems with the importunate Western merchant powers. I perversely chose an eighteenth-century topic—thereby validating a wise point made in this wise book, which is that the first focus of research, given the historian's instinct to ferret out causes rather than consequences, is likely to be as close as he ever gets to the present, at least for a very long time . . . .

". . . In consequence, I have watched most of what Fairbank has given his life to from a very respectful distance, mindful that I am watching a man who sometimes lightly remarks to friends (not in this book) that 'anything earlier than 1949 is ancient China, and anything earlier than 1840 is ancient-as-hell China.'

"Yet we share an ideal, quite simply because I was his student and that ideal stuck. There was a time when Western attention to China was schizoid; some scholars wrote or talked about modern history on the basis of a treaty-port or missionary experience, often without being able to read Chinese or knowing much about China's earlier history. Others, scholars who did possess these abilities, dealt with philological problems of the sort that often had engaged Chinese scholars for centuries, but never succeeded in writing about China as an entity that still existed. The need, of course, was to combine the virtues of the two approaches and so attain a true stereoscopic vision of China; and in doing this, to exploit all of the resources that a historian of, say, nineteenth-century Europe would expect to use in understanding an incident or a life—letters, essays, diaries, local records, state papers—in whatever language they are in. The opportunity to do this, while looking both ways, toward the present and the past, was what made the 'trade and diplomacy' of mid-nineteenth-century China fascinating to Fairbank. His students and younger associates picked up the idea and went their own ways with it.

"This meant, especially, that the historian had to put together in a way that could be seen to matter, virtually all aspects of history, always keeping in front of him how they would seem to a thinking Chinese as he was moved to act: that would be intellectual history in the fullest sense. The ideal took shape in one of Fairbank's most fruitful organizing efforts. In 1951, following a suggestion from Mortimer Graves of the American Council of Learned Societies, he began to talk with a few other scholars interested in experimenting with new approaches to the history of ideas in China.

"The result was the formation of the 'Committee on Chinese Thought,' later attached to the Association for Asian Studies. This group held five conferences of a week or more between 1952 and 1960, publishing five volumes of conference papers. The story reveals what is probably a key to Fairbank's organizing success. He did not try to do everything himself. He was able to see an important idea, find others who could see it too, nudge an enterprise into being, and then be himself simply a participant. Younger members of this group such as myself look back at our experience with a grateful sense of having been there at the beginning, when the study of Chinese intellectual history, and our own thinking about it, were transformed and enriched . . . ."

Of course there is more in my own association with John, even though my own life has followed a quite different track. I have not mentioned John's encouragement and his efforts to help me when I was young and sometimes desperate; he never forgot a student or friend, and one's focus being "ancient-as-hell China" made no difference. He sometimes visited Stanford (staying with Arthur and Mary Wright; it was Arthur who involved me in the Committee on Chinese Thought). In later years our meetings were rare: Monday morning, 5 June 1989, found me in town (for a Harvard class reunion) just after the Tiananmen massacre, and with scores of others I sought out the inevitable meeting at the Fairbank Center, chaired, of course, by John. In a crisis, everyone knew, without a word, that John was the man we needed.

We need him still. It was the last time I saw him.

Marius B. Jansen
*Princeton University*

I first met John Fairbank in the summer, I think August, of 1946. I was just out of military service, and had served for ten months on Okinawa and Japan in the Counter Intelligence Corps after having had a year's training in Japanese in the Harvard Army Specialized Training Program. I had decided to change my graduate training from Renaissance and Reformation, the field of my undergraduate specialization at Princeton, to East Asian history. When I contacted the History Department for advice on program I had been referred to Fairbank. John had recently returned to Harvard from nine months in China, where he had been director of the China division of the United States Information Service in the reorganization of the Office of War Information that followed the Japanese surrender.

Deeply concerned as he was with the deteriorating situation in China, John had immediately dug in to create a new program called "Regional Studies - China." It was not clear to me that with training in Japanese and experience in Japan I was destined to be a member of a new China program, but of course it was to John. "You have a great opportunity," he said quietly; I should bring my training to bear on the understanding of China, and I could utilize Japanese language materials for the study of China. It was my first encounter with his sense of the urgency and primacy of China study and understanding as a prerequisite to any intellectual endeavor. Other disciplines, languages, and areas were of importance chiefly for what they could contribute to the understanding of China. In later years, as my work became increasingly Japan-centered, John would reproachfully remind me of the desirability of returning to my earlier focus of Sino-Japanese relations, sometimes with an urgency so pressing that in self-defense I proposed that he in turn find meaning and application for China in the study of the Meiji Restoration.

That initial meeting was nevertheless pivotal in many ways. The Regional Studies-China seminar I joined met every Thursday morning and five days a week from 3 to 5 in a drafty room on the second floor of Boylston Hall. Many of these sessions were centered around visitors from social science disciplines who reported on their methods and approaches, followed by a discussion led by John that related this to the study of China. The intensity of this program made for a high degree of cohesion, and occasional dismay. John would try to counter this by scheduling what he called "Whither have we drifted?" sessions. The "regulars" of the Harvard Yenching program thought us somewhat odd in our contemporary focus and disciplinary ubiquity and suspected that we were not very scholarly, though of course we studied side by side in the language courses that brought us all together. John later wrote that the seminars "were a focal point where many things came together, for me at least, in an incandescence of exciting ideas," and I think that this was true for most of us much of the time. With a constituency that included Ben Schwartz, Rhoads Murphey, Bill Nelson, Carl Bartz, Bob Barzilay, Conrad Brandt, and Joseph Levenson and Marion J. Levy Jr. as auditors (although the word lacks all precision when applied to Marion), it could hardly have failed to be a lively and at times uproarious group.

Those sessions brought me into close contact with JKF as person, doer, and mentor. He was himself, as he later wrote, feeling his way, somehow combining with this schedule work on *The United States and China*, organizing with Edwin Reischauer what would become the famous "Rice Paddies" history survey, keeping close tabs on the disastrous news from China, rushing off to Washington to discuss it there, and forging the seminar program in Ch'ing documents and history that would become the staple of the future graduate program. Nothing better showed the man than the way he taught. With our first contact there began a series of notes, first scribbled and scrawled, and later dictated and typed, that combined encouragement with exhortation. Nothing, then or later, ever went unread, or failed to have his comment and suggestion. He never tried to dominate or direct; once I thought I saw something I wanted to do, whether or not it followed the lines of his preference, he was supportive, asking only that it be done well. From that Regional Studies-China seminar came early gropings toward the ties between Sun Yat-sen and his Japanese friends, soon to be published in the Regional Studies *Papers on China* and ultimately the subject of my dissertation.

It was essential for John that, in a field in which so little had been done, whatever was developed be made more widely available as soon as possible; preferably, in fact, immediately. So it was with the seminar papers that went into the mimeographed *Papers on China* series. Ten years later, when I came back to Harvard to do a summer school version of Rice Paddies, it was in relation to a program launched with the School of Education, then headed by Francis Keppel, to include a seminar for secondary teachers. John worked out the details with us, and then left us alone to put it together. Once again daily seminars led to reports that were to be "nuggets," capable of insertion in a curriculum that still had no tolerance or slack for what is now called multicultural content; within months these reports, which received their editing on a Japan-bound freighter (after which the originals were ceremoniously deposited in the Pacific), saw light of day in *Major Topics on China and Japan* edited with Harold Hinton and brought out under the imprint of the Institute of Pacific Relations. John was one of the great planners, proselytizers, and propagandists of our field.

Wilma was at all times an active partner in everything he did. The strain of daily seminars was lightened by Thursday afternoon drinks and teas at Winthrop Street, when those narrow rooms were filled with students, colleagues, and visitors from China. We became wary of having John catch us off guard and match us with an unknown dignitary with whom we might or might not share a common language, say "Marius, have you met Mr. X.?" and disappear as suddenly as he had arrived. It was another way of learning by doing.

At the end of the second year we decided we should celebrate our survival and endurance by having a party. John did not have a proper American Ph. D., we knew, having been a Rhodes Scholar at Oxford, and the thing to do was to give him a proper oral examination.

Annalee Jacoby had recently hailed his book in a front page review in the book review section of the *New York Times* that spoke in awe-struck terms of John's ability to read Chinese at a clip of forty pages an hour, and I recall that my contribution to our cleverness was to ask how long it would take to get through the thirteen classics at that speed. "Think nothing of it," John responded blandly. But a few minutes later he donned what became his famous beard and read a carefully and brilliantly prepared parody of all the afternoon seminars we had attended, combining smoothly Gorer's themes of infant toilet training, Northrup's "undifferentiated aesthetic continuum," and Karl August Wittfogel's water control in early dynastic history in a way that had us convulsed with laughter. He won, hands down, and provided one more example of the wisdom of preparation and foresight.

John found it difficult to relax, to be informal, and to be personal. There was a kind of reserve that was part shyness, part pride, part professionalism. Despite this he projected a kind of personal warmth and interest and encouragement that left no doubt of what he thought and what he hoped for all his students. We shall not see his like again.

Martha Henderson Coolidge
*Cambridge, Massachusetts*

One winter day in January 1948 I went to work for John Fairbank who was then mid-way through the second year of the initial class of the China Program. I was just turning twenty-three and a year and half out of Radcliffe. The class was virtually all made up of veterans, extraordinarily able and scarcely to be described as shrinking violets: Ben Schwartz, Marius Jansen, Rhoads Murphey, Conrad Brandt, Andy Rice (later head of the Society for International Development), Bill Nelson (subsequently rumored to be a chief spook), Bob Sheeks, who was to work all over the Pacific area, Davy McCall of the World Bank, Bob Barzilay, a *New York Times* reporter, and associates like Bud Levenson. To put it mildly, they were lively. John was not that much older, but they still treated him as their leader.

John decided I should attend the "Joint Seminar" with them. This was a joint gathering with the Russian Program in which interdisciplinary approaches were to be gained by listening to the great leaders in different social science fields—with occasional unexpected results. The day of my introduction, J. K. Galbraith's predecessor was dilating upon agricultural economics. He distinctly lacked the wit and humor of his successor. His audience drifted off until he suddenly said that if you fed a hen so many pounds of feed, it would lay so many eggs, and so many more pounds, so many more eggs, etc. The entire group got the giggles. I remember having my head under a table with Bill Nelson laughing until we were weak, only to be undone again upon poking my head up and discovering Ben chortling. John, meantime, sat in the front chewing chiclets with a singular expression of Mandarin calm fixed on his face.

A little later we almost managed to shatter that equanimity. This time the lecture was on political science by a distinguished German professor in our midst. On his left, flanking me, sat two foreign service officers assigned to Harvard for a year: Dave Osborn, who ended his career as Consul General in Hong Kong, and Ed Seidensticker, whose career ended far more quickly when he taught the Japanese secretaries dubious language and retired to life as a professor and famous translator of Japanese novels.

The lecture was extremely serious. Bureaucracy was explored at some length. Ed drew a picture of a mule all tied down with a network of ropes. When we progressed to charisma, Ed drew a dreadful mask with its mouth turned down. By this time Dave, Ed and I were unable to suppress our laughter. Seated opposite us, John's face recorded two looks. One said, "Will you please stop behaving like high school students," the other, "What's the joke?" When the lecture ended, without consultation we all rushed over and showed him Ed's pictures since we knew he'd laugh. He did.

The class soon realized I made a safe go-between. They would tell me their problems with the program and I would recount to John. "Strong character or weak one?" he'd inquire. Since they were about 95% strong, that answer was easy.

His comments enlivened the scene. Clyde Kluckhohn was head of the Russian Program. When I asked why a Navajo expert took this role, John said, "Scratch an Indian and you'll find a Red." One student presented his M. A. thesis complete with gold paper and tassles. "Prose or poetry?" John queried innocently.

These were the happy months before McCarthy gouged into the scene. I think all of us remember them with a kind of glow.

In the mid-fifties John and Ed Reischauer supported my application for the M. A. Program. Since I had by then held administrative and research jobs concerning both China and Japan, with China closed, I decided to work with Ed and pressed on for a while toward my Ph. D. Although I took courses on China, I did not study with John, who was struggling to keep the China field afloat. I was also under stress, and we did not fare well together. Our paths diverged, and it was to be many years later, when John had become the paramount leader of the modern China field and was close to his retirement, that we finally unscrambled our difficulties and returned to our earlier harmonious relationship.

Sometime after my husband's death in 1985 I heard about John's biography of the distinguished historian, Hosea Ballou Morse, of the China Maritime Customs Service, and offered a few suggestions. Eventually John asked me to help with it, and my work resulted in his inviting me to coauthor the biography. It is the one book he did not have time to finish, but its completion has been arranged, with Professor Richard J. Smith of Rice University serving as editor. He collaborated with John earlier on two Hart volumes.

The past two or three years working with John have been busy and productive although his health became increasingly complicated. By leading a highly disciplined life of work, walks and frequent rests, both in Cambridge and his beloved Franklin, New Hampshire, he put the finishing touches on the final Hart volume and on his editing of vol. 15 of the *Cambridge History of China*. His chief effort was to conceive and finish his *China: A New History* for which he accomplished an enormous amount of reading, adapted many solicited commentaries and revised a troublesome chapter the week he died, seemingly holding death at bay by sheer will power. For me, a time with the Morse book of rediscovering the pleasures of research and writing became at John's request deflected into helping with the PRC section of the bibliography for the *New History*. Having gone full circle, in these years I found again the joy and laughter of associating with John. His death leaves a great gap.

DONALD B. COLE
*Phillips Exeter Academy*

John King Fairbank was an imposing figure even then—certainly through the eyes of a new graduate student, enrolled in History 83b to uncover the mysteries of China and Japan. As John Fairbank wove his magic that winter in 1947, the young student learned that East Asia was not so mysterious after all and that his professor could cut through the mists of the past as no one he had ever heard before. He also learned that the imposing professor was a man of uncommon kindness and rare common sense, who made even a new graduate student feel comfortable. This was never more apparent than when the student naively asked why his professor had not included some history of India in the course, to which he replied, "Because I don't know anything about India."

Unlike many of those who are writing remembrances, I did not follow John Fairbank into the mysteries of China, but pursued instead a doctorate in American history. Our lives, however, continued to intersect, because I chose modern China as a related field of study and also because we shared a common affection for John's old school, where I taught, Phillips Exeter.

In my own teaching, I tried to put to work what I had learned from John. He had based his lectures on a solid foundation of fact, often calling our attention to the assumptions surrounding the facts. In the opening lecture he had held the assumptions of American policy in East Asia up against the revolutionary and nationalistic assumptions of the Chinese and Japanese, suggesting at the end the problems and opportunities the mix could produce. To make sure that the facts were clear, John handed out meticulously organized lists of names and events. He also made us prepare maps, and went to the trouble of placing model maps under glass in the library for our guidance. Throughout the course, his wit and dry humor—which I could never match—brought out the ironies of history. Most important, he gave life to the subject and assumed that we loved it and believed in its importance as much as he did.

In preparing for my oral examination, I had the good fortune to have John as my mentor in a reading course on China. The names of books that he had me read, such as Morse's *International Relations of the Chinese Empire* and Wright's *Hart and the Chinese Customs*, still bring back memories of China. They also bring back memories of John—in his forties at the time and as imposing as ever—occasionally striding into his office in his riding boots.

On my oral examination he was characteristically kind yet demanding. Observing that a lamp was shining in my eyes, he carefully adjusted it. Then he asked me to offer some broad question of my own about modern China and give an answer. It required more thought than the more direct questions coming from the other examiners, but I felt more comfortable answering it. When Samuel Eliot Morison asked me why a conservative like George Washington had become a revolutionary, John gave me a breathing spell by getting into a discussion with Mason Hammond on ways in which the question applied to Chinese and Roman history.

During his several visits to Exeter over the years, I caught more glimpses of John's teaching skill and his humanity. Once when I was late for a class on Chinese history that John was visiting, I arrived to find the old master standing at a map and delighting my students with tales about the Taipings. In another class I watched a group of my students sit entranced while John talked informally with them about China. Several of them went on to study China in college the next year. When John spoke before a large audience about the Vietnam War, his observations on American policy reminded me of that first time I had heard him—in History 83b—commenting on an earlier crisis in American policy toward Asia. The wit, the irony, and the clear sense of history were the same as always.

John was at his best on that happy occasion when Exeter honored him with the John Phillips Award, given annually to a graduate who had performed great public service. In his gracious acceptance he said that he had never missed an opportunity to give a sales pitch on the importance of East Asia, and proceeded to keep his record intact.

When John finally relinquished his office in Widener, he gave many of his books to Exeter. On visiting the academy soon afterwards, he spent part of an afternoon roaming through the library stacks, noting with approval how his books had filled gaps in the holdings on China. He was pleased, I think, that young students would continue to use them.

As I drove him back to his summer home in Franklin after one of his last visits, John showed his down-to-earth delight in the glories of an early spring day in New Hampshire, but when he arrived he said that he must go indoors, for he had work to do. It was typical of this humane scholar that he worked down to the very end.

## Ellsworth C. Carlson
*Oberlin, Ohio*

John was great in so many ways that I shall limit my account to one aspect of the man. I shall let others speak to his scholarship, his teaching, and the wisdom of his pronouncements on the issues of the day.

Personal experiences lead me to speak of John's great personal sensitivity and generosity. I look back with gratitude to an incident in my second year as a graduate student at Harvard. I was enrolled in the Ch'ing documents course. Not feeling well, I went to the Harvard student health offices to see what the doctors there could do for me. The doctor who helped me pronounced that he thought that my trouble was simply that I was very tired. The next day I was working in the Regional Studies reading room in Boylston Hall, and John came into the room and spoke to me. He said, "Ells, you look very tired. Your oral report in the documents course was fine. Don't bother to write it up."

A year later I was working on my dissertation. On encountering John in Harvard Square, I asked whether he had had a chance to look at the last chapters I had left at his office. The response was that he had and that we should talk about them. He went on to say, "Wilma is away. Why don't I buy some ice cream and come to your place for dinner tonight." He came and gave us a very happy evening. Imagine the distinguished John Fairbank coming to my humble abode!

Preparing me for my faculty career at Oberlin was not the end of the story. At times when I was discouraged he offered encouragement and support.

I shall never forget my great debt to John Fairbank.

LEA E. WILLIAMS
*Brown University*

The admiration, gratitude and friendship felt for John Fairbank over almost half a century—since our paths first touched in China near the end of the second world war—can but be briefly suggested here. Perhaps recalling a few episodes, randomly chosen but typical of the man, will help bring out his character and his qualities.

Our academic relationship began in 1950 when my wife and I were invited to breakfast at 41 Winthrop Street upon our arrival in Cambridge. It was a gracious introduction to graduate student life, one that in my naiveté then I took as routine but now I recognize as quite special. Later, my move into the study of the overseas Chinese was made possible by being put in touch by Professor Fairbank with the right people—those with research grants to distribute. That single act of thoughtfulness has shaped my career ever since.

Further support was never absent at critical points. Once, quite awed, I found myself the lone student in a seminar involved with the reading and analysis of documentary Chinese from the last dynasty. When Professor Fairbank was the only person to join me in the room the first day of the seminar, out of politeness and apprehension, I suggested that the whole undertaking be postponed. "No, the seminar is offered and you've signed up for it," was the reply. Never have I worked so hard and never have I learned so much. At the end of the term turning in a paper of dubious merit, I feared the worst; but a top grade was awarded with the straight-faced explanation that mine was the best piece of work submitted that year.

A far more meaningful illustration of Professor Fairbank's sustaining students in the graduate school jungle involved a fellow student who for obvious reasons must be anonymous here. Confused by an intimidating environment and unfamiliar with the routines and pressures of his new life, the young man did not do well in his studies in his first year. Accordingly, he was advised to reconsider his plans with a view to withdrawing from the program. The suggestion, thoroughly justified though it seemed at the time, was ignored or, more accurately, overcome. The student went on to earn an enviable record and qualify for a doctorate. At that point, Professor Fairbank wrote him a sincere apology for the earlier, negative assessment and wished him success in his future career, which has been brilliant. It is a sad truth that not many eminent, very busy top figures in the academic profession would take time for such a gracious gesture and, even sadder, fewer still would acknowledge a previous error of judgment.

A further incident, one selected out of many, can be recalled in conclusion. In my first year of teaching, my then departmental chairman asked me to recruit a China specialist to give a public lecture, adding that Professor Fairbank would be a good choice. That was fine, except that the honorarium proposed would have been laughable had it not been insulting. Untenured and habitually insecure, I had to send an invitation up to Cambridge. I mentioned that there might not be departmental funds available for a proper lecture fee but a round-trip train would be covered. A letter of acceptance came almost by return mail. The lecture was of course a great success and, some years later, I confessed that I had decided to offer nothing rather than risk great embarrassment. Professor Fairbank replied that he had suspected the truth and reassured me that I had done the right thing.

It ought to be kept in mind that the events presented here for the most part took place early in the decade of the fifties, a time of obscene political persecution in this country when Professor Fairbank was one of the many victims. The brutal pressures under which he then operated were never permitted to interfere with the concerned and conscientious guidance of his students. More than anything else, his grace under attack revealed his stature.

It may have seemed odd that throughout these recollections, I have referred to Professor Fairbank with precisely those words rather than with less formal language. Through nearly fifty years, that was how I addressed him and there is no wish to change now. As May Sarton once observed, no matter how old one becomes there is always an urge to stand when one's honored and admired former teacher enters the room. I continue here to stand in grateful salute.

MERLE GOLDMAN
*Boston University*

John Fairbank was not only a teacher, scholar, founder of the field of modern Chinese studies and public policy spokesman, he was also a great mentor.

In the days before women's liberation he unfailingly encouraged me in a career that encountered daunting obstacles. In 1953, I was to enter the M. A. program in Chinese studies at Harvard of which he was the director. But my husband Marshall was drafted and as a dutiful wife I accompanied him to an army base in Texas. Even though John had met me for the first time when I told him about my withdrawal, he urged me to continue my studies and gave me a list of books to read and critique while in Texas. Once a month I sent him a critique and shortly thereafter I invariably received a response along with words of encouragement.

When we returned to Harvard in 1955, I was pregnant with my first child and once more feared an end to my plans for a career. Again John came up with a solution. He negotiated with the Harvard-Radcliffe bureaucracy so that I became the first graduate student to be able to go part-time. Even though I was to have three more children before I received my Ph. D., John never questioned my commitment or treated me any differently from my male colleagues. When I gave him a chapter of my thesis, I received a response either that night or the next day, followed a few days later by a note telling me how much he was looking forward to the next chapter.

Even when I finally became a professor, he continued to provide support. Whether I published a short article or a book, I would receive a phone call from him, usually at 7 a.m. on a Sunday morning, to express his congratulations. We did not always agree and my work on the role of the intellectuals in Chinese Communist history was not close to his area of research, but that never diminished his interest in and encouragement of my work.

It is said that women of my generation had difficulty in pursuing successful careers because they were unable to establish a mentor relationship with their male professorial advisers. My experience with John Fairbank was just the opposite and one for which I will be forever grateful.

LLOYD E. EASTMAN
*University of Illinois*

For us students, a major part of Fairbank's universe was his study on the fourth floor of Widener Library. There the window faced out onto Mass. Avenue. The walls on three sides were lined with books; his desk sat kitty-corner near the window and faced a low couch against the opposite wall. This was the couch on which he took his famously regular naps. At the other end of the room was the seminar table, large enough for eight people to sit around. We students usually had our private conferences with Fairbank at his desk. During our talks, John sometimes had his feet up on the desk; frequently he whisked his jaw with an electric razor; and sometimes he snacked on a chocolate candy bar spread in front of him. The impression this imparted was of a man enormously busy, for whom every moment counted. I tried not to waste his time.

It was at the table in the study that we studied Ch'ing documents. John reveled in Ch'ing documents. In seminars, we pored over those documents, reading two or three lines at a time explicating every phrase, character, and signpost. And, as often happened, when we encountered some example of a Ch'ing official's bureaucratic obtuseness, or distinctively Chinese sense of superiority over the foreign barbarian, John would roar with laughter. Ch'ing documents for him, and thus for us students, were not merely a means of studying Chinese institutions. They were also a window to a whole other world that was vibrant with human idiosyncrasies and with ways of looking at the world that were distinctive of Chinese officials in the late nineteenth century. After graduation, some of us returned to Cambridge during the summers to do research, and John so enjoyed reading Ch'ing documents that he organized weekly sessions during which we devoted an entire evening or large part of a summer afternoon to *explication de texte*. Ch'ing documents were fun, for him and for us.

John was more than generous with the books in his study. We were given access to a key, and could pursue our research there. Pinned by the door was a note, in typical Fairbankian idiom, slightly oblique and tinged with humor: "People Sometimes, Books Never." I was never sure precisely what that meant, but I think I got the message.

I had not yet come to Harvard during the McCarthy era of the early 1950s, but I came to see how John had been seared by the political flames of that period. One time in about 1963 I showed him a book I had just purchased (it was, I think, *The Red China Lobby in American Politics*), which renewed the McCarthyite attacks on "liberals" like John. He looked at the book briefly, and, with tears welling in his eyes, said, "Are they going to start that again?" On another occasion, he encouraged me to keep a journal so that I would have a record of everything that I did—and why I did it. Memory fades quickly, he warned, and such a record of acts and motives would be of incalculable value should I ever need to defend my actions. He obviously wished that he had had such an *aide memoire* during his appearances before the Senate Internal Security Subcommittee.

My relationship with Fairbank evolved over the years. While I was a student, he was like a Chinese father: supportive, but remote. He signed his communications to me "JKF." After I received the Ph. D., he signed himself "John," and treated me more as a somewhat distant friend and fellow professional than as a student. We became very close only during the last year of his life. In December 1990, I became seriously ill, and he was the first person to call me at the Mayo Clinic. He was seriously ill at the time, too, and this created between us, he remarked, a special bond of interest. Thereafter, he and I telephoned each other every week or two. We talked about everything: China, of course; the progress of the book manuscript he was then completing; gossip about people in the field; and some very personal things. He seemed to enjoy these conversations which in earlier days I would have avoided, fearing that he would think he was wasting time. I was pleased when he wrote me that these conversations were a "boon" to him. We talked to each other only two days before his final heart attack. By that time we had moved well beyond the teacher-student relationship although I would and could never forget that he was My Teacher, My Mentor, My Role Model.

John's influence on me was, however, only slightly in the realm of ideas. I did, it is true, write my dissertation on the Sino-French War of the 1880s because of him. I had wanted to write the dissertation on the Republican period, but he had other ideas. Each time I mentioned a possible topic, he claimed to foresee some difficulties, suggesting: "Why don't you work on the Sino-French War?" I had written a seminar paper on Chinese nationalism during the Sino-French War, and he saw this as a period woefully neglected. Eventually, because time was awasting, I gave up and accepted his suggestion. I guess it was in some such manner that he filled the cracks and crannies of the history of modern China.

Years later, after having read his *Chinabound*, I realized that my sometimes critical views of the Chinese Nationalists were very close to his. I am sure that party historians in Taiwan would say this coincidence of views was because I was Fairbank's *ti-tzu*, or disciple. In fact, my work on the Nationalists originated and developed entirely independently of John. We never talked or corresponded about my work, and it was only once or twice after I had published a book on the subject that he wrote applauding my efforts. Clearly John's profound influence on me lay elsewhere.

I once wrote in the inscription to one of my books which I sent him (I do not remember the precise words): "With your dedication to the study of China, your generosity in helping others, your political objectivity, and your sense of humor, you have provided me with an ideal, which I could never hope to attain, but that has been an inspiration to me always."

John Fairbank was a *chün-tzu*. Therein lay the source of his influence.

YING-WAN CHENG
*Sayville, New York*

Mr. Fairbank was the last in a series of wonderful teachers I was fortunate enough to have in my life and the one who helped to shape my career. Having spent seven years in England and a year of internship at Vassar, I returned to Radcliffe to work on the dissertation. At the time, Mr. Fairbank had just organized the Chinese Political and Economic Studies Project at Harvard and my application for a position was accepted. I was assigned to translate a volume of a work on Ch'ing economy, while my friend E-tu Zen Sun was to translate another volume of the same work. It was most thoughtful of Mr. Fairbank to arrange things so, as E-tu was more experienced in the field. My switch from European and English to Chinese history was greatly facilitated by working on the research project.

It was Mr. Fairbank who got me interested in Robert Hart and helped me choose my dissertation topic. He let me use the Chinese Postal Atlas in his office in order to trace the routes of the I-chan, the old postal system. Weeks were spent locating stations and substations. Sometimes Mr. Fairbank also worked in his office, but I can't remember that we ever talked to each other while we worked. In spite of his busy schedule, he was always available for consultation and advice. I was particularly touched by his response to seeing the first chapter of my thesis. His face lit up and he said in Chinese: "*Hsieh ch'u-lai-le*" (You have written it!).

There is no need for me to elaborate here on Mr. Fairbank's many qualities as a scholar, teacher, and friend and his enormous achievements in developing the study of modern China, placing it always in its historical context. I would like to mention, nevertheless, one incident which left a deep impression. Many years ago when, in a casual encounter, I presented to Mr. Fairbank a friend of mine in Chinese history, Mr. Fairbank asked me to repeat his name and write down the characters. Attention to details as well as to larger issues probably constitutes one of the ingredients in the making of a great man. So many of us owe so much to this one person; we can see him no longer, but I feel he will continue to inspire us to greater endeavors and to pass on the benefits we have received to others.

ROBERT L. IRICK
*Taipei, Taiwan*

Perhaps it was my many years in Taiwan, but I believe it was due more to the stature of the man than anything else that I could never call him "John," as so many of my colleagues did. He was always "Professor Fairbank."

One of my earliest recollections is of his habit of getting me out of bed at 7 in the morning to suggest another research topic involving the missionary movement in China. I stuck to my guns and remained determined to study Sino-American relations. I recall him accusing me at one point of really wanting to rewrite Morse. His accusation of course was without basis. I'm sure he realized this when he discovered how hard it was to get me to do the simplest of revisions on my thesis on the coolie trade so that it could be brought into print.

I've heard many tales of how Professor Fairbank extracted theses from procrastinating students, including the use of threats and other stratagems. I believe he had an uncanny ability to analyze the temperaments of his various wards. In my case, he never resorted to threats because I think he realized it would have the opposite result. As some of my friends know, I spent three years on a Fulbright in Taipei, went back to Harvard for a year, and wanted to return to Taipei so much that, with the help of Professor Fairbank, Mary Wright, Knight Biggerstaff, and several others, I founded the Chinese Materials and Research Aids Service Center in that city. I brought my research notes back with me to Taipei, determined to spend my evenings working on the remaining three chapters of the thesis. After a couple of years, when I still hadn't finished, I started getting those notes from Professor Fairbank telling me how he would wait for the postman to see if he had brought the Irick thesis, or would watch the postman trudging up the walk covered with snow and wonder if he had the Irick thesis.

The few times I saw Professor Fairbank in Taipei after I left Harvard, he never failed to remind me that I should be keeping notes, because they were the materials for future books. I could never bring myself to do it, and I greatly regret it now.

One of my most treasured memories is of my graduation day. I had finally finished my thesis, but had had heart failure a month later. I was able to leave the hospital accompanied by my friend and partner, Larry Huang, to make the trip back to Cambridge to receive the degree. Professor Fairbank spent the whole day with me, taking me to the clinic for a blood pressure test, etc. I will never forget his concern.

Professor Fairbank, for all his love of China, ended up being attacked on both sides of the Taiwan Straits. I always found that difficult to understand. In all of my contacts with him, he never tried to influence me politically. I believe to this day that he was not so much concerned with politics as with wanting the best for the Chinese people.

FRANK H. H. KING
*University of Hong Kong*

In 1952 I had unwisely accepted a University of Hong Kong lectureship in economics, a tenured post, before I had a doctorate. This was still possible in the British system, and it proved a deadly temptation. John Fairbank was at the time visiting a fellow Rhodes scholar, Sir Lindsay Ride, the Vice-Chancellor of the University, and understood my dilemma. Soon after his departure I received a cryptic note which ran something like this: At Harvard we are interested in China. Are you?

I frankly didn't know what to make of this but kept it in the hope of someday breaking the code. Indeed, I showed it some months later to a wandering scholar who said in effect: it means Fairbank is offering you a position in the Chinese Studies center. Somewhat skeptical I nevertheless wrote saying that despite a youthful resolve never to live east of the Mississippi, I would be delighted to come to Harvard and I enclosed a full application. This time the reply was detailed and no doubt legally correct. I gave up all plans to build a home in the New Territories and set sail back to America.

My task as a research associate was to (1) learn Chinese and (2) write a history of the Ch'ing monetary system. I never seemed quite to grasp the first, although Fairbank was patient and we used to read over the relevant documents together. My instructor said I was doing well for one of my advanced years—I was not yet 30—and I did learn how to assess and make use of the documents in analysis—which was, of course, Fairbank's making over of me from a monetary specialist to a monetary and banking historian. I had the key to his room in Widener Library and could use it even in normally prohibited hours, that is when he was present, provided I did not speak to him—I was especially forbidden to say, "Good morning." If I had said, "Have a good day," I think he would (quite rightly) have asked me to leave the university. On occasion he would himself break the silence and call me over to check my progress, and those were inspiring moments.

At this point I found myself unable to afford to be a Harvard graduate student and consequently I applied to Oxford, requesting permission to do the first year in absentia. This I was to learn was unprecedented, but the Oxford faculty, realizing Fairbank was an Oxford man, simply appointed him my supervisor (without asking, of course) and he was too amused to refuse. I think he was entitled to a fee of about twenty pounds sterling. Executors take note—as far as I know he never made any claim; it may be owing yet.

Fairbank's contribution to my career and I am sure those of many others was not subject to temporal change. He taught by example the principles of integrity—even if this at times became precision in a romanization alas now dying. But precision in documentation, care and concern with interpretation, understanding of the period and people—if I have become a historian (even a hyphenated one) it is because of this instruction.

That is why I have remembered with amusement the protests of an old-style Sinologue: "I tried to tell Professor Fairbank that it took a lifetime with the classics before you could write anything about China. And do you know what he replied? He said, 'Not at all. Suppose my student is concerned with naval history, he just learns the character for ship and then searches it out in the collections. Quite simple, really.'" Those who remember the Ch'ing documents seminar will detect a slight touch of humor in what was then a rather serious battle among China scholars. Indeed, his continued interest in my work despite my own negligible knowledge of the Chinese language was an exception and a witness of his tolerance.

And I suppose that it was this tolerance, his scholarship, his sensitivity, and his integrity which made the mindless criticisms of Fairbank in the "concerned scholar" period so intolerable. He stood erect at meetings, made sensible proposals, and was abused. His ability to withstand this from Right and Left was both a factor in and a witness to his greatness.

MARTINA DEUCHLER
*University of London*

Each of JKF's former students may have different reasons for remembering the great master, but I think I have a very special one. It is no exaggeration when I claim that no teacher, or for that matter no other person, has had a more decisive influence on my professional, and by extension private, life than JKF. He guided me at every crucial juncture of my career, and he guided me well.

I first met JKF at the annual conference of the Junior Sinologues at Leiden in the early summer of 1955, when I was an undergraduate student in Chinese at the University of Leiden. John gave an enthusiastic talk on developments in Chinese studies at Harvard, and afterwards I mustered the courage to approach him to ask about the possibilities of studying there. He encouraged me to apply, on the completion of my Leiden B. A., for graduate studies at Radcliffe, and this I did. Through John's good offices, I received scholarship aid from Radcliffe and in the fall of 1959 enrolled in the Regional Studies - East Asia program at Harvard. For someone coming from a small European country, this was indeed a big step into a new world.

John's seminar on Ch'ing documents was my first introduction to Chinese studies at Harvard—an initiation I survived only because John gave me credit for my command of classical Chinese that surpassed my ability to write intelligible English. A memorable event (documented in a well-known photograph) was the visit of Mary Wright of Yale to one of these seminars.

John was a demanding teacher, but at the same time a compassionate and caring adviser. He was always ready to meet his students, and he was quick with writing recommendations. I remember with particular fondness the Thursday afternoons when his house on Winthrop Street was open to anyone who wanted to see him on scholarly matters or just for a chat over a cup of tea with a brownie in hand. John had a phenomenal memory for names and facts which enabled him to pick up a conversation where it had been left off earlier. He also took delight in introducing people to each other and finding common ground, whether for lighthearted talk or serious discussion.

When the time came to think about a topic for my doctoral dissertation, it was John who suggested a study of the opening of the Korean ports to Western traders—a topic that, in contrast to the opening of the Chinese ports, had not yet attracted scholarly attention. At first I was reluctant to take on this assignment because I knew nothing about Korea. It was perhaps partly my admiration for John's work on the Chinese ports, and partly the exciting prospect of exploring an as yet completely uncharted field of historical research that eventually persuaded me to begin working on Korea. John had unwittingly launched me on a track that led to another decisive turning-point in my life: my involvement with Korea.

After completing my Ph. D. with a dissertation on the opening of Korea, 1875-1885, on John's recommendation, I went to Korea to continue my research on the country's late nineteenth-century diplomatic history. Under John's long-distance guidance, I searched through Seoul's archives and libraries for two years and eventually collected enough additional data to expand my dissertation into a publishable monograph.

I achieved what I had set out to do, but during my stay in Korea I lost some of my enthusiasm for diplomatic history. I think John understood that I was completely fascinated by Korean life, and my decision to switch to Korean social history did not come as a surprise to him. Korea in the late 1960s, just before its rapid economic take-off, was a veritable treasure house of old traditions and customs. I started to collect written and oral materials on Korean traditional life and Choson dynasty history. John and Wilma visited Korea in the summer of 1978, and we spent a delightful couple of days driving through the countryside and taking a dip in the Yellow Sea. John was especially interested in the rapid transformation of Korean agriculture, while Wilma tried to peek into every courtyard we passed.

The switch to Korea was accomplished, but whenever I passed through Cambridge or spent a few days in the Harvard-Yenching Library, I visited John and Wilma. It would have been unthinkable to leave Cambridge without looking them up. Both always took a lively interest in my teaching of Korean history, first in Zurich and later in London. John was a Corresponding Member of the School of Oriental and African Studies—a fact that seemed to keep us in close touch.

The most appreciated legacy of John's teaching and scholarship in my own work was the broadness of his intellectual approach to East Asia. John was not a parochial thinker, concentrating on China alone. Rather, he appreciated the historical interconnectedness of the whole region. This was for me an insight of enduring value and a constant stimulation.

JOHN ISRAEL
*University of Virginia*

In 1954, as I entered my senior year at the University of Wisconsin, I began to explore ways of pursuing my interests in history after graduation. Hearing that the Ford Foundation might underwrite a pursuit of one or more advanced degrees in the field of modern China, I went to see Eugene Boardman, a kindly soul with whom I had taken a year-long course in the History of the Far East. "Where should I apply?" I asked.

"Harvard," he replied.

"Why Harvard?"

"Because that's where John Fairbank is."

"Who is John Fairbank?"

With his letter of recommendation, Boardman took the first step toward dispelling my monumental ignorance.

Getting into Harvard had been easy. Finding out who John Fairbank was proved more difficult. During my first year in Regional Studies, I sat in on Fairbank's famous "Rice Paddies" course, and I still recall his monotone voice accompanying the lantern slide of the bearded old men stooping over a microphone: "The New Life Movement. Next . . . ." But I was so preoccupied with first-year Chinese (taught by the unlikely troika of Rulan Pian, Francis Cleaves, and Yang Lien-sheng) that I recall little else about Fairbank beyond this display of understated wit.

In the spring of my second year, while writing a paper for Fairbank's Regional Studies seminar I quickly discovered that the best way to extend a tightly scheduled appointment with the great man was to get myself scheduled for the final ten minutes in his Thursday afternoon office hours so that we could continue our discussion en route to his weekly tea party.

During the last session of the seminar, Fairbank Remotus suddenly became Fairbank Ludens, presenting a hilarious spoof on our collective efforts entitled "Nietzsche-Nietzsche and His Student Movements." Opening with "Nietzsche-Nietzsche began to have movements at an early age," Fairbank continued his slapstick presentation during which he pulled a half-eaten sandwich and a banana from an unwieldy stack of notes.

Fairbank encouraged my continued interest in Chinese student movements, but I assumed that Ben Schwartz, with his expertise in Chinese Communism, would direct my doctoral dissertation, innocently taking Fairbank's domain to be limited to the nineteenth century. At Fairbank's behest, however, I submitted chapters to him as well. Each of these was returned within 48 hours with marginal annotations and a page or two of single-spaced typed comments. Somewhere in the process I realized that I was writing the dissertation under Fairbank.

By 1963, as I embarked on my first teaching job, fortified with duplicates of a hundred or so of Fairbank's lantern slides and page proofs of *East Asia: The Modern Transformation*, I was aware of the enormous debt I owed to my teacher, whom I respectfully called "Professor Fairbank." Of my contemporaries, I think that only Mark Mancall was intrepid enough to call him "John" before leaving Harvard.

I am not sure when I finally summoned up the courage to call John "John"—but it was sometime after I realized that I was splicing my lectures with bits and pieces of dry Fairbankian humor including, no doubt, "The New Life Movement. Next . . . ."

Every time I saw John over the years he was working on something. In 1960 while I was studying Chinese and collecting dissertation materials in Taipei, he came to visit, armed with a self-taught Russian syllabus to absorb leisure moments during his travels. In the early 1980s, when we invited John and Wilma to come to Charlottesville to relax after a Washington convention, he arranged to speak to the local chapter of the Council on Foreign Relations while he was here. The first thing he did once he and Wilma had settled into their hotel room was to ask for completed portions of my manuscript on Southwest Associated University (Lianda), 1937-1946. Before he left, he gave me a detailed critique.

John kept a hand in all my work, as he did with that of his other students, but none more so than my longtime-a-borning project on Lianda, on which I focused on and off from 1973 to 1991. The Lianda years in Kunming represented a high point of Chinese liberal education, a cause in which John had something of a missionary interest. He knew many of the faculty from his Qinghua days, and he and Wilma had done what they could to keep them physically and spiritually alive during the arduous years of wartime exile in southwest China. When I went to Beijing to pursue my work in 1980, John armed me with introductions to his old friends Jin Yuelin, Qian Duansheng, and Chen Daisun. I continued research in Kunming where, I was amazed to discover, a younger generation of historians had read a "restricted circulation" translation of the third edition of *The United States and China* and were warmly receptive to Fairbank's message: Not even Mao Zedong could break the stranglehold of Chinese tradition.

As my Lianda project stretched into its second decade, John alternately cajoled and encouraged me, invariably employing the right tactic at the right moment. As Mary and I prepared for a visit to the Fairbanks' New Hampshire dacha in August 1989, I feverishly finished a series of chapters over which I had procrastinated for years so that I would have a tributary offering to present upon arrival. Our brief visit was a Fairbank-style work holiday. I went through his archives looking for materials on wartime Kunming, he appraised my chapters, and Mary and I read Wilma's manuscript on Liang Sicheng and Lin Huiyin.

When I finally finished the manuscript in May 1991, two days before departing for China on a new research project, John gave me the green light to submit it to Harvard's Council on East Asian Studies. One of the reader reports, a generous appraisal mailed two weeks after John's death, bore his unmistakable imprimatur. He did not live to see the book, but he spent countless hours of his later years making sure there would be a book. Without my mentor and friend looking over my shoulder, God knows when I would have finished. Even now, as I prepare the manuscript for publication, I can feel his presence.

JAMES C. THOMSON, JR.
*Boston University*

I first heard of John Fairbank when I was a 17-year-old wandering with a friend through West China. It was January of 1949, and someone in a dreary Chengdu hostel had given me a copy of *The United States and China*, just out. In the next two months, as we struggled to get eastward to Canton—by truck, postal bus, long-distance rickshaw, and even bits of railroad—I buried myself in that book. I was desperate to understand what it was all about, this revolutionary convulsion that had ousted us that winter from my parents' Nanjing University home. Fairbank's book produced for me illumination, and I resolved then and there to study with the man.

It took me six years to get from China to Harvard—four at Yale, and two in Cambridge, England—but I never lost the resolve. Actually, it almost vanished in September 1955, during my Regional Studies Committee interview, when Francis Woodman Cleaves tried icily to prove my illiteracy in Chinese by shoving a piece of text in front of me to read out loud. But the tall, bespectacled and balding chairman ("Fairbank," he had said, as he shook my hand) quickly seized the text before I could show my total ignorance, and then assured Cleaves that he would "work things out" with the candidate. I had found, it seemed, a protector.

To those many of us who have known it, the mysteries of a Fairbank protectorship require little explanation—only breathless and sometimes hilarious exchanges about recent episodes. To those who have not known it, the subject is almost unfathomable. Each case was exquisitely different, with the master bringing to bear on the protégé the appropriate means from his limitless arsenal of techniques to induce production. Many would-be students of Communist China he cajoled far back into Qing dynasty studies. Many who came only for the M. A. he deftly seduced into that long and dry trek, the Ph. D. in one thing or another, with China at the center. He was not actually a bully; rather, he saw in his mind's eye what you *ought* to want to do, sometimes better than you did, and eased you onto that track. Research and publication were the highest goals. But those who had a yen and talent for journalism, foundationing, deanships, or government service he not only forgave but wholeheartedly supported. To understand China—his consuming passion, and a mammoth undertaking—would require, he knew, all sorts of well-trained people strategically positioned throughout the nation and overseas. Thus the creation, incrementally, of his dominion.

No single case proves anything much. But here, nonetheless, is mine.

Fairbank knew about my China missionary childhood and all that—especially, as he would tell audiences in later years, that I had been "fondled" on the lap of our Nanjing next door neighbor, Pearl Buck. He also knew that I was originally headed for the Foreign Service and wanted a quick M. A., having tired of endless schooling. But he soon learned two important things: that I was involved in the out-of-office Democrats through the former Connecticut governor and ambassador to India, Chester Bowles; and that I was courting a young and beautiful Cambridge poet named Diana Butler.

As it turned out, those were the only two things Fairbank needed to know in quietly shaping a definitive part of my career. When Bowles beckoned for the Stevenson presidential campaign of 1956, Fairbank let me go on leave, then welcomed me back (after the Democratic disaster) to complete the M. A.—"and why not, while you're at it, get the course work done for the doctorate?" When the Foreign Service beckoned, Fairbank found Diana at a dinner party, bluntly informed her that she and he had a common interest in "keeping Jim Thomson in Cambridge"—and said to me, after they had arranged things, "so why not get the Ph. D. orals out of the way?" Then when Bowles summoned again, newly elected to the House of

Representatives, Fairbank got the Congressman to urge that I stay another year at Harvard to do the first draft of a thesis. So it went: the protector conspiring quite shamelessly behind the back of the protégé.

I have few regrets about the course he shaped for me in those years. I went to Washington in 1960 (now married to Diana) with his hearty blessing—to work with Bowles in the Kennedy campaign and administration. And six years later, with Kennedy dead and the Vietnam War consuming us all, it was Fairbank who engineered my return from Lyndon Johnson's NSC staff to teach the history of American-East Asian relations at Harvard.

To become a junior colleague in your mentor's department can be an awkward thing. It was increasingly so for me, in the late 1960s, as both of us got swept into the tumultuous national and campus politics of that era, and his plans for me seemed inscrutable. One high point of those six years was my emceeing of his 60th birthday dinner, with all his special progeny present—Teddy White, Mary Wright, and others. A low point was the day when, in response to the plea that yet another year spent on the draft of my second book might destroy my marriage, he said, "Well, some people care about people; I care about manuscripts." Most of the time his aphorisms were less chilling—such as his reassurance to me that "guilt is for those who enjoy it," or the famous old sign as you left his Widener study, "People sometimes. Books never." But overall he hovered enigmatically; I spent much time resisting.

My liberation from Fairbank's protectorship, and the true beginning of our adult friendship, finally came in 1972 when I, let go by the History Department, was made Curator of the Nieman Foundation. One autumn day I invited him to lunch—not, I specified, in the quickie-food basement of the Faculty Club, and not at his house (he was a terrible cook!), but at that dim-lit and moderately posh Cambridge eatery, Chez Dreyfus. *On me*! Well, we had a marvelous two-hour lunch, and from then on things were nicely different.

Many of John Fairbank's admirers revered his self-discipline, his productivity, his entrepreneurship, and of course his mentorship. What I like most to remember is his playfulness, expressed in so many ways. He had a dry, deadpan wit as a lecturer that went over the heads of all but the best students. His Asian bowing and smiling seemed often to drift into mimicry. He had an adolescent delight in puns, costumery, and slapstick antics. He had an appalling habit, when we were at large stuffy dinners together and nothing much was happening, of clinking on his glass, then rising to introduce me as the featured speaker (there was no featured speaker, of course), and I would try to be on my toes for these things. He always wanted to tell the assembled crowd not only about me and Pearl Buck, but about my having gone to Yale, "just like Mac Bundy." (I would try to counter by introducing him, as General Marshall once did, as "Professor Fairchild of Yale.") Way back, when I was a Teaching Fellow in Rice Paddies and had to show slides for my sinecure, he had slipped into my projector box two identical photos, in close succession, of Mongolian sheep dung—and then told the giggly throng that he could not really explain Mr. Thomson's infatuation with sheep dung. He even made reference to that event in his retirement lecture—the one in which he, garbed in Oxbridge colors, was (as he put it) "dressed like a sunset in order to walk into the sunset."

John Fairbank died on my 60th birthday, September 14th. Four days before he died, he wrote me a birthday letter. Its opening paragraphs read:

> When you first came to see me in 1955 you said you had edited the Yale Daily News and now wanted to study China as a way of finding your amah.
>
> I said I also had been searching for an amah, but good ones are hard to find.
>
> I also told you that I was waiting to be Emperor of China while you said you were the only sinologist who had sat in the lap of Pearl Sydenstricker Buck.
>
> We got on well from the start and it was subsequently a pleasure to take our show on the road among the local yokels.

He then suggested I write a new book. "You see," he concluded, "I continue to plan careers."

John Schrecker
*Brandeis University*

In the spring of 1958, toward the end of my senior year at Penn, I went to my first meeting of the Association for Asian Studies. I was eager to see the field in action and wanted particularly to meet John Fairbank, with whom I was to begin studying at Harvard the following year. As it turned out, I didn't have the courage to approach him. I did, however, catch a glimpse of him in a hall and I've never forgotten my first impression of the man: poised for action, surrounded by people, in control, elegantly dressed, directing everything.

What I remember most from graduate school was the excellence of John's seminars, History 282a/b. His goal in the courses was to propel us into serious research and to teach us to write. We worked on quite a diverse set of topics but JKF had rules to keep things organized: a paper would be presented and then we would go around the table making comments, there were no questions allowed of the speaker—only observations to help improve the paper—and the paper-giver was not supposed to respond to any of the comments, but simply to use what seemed helpful for revision and to ignore the rest. JKF's turn came at the end. How proud we were if we had been able to make comments he chose to emphasize, and by the end of the semester, as he needed to say less and less, we really knew we had learned something. I've used his format ever since in my own courses.

It was in these seminars (with some final touches from Libby Matheson and *Papers on China*) that I first learned the basics of writing—something no English teacher had previously seemed able to teach me. John's ability to teach many subjects that were usually considered to be specialties was one of his most impressive traits, a perfect example of the generalist ideal of Confucian China. For example, in those days, classical Chinese was generally taught in a rather informal way, by simply reading. We never used textbooks, as the grammar was considered too subtle to be directly presentable. But JKF, writer, historian, student of Chinese, did produce a textbook, his wonderful *Ch'ing Documents: An Introductory*

*Syllabus*, certainly the most helpful approach to the classical language I ever used.

When I began teaching, my most vivid memory of John was at the AAS meetings of the late sixties when the Vietnam War dominated all other concerns. There were frequent attacks on senior scholars including JKF. I was very opposed to the war, but also strongly against the attacks, and most of JKF's pupils, I think, shared my feelings. At one bull-session of antiwar people, someone from another school said that all the "Fairbank people" seemed odd, talking about him as we did in such an affectionate, even reverent way. One of us (someone with quite a radical reputation as it happened) said, "Well, you just don't know him. He's such a good teacher; he's really very special," and it made us all feel very proud of our connection with John.

When I returned to the Boston area in the seventies, I began to see John more as a colleague and to assess him in the light of my experiences in university life. I was struck anew by his exceptional politeness, a politeness that made him instantly and constantly a model of good behavior. He treated people the way he once said a Confucian gentleman did, in terms of *who* they were, not *what* they were. In a group of people John would talk to the most appropriate person or to the one closest at hand, and he would speak directly to that person and not, as so many of his station might, to a larger audience of those around.

Once, I heard that he had been at a White House banquet, seated at the head-table with Deng Xiaoping and President Carter. When I saw him later I said, "What in the world do you do in a situation like that?" He replied, "First you talk to the lady on your left and then you talk to the lady on your right." It was typical of John, however, not to have even mentioned the dinner until I brought it up. In conversation, he always spoke to the topic and never referred to his own writings or dropped names or meetings he was attending. This subordination of his own ego, so unusual in the academic world, seemed to stem from his amazing, though completely justifiable, sense of personal security.

In the eighties, when my own views of Chinese history began to diverge sharply from John's, he taught me his final and toughest lesson. We kept up warm relations despite our differences. But, perhaps even more than for most, John was as much a father figure for me as a teacher. So I was endlessly concerned about his opinions of my views and eager to convince him of their worth. One day he gave me the lesson I most needed, by saying simply, "John, you're on your own."

Now we're all on our own, but the lessons JKF taught us and the example he set for us will, like the memories of this great man, remain with us always.

Shirley Garrett
*Millersville, Pennsylvania*

Life washed me up at John Fairbank's office one January day at the age of thirty-four, refugee from ten years in the advertising business and from a severe personal loss, and veteran of several months in Asia, about which I knew precious little. I wanted to enter the Regional Studies program. We talked for fifteen minutes and he said "Sure, come on in." Not until a stiff letter arrived from the admissions office did I realize how much red tape he had simply cut for me. Powerful man, of course, but also unorthodox, a gambler on people and ideas, because you never knew what might come out of it all.

The following week I got a handwritten note inviting me to the Fairbank afternoon teas. I went whenever the anonymity of graduate school became overwhelming, and he always seemed to recognize me. As months passed it was clear that he made a point of knowing who students were, both personally and professionally. He listened to our complaints, he read our exams and papers carefully. I remember not only the occasional mark of approval, but also an acid "Don't write for housewives" —a stab presumably aimed at my previous career. (It was not a dig at women; to Fairbank a mind was a mind, whatever the packaging. Years later he told me that the faculty members resisting appointing a woman to the History Department were "old dodos.")

In time, he backed my entrance into the doctoral program and eventually I took my orals. The questions from other examiners were decent; the minutes passed. By the time we got to Fairbank I was relaxed, preening a little. His first questions were pedestrian enough. Then, I can remember quite distinctly, I saw a glint in his eyes and he asked a Killer Question, the kind you dream about twenty years later during a Harvard Examination Dream. There was stupefied silence and more silence. I stumbled along and the inquisition ended. Well, he had shown me what scholarship really involved. An hour later I was bold enough to ask "How could you do that?" He laughed and laughed, a very big cat watching with amusement a mouse too small to eat but big enough to tease.

During the thesis years I learned more about his way of dealing with students. His style consisted of leaving you alone except for an occasional prod to see if you were alive and working. No demands for master plans, outlines, bibliographies. You were supposed to figure all that out on your own. When I asked him what kind of thesis he wanted, he said "About a two-hundred-page kind"—certainly one of the most practical pieces of advice I have ever had about writing, one that forced me to select, organize, throw out, and rewrite. Eventually I began to disgorge chapters. I would mail one off, and within a week—a week!—it would come back with comments in red ink in the Fairbank scrawl. I was surprised to hear in later years that this courtesy, this promptness, was the mark of a Fairbank and not of the entire subspecies of thesis advisers. When my final version went off he responded immediately, addressing me as "Dr. Garrett" and asking how soon the manuscript could be ready for publication. And signing himself "John." With similar efficiency and kindness he answered later requests for job recommendations, grant proposals and conference participation. I know he did the same and more for others.

Considering his teaching, his scholarship, his administrative work, where did he find the time? He had a marvelous staff, of course, and a marvelous colleague in Wilma, and he wrote things down in his little notebook and followed up on them. In addition he had the ability to focus completely on what he was doing. Once as I hurtled down a corridor at O'Hare Airport, dizzy from the roar of planes and public address systems and people, I caught sight of him. He was sitting on one of the spine-crushing airport chairs, suitcase propped on his lap, and he was reading—as deep in concentration, as isolated from the turmoil as if he were in his study at Widener. I did not dare to approach him to say hello.

But there is another picture at another airport—a chance meeting at Logan. He was wearing a well-cut suit, much unlike the ancient tweed jacket of classroom days. I congratulated him on his splendor. He was out to raise money for Harvard, and had dressed for the world of high finance. "I'm off to have lunch with David Rockefeller," he said. "Notice the tie" and he chortled, vastly amused at himself.

So I am lucky enough to remember John Fairbank both ways, working hard and laughing hard. He had the secret, all right, and he tried to pass it on. Bless his memory.

John E. Wills, Jr.
*University of Southern California*

My memories of John King Fairbank are very much tied to his big study/office/seminar room on the top floor of Widener Library. There we sat around the long table and tried to read Ch'ing documents. There we got acquainted with distinguished visitors. I especially remember Mary Wright's visit to our seminar in the fall of 1959; the photograph of her in *Chinabound* was taken that day. There we reviewed the literature of the field, far less voluminous then than today, in preparation for the dauntingly brief ordeal of an hour and a half of oral examination that was the only qualifying examination for the Ph. D. in History and Far Eastern Languages.

With his usual relentless practicality and generosity, John arranged that any of his graduate students could pick up a key at the south entrance to Widener and use the collection of published documents, reference books, and monographs in his top-floor study any morning, but not afternoon. One time I got casual about the limitation, picked up the key in the afternoon, saw no light inside, opened the door, and turned on the light. John rose from the couch in his private end of the study, where he apparently had been napping. I apologized, beat a hasty retreat, and began to review my options to take an M. A. in Teaching or to go into the travel business. But of course I never heard anything about it; John was too busy and too realistic to be upset by the low-grade idiocies of ambitious and inconsiderate youth.

Then there were the Thursday afternoon teas at 41 Winthrop Street. You met all kinds of people there: I especially remember General Samuel Griffith's tales of Beijing in 1945-46. If you hadn't managed to get an appointment during the week, you could always go to tea and get John's ear for a moment of business; you would get attention, a sensible response, and action if necessary.

The last time I saw John was in the living room of his Winthrop Street house in the spring of 1987. As usual, he was thinking about things to be done for the advancement of Chinese historical studies, and in particular things for which he thought I should be the point man: Western sources, maritime connections. Not having John's gifts for prioritizing and completion, I'm still trying to figure out how to do those things. I know now I'll never get another very brief letter asking me how I'm progressing on them. But I also know that I won't stop trying, and that eventually I'll have something I wish I could report to John. That's what he did to you. That's one important reason why our field has come so far since he began prodding it along. My generation has some impressive followers of his examples in scholarship and professional promotion, but I think all of them would agree that we will not see his like again.

Alexander Woodside
*University of British Columbia*

John Fairbank was a prolific producer of Chinese history for the common reader. Yet the parts of his most famous book which I found the most moving, even before I became his graduate student in 1960, dealt with the Chinese intellectuals, past and present, who created positions for themselves out of nothing but their moral self-possession, and then took their stand in what was all too often a politically condemned world. They were the "brave scholars in Chinese history" who had "corresponded to tribunes of the people and martyrs for personal faith in the West" (*The United States and China*, 1958 edition, p. 197). Their company included the Tung-lin Academy scholar "heroes who attacked evil in terms of principle," criticizing the rule of the late Ming eunuchs and "suffering torture and death accordingly" (ibid., p. 103); above all, it included the modern "Chinese liberals" of the 1940s whose children died of tuberculosis, whose university faculties in southwest China "preserved themselves by their pride, patience, and fortitude, " and who themselves—like T'ao Hsing-chih or Wen I-to—might be suppressed or murdered by unsympathetic politicians (ibid., pp. 202-203). Not being a specialist in the history of thought, John was most comfortable describing such figures in terms of their moral identities, not their philosophical theories. Yet this may well have brought him all the closer to most of them in spirit. And what other writer of a history of modern Sino-American relations, approaching this subject in the late 1940s, would have looked so hard for "liberal" political inspirations in the vanished pieties of medieval Chinese humanism?

Obviously, John himself had much of the patience and dignified self-assurance of the traditional Chinese scholar. He certainly lived in a period of warring states, and of undeclared civil war between right- and left-wing Americans over U. S. Asia policy in general, and U. S. China policy in particular. Surely no other English-speaking historian was so much our own era's repeatedly thwarted "uncrowned king" of Confucian legend, feeling himself bound to reprove diverse presidents in Washington, D. C. about their latest policy-making disasters, and suffering more snubs from the shallow courtiers and crumbling public men who surrounded them than Mencius had ever had to receive from the unlovable King Hui of Liang. More than once, it all became so painful that John, like Chinese literati before him, was driven to fall back upon the position that learning and teaching were, in the long run, more important than rotting dynasties and the eunuchs who had temporarily seized them.

In the spring of 1970, during Richard Nixon's invasion of Cambodia, John called an emergency meeting of the members of the East Asian Research Center to discuss the crisis. He predicted, hopefully but wrongly, that Nixon would lose the presidency in 1972. Then he reminded us that "Harvard is twice as old as the United States and may well survive it." We still had to get on with scholarship.

He was even more an Americanized image of the traditional Chinese scholar in his relations with his colleagues and his students. As everyone knows, he was the center and the fountainhead of a prodigious network of correspondence with them by letter and by memorandum, even while he wrote his own books and addressed congressional committees. Here he reminds me a little of someone like Tseng Kuo-fan, diligently pouring out elaborate instructions by letter to his sons about how to read the classics correctly, even while he was marshalling his soldiers for another battle with the Taipings. The ironic playfulness in John's letters could be surprising and affectionate enough to smooth out the angularities of most of their recipients. Trying to build new bridges to a difficult junior colleague of vaguely British (that is, Canadian) background whom he feared felt unappreciated (I was then considering a job elsewhere), John began his letter this way: "Dear Alex: In Victorian novels, the young people are secretly devoted to each other, but never get into communication because they meet only at the Epworth League. The tragic result is that he goes off to join the Queen's Own in the Khyber Pass, while she marries the decrepit Mr. Smidgin, an old friend of her father's." Very rarely, the networking failed. John once wryly told me that he had tried to win over one extravagantly unpleasant colleague in the Harvard History Department, but had run up against an immovable obstacle of inexorable good common sense which even he could not overcome: "Wilma refuses to let him set foot in our house." Thank God (as we all did) for Mrs. Fairbank.

S. A. M. Adshead suggested recently that John founded an academic school whose "only comparable analogue in twentieth-century historiography" is the school of the *Annales* in Paris. But he adds that the Fairbank school's "unity is one of method rather than conclusion" (*Pacific Affairs*, Winter 1990-1991, p. 552). The qualification is crucial. John was not a theoretical system-builder of the Parisian sort. Although some political opponents have regarded him as arrogant, he was in fact modest to a fault about the intellectual substance of his work as a historian. I have a letter from him of March 1974 in which, pondering the future of Chinese history in the Harvard History Department, he wrote: "I shall not be here much longer, and in fact may disappear at any time . . . . An effort should be made to find a competitor for my post who might, for example, deal with Chinese socio-economic history in general, parallel to Ben's interest in the history of thought. This could bring Chinese history more into the mainstream of historical thinking . . . ." Only partly because I thought that much of the alleged "mainstream" of postwar "historical thinking" was conceptually and spiritually impoverished, I felt that John was much too hard on himself. But I was touched by his anxiety that he was marginal to this mainstream, whatever its value, and I was grateful that this anxiety coexisted with such openness to the intellectual contributions of scholars who embarked upon very different approaches to China than John's own.

About literary form and structure he was less accommodating. John cared about the way he and others wrote whatever they wrote. Again, he reminds me of the Chinese literati who believed that the achievement of a pure literary form might compensate a little for a distempered political landscape. After reading the chapter of a book I was writing, John told me: "Your style is muddy. The flashes of cultural insight are obscured by the language, like gold fish flitting through a bowl of soup. Your crystal ball needs to be wiped off on the outside." For him, subheadings were a touchstone of analytic sincerity as well as of structure. Without them, he once told me in another note, this time about a particularly muddy article I had just finished, "social scientists will disparage [your article] as humanistic lore, no more." I also received memorable warnings not to imitate the exuberant inflated prose of his otherwise much admired and beloved early student Theodore White.

For John, all history was contemporary history. Washington policy-makers could be despised for many reasons, not least because they knew nothing about the Ming dynasty. The future of China's relations with the West was at stake in the classroom and the library. The self-limiting vocationalism into which so much professorial historical study could subside was never for him. Late in his life my father, as the provost at the University of Toronto, presented John for an honorary degree at that institution. He concluded his citation of John with the quotation from *The Analects* which seemed so obvious: the person "who reviews the old so as to find out the new is qualified to be a teacher of others." Nobody worked more tirelessly than John to make a richer understanding of the past illuminate and reform the purposes of what was often a terrible present.

YEN-P'ING HAO
*University of Tennessee*

In 1960 I applied to Harvard for graduate studies, sending along a copy of my Taiwan University B.A. thesis on modern China's cultural conservatism. Subsequently I received a scholarship and became one of John K. Fairbank's students—an event that has changed my life. Twenty-seven years later, at the request of the editors of *Chin-tai Chung-kuo shih yen-chiu t'ung-hsun* (Newsletter for modern Chinese history) at the Institute of Modern History, Academia Sinica, Taipei, I wrote a biographical article on Fairbank for the September 1987 issue. Fairbank wrote me (with copies to Philip Kuhn and Paul Evans) on March 28, 1988:

> Your article on my career and recent book together with bibliography in the IMH *Newsletter* 4.64-79 is remarkably comprehensive yet succinct, intimately conversant with the subject, and discriminating in its choice of ideas and remarks to quote and comment on. In short, I could not have done better myself and I feel immensely indebted to you for writing it. When the Harvard Faculty get around to composing a Memorial Minute, they would do well to have this article at hand.

With China specialists in mind I discussed in that article Fairbank's contributions to the China field as a whole. This piece of reminiscences amplifies, with personal testimony, one aspect of Fairbank referred to in the article—his role as teacher.

After an exhaustive oral and written critique, my paper for Fairbank's seminar was published in *Papers on China* in 1961. On June 18, 1962, having read a paper I wrote for Professor Benjamin Schwartz's seminar, Fairbank graciously advised me to revise it for publication: "I think you might find it a useful experience to make such a revision, since it would be a kind of self-training which all writers have to give themselves . . . . The task is to give it some integration and synthesis." For me, the most revealing part of his comment was his differentiation between a historian and a Sinologist: "One point of method—your text should be essentially self-explanatory while the notes give the apparatus of sources rather than further material of substantive nature. I realize this is not the Sinological tradition but I assume you aim to be an historian, not an out-of-date Sinologist only." He then spelled out at length the specifics of revision. I followed the advice accordingly and the paper was published.

Under his guidance and with valuable help from Professor K. C. Liu, I started in 1962 my dissertation on the nineteenth-century comprador. During my research trip around the world he gave me letters of introduction everywhere. When at the writing stage I finished a chapter, he would take it home and returned it to me the following morning with extensive comments, ranging from punctuation and romanization to the entire framework of the dissertation. After completion, in 1965, he arranged for me to do further archival research in England before submitting the manuscript to the Harvard University Press. In May 1968 he urged me to make some final revisions (as suggested by the two outside readers): "You can make it a very good book indeed and these little additional efforts may make all the difference between a book that is 'good' and a book that is 'very good.'" After reading the final, revised version, he was elated and wrote to me: "I am immensely impressed with your manuscript . . . . It is a real achievement and I congratulate you." But much of that achievement I owed to his care as a teacher. It was finally published in 1970, five years after I began to teach at the University of Tennessee.

As a teacher, Fairbank was "most anxious" to see that the collections in his Widener Library study be fully utilized. Prior to his Asian trip late in 1972, he wrote me: "I propose to clear up my desk to give you working space and give you the extra key . . . to use Room 745 as your own study." This arrangement also benefited his other students because they could continue to get access to the collections there. Upon returning he wrote: "I do not want to disrupt your working there by my return . . . . If neither of us talks while we are working, there is no reason we could not jointly use such a big study." Unfortunately, this arrangement never materialized because I had to return to my teaching at Tennessee. Nevertheless, the physical experience of working at his desk has left an indelible mark upon me, and, on the eve of my departure, I wrote in my diary in Chinese: "It has been quite an experience to use the personal desk of Teacher Fei to do research in the past three months. To be able to write history in front of the portraits of such giants as H. B. Morse and William Langer—what a joy (*i-le-yeh*)!"

As a teacher in a larger sense, Fairbank was keen on sharing his knowledge about China with the public. In the wake of U. S. recognition of the PRC, we at the University of Tennessee invited Fairbank and Patrick Buchanan each to give a public lecture on this issue. However, Buchanan hardly talked about China except to attack President Carter personally and to complain that Carter had not been tough enough with Teng Hsiao-p'ing, and devoted the rest of the lecture to right-wing statements.

In contrast, Fairbank's remarks were moderate and scholarly, emphasizing that U.S.-Chinese relations should rest on mutual respect. Giving some examples of basic cultural differences, he pointed out that due to overpopulation, "the Chinese don't make any bones about abortion," and further, the Chinese do not regard as absolute truth the concept of an eternal soul and heaven. In short, the speech was lively and provoked even more lively discussion. Here I saw Fairbank the teacher-popularizer at his best.

It was an entirely different matter, however, for Teacher Fei to introduce his Chinese students to the American way of life. In 1962 he invited Chang Hao, Winston Hsieh and myself to stay at his "primitive guest cottage" in New Hampshire for a weekend. His letter of July 16 testifies to his meticulous attention to details:

> So as to see the last vestige of the great Railroad Age before it vanishes entirely, turn to table 11 of the Boston and Maine Railroad Timetable enclosed and arrange to take Train Number 31 which leaves Boston North Station (note that this is not the South Station) daily at 12:45. Taking this train at 12:45 on Saturday, July 28, you should reach Franklin at 2:33, where we will be waiting for you. Our phone is Franklin 92W3 [sic].

In his typically fatherly manner, he reminded us to bring old and warm clothes, bathing trunks if available, and, for us three Chinese *shu-sheng*, "tennis shoes with rubber bottoms rather than leather," and he concluded by saying that "we try to live close to nature."

That he certainly did. When the three of us arrived at the Franklin station, we could not immediately find our host. But soon a tall, husky man dressed like a local farmer briskly walked toward us. I could not believe my eyes—this "peasant" was none other than our venerable teacher, Professor Fei Cheng-ch'ing! During those two days we picked wild blueberries and talked about various subjects while strolling in the woods. It was not unlike a typical outing of Confucius and his disciples in the state of Lu some twenty-five centuries ago. One difference was that physically Teacher Fei was obviously stronger than Master K'ung. With a big knife in his hand he led us on a hike, making trails in the thick bushes in the woods—a true "trailblazer" at work. On Monday, Mrs. Wilma Fairbank drove us back to Cambridge. For me this was a most memorable experience, because even today I still remember vividly how I was surprised to find that so much of New England's level, fertile land was "wasted" agriculturally—a far cry from the terraced rural landscape of my native Chung-wang Village on the Yellow River. Thus, Fairbank not only patiently trained me to be a historian but also showed me what my own cultural heritage meant.

Fairbank was a teacher by profession, but he was not an ordinary teacher. He was truly a teacher with a missionary's zeal, spreading the message with personal care, faith, and perseverance.

Jon L. Saari
*Northern Michigan University*

I was a graduate student in the Department of History from 1964 to 1971, until I headed back to the Upper Midwest to teach at a regional university. My forays back to Cambridge became less frequent as the years wore on: two stints as a research associate at the EARC in the 1970s, to convert the dissertation into a book. My guilt made it increasingly harder to return. I knew what Fairbank wanted: he consumed manuscripts with gusto, and I always felt that mine was there in the back of his mind, awaiting presentation on the platter. After my last stay at the EARC (by then renamed the Fairbank Center), I had vowed never to return to Cambridge without the manuscript in hand. Enough had been invested in me already, I reasoned, and without production of a book I was not worthy to show up and be recognized as a peer in the society of scholars. It was 1985, seven years later, before I showed my face again.

I need not have taken it all so personally, or so it looks in retrospect. Rereading *Chinabound* I can see that I was just one project among many. Graduate students were the crucial raw material in a "training assembly line" intended to produce a "corps" of teachers and researchers. Mentors needed to "grease" egos to make sure we stayed on track, that we did not get overly discouraged, that we did not—worst horror of all —leave the China profession. And China was a profession, a calling. Industrial production metaphors mix uneasily in my memory with religious ones, for we were called by Fairbank to participate in a secular mission. It was a mission to educate the American people about China because China mattered in our—their—future, in the world's future. We were not just numbers, because the importance of China gave all our efforts significance. In a kind of parody of Milton Theobald Stauffer's 1921 survey *The Christian Occupation of China*, I can see now that I was part of the "Numerical Strength and Geographical Distribution" of the Harvard-trained China forces in America. It was right and proper, even heroic, that I was a lone China specialist in the remote Upper Peninsula of Michigan. The China message needed to be spread there, just as much as the Christian gospel needed to be heard in Kansu, Chinghai, and Yunnan.

If the Christian occupation of China was a myth, so has been the vision of America being enlightened about China by scholarly writing and teaching. We reach so few in a society where people read less and less. Our classroom efforts are at best vicarious learning, where the lessons are easily eroded by the pressures of actual experience. The Vietnam War infected millions with stereotypes and bitter memories about "Orientals," recent economic competition has led to Japan-bashing and distrust of foreigners and immigrants. Beyond the major research universities and liberal arts colleges, our scholarly enterprise in modern Chinese history is still fragile, resting on the sufferance of colleagues, administrators, and society at large. While hard to do in practice, enlightening America about China was a desire bred into me through my graduate studies at Harvard, in part through Fairbank's example of the engaged scholar, in part through the antiwar movement, in part through my own need to be useful.

In the Epilogue to *Chinabound*, Fairbank wrestles with this nexus between knowledge and action, with the idea that knowing more will help us act better in history. It is the core issue of his work and life, as it touches his own sense of purpose. First he puts his own apparent "success story" into a larger context. He cites the limitations of China studies as part of the general effort at world crisis management, and is all too aware of how the Vietnam War "conferred little glory on our mental processes, either official or popular." He knows the thinness of our intellectual resources. Yet he retains "some faith in the efficacy of historical perspective" and a belief in the trickle-down theory of knowledge. Faith and belief are key words here, for "cool logic" seems to defy them. His examples of why we should be optimistic are typical Fairbankian jesting: The Chinese, after all, would be prime candidates to rebuild a world "ill-advisedly" destroyed by nuclear blasts, and they have long experience in techniques of social management, such as mounting criminals' heads on pikes for thoughtful viewing by the public.

Beyond the jesting and being his own devil's advocate, Fairbank in this epilogue sees the final task of scholars as facing down gloom and doom, overcoming negativism, and of course continuing to try to understand China and ourselves. As a people we must, he says, study our problems more wholeheartedly, and take "religious faith as a motive but not a principal means of salvation." This prescription for others was his own credo of wholehearted and conscientious study. Acquiring and applying knowledge had the aura of a religious obligation for Fairbank. If we cannot understand how the sixteen volumes of the *Cambridge History of China* relate concretely to the survival of a humane world, we can at least know that "knowledge" for him was understood as a religious quest into what it meant to be human and humane. This quest was open-ended: He had more faith in the rationality of individual human persons than in technological gadgetry or ideological truths. America and China, the poles of his world, were in the end framed by the human story, as they should be.

My trip back to Cambridge in 1985 was a pilgrimage. The offering for my guilt and indebtedness was a manuscript. And I departed for the hinterlands once again, trusting in the belief that I was doing good works for two parts of humanity. John Fairbank and I were never close, but we were made for each other.

Suzanne Wilson Barnett
*University of Puget Sound*

John Fairbank's ideas had a way of moving the profession in far-flung places through circuitous routes. My college teacher in Ohio in 1960 was not John's student, but his connection with John's students and colleagues Mary and Arthur Wright at Stanford must have influenced David Sturtevant of Muskingum College. He fashioned a research seminar on Protestant missionaries in China and the Philippines that unwittingly led me along Fairbankian lines before I could recognize the territory. My assignment was the missionary printer Samuel Wells Williams, whose life and work focused my attention on nineteenth-century China and set the course of my career. Not until I was on my way to Harvard to do modern Chinese history did I learn that missionaries were an intellectual interest of John's as well. My preliminary work on Williams helped me understand why. After my first encounter with his *Middle*

*Kingdom* (1848), never again would I assume either the superiority of "the West" or the right of missionaries or other outsiders to seek to impose their values on the inhabitants of China.

In all this, JKF was ahead of me, of course. When eventually I read "Patterns Behind the Tientsin Massacre" (*HJAS*, 1957) I could appreciate the brilliance of John's angle of inquiry, understanding the missionary enterprise but assessing missionary habits and values from the Chinese side. When John produced his 1968 AHA presidential address (*AHR*, 1969) and spotlighted American China missionaries and merchants as ready means of access to China's complexities, I already was on board.

In retrospect I know that my path to Harvard, the American Board collection of Chinese-language tracts and textbooks, and the privilege of working with John on the Luce project on early Protestant missionary writings derives from some academic moment in my senior year in college. In a broader sense, however, my scholarly odyssey, like that of so many others, has rested on John Fairbank's vision, energy, and constant concern neither to deny the complexity of Chinese history nor to cast it as esoteric. John's approach and example reach my own students at a distant undergraduate university through both his prodigious writings and my efforts to emulate and extend his style of insight and instruction.

Ellis Joffe
*The Hebrew University of Jerusalem*

My last meeting with Professor Fairbank, several weeks before his death, was similar in one respect to the first, some thirty years earlier: I came for advice and he gave it thoughtfully and generously. In the years that followed that first meeting he gave much more—knowledge and guidance, inspiration and encouragement, kindness and consideration, understanding and material support. All I could give in return was an uncertain commitment to the study of China in a far-off land.

You'll notice I said "Professor Fairbank." I never could bring myself to call him by his first name despite his friendliness and informality. Attribute this to awe or reverence; I think hero worship would be more appropriate.

For countless reasons. Like the invitation to breakfast to unravel what seemed like an insurmountable thesis problem. Or to a game of frisbee in order to lift what he discerned as a sagging spirit. Or the effort he personally exerted with the bureaucracy to overcome a visa difficulty. Or his quick and crucial approval of a contemporary topic for a history dissertation. Or his unfailingly good-humored responses, even after I passed the age he was at when I first came to Harvard, to my numerous requests for that bothersome fixture of academic life: letters of recommendation. Seemingly small gestures, perhaps, but only the receiver can know what great significance they carried.

For thirty years I've tried to fix in my mind, surely not too successfully, what he wrote on my first seminar paper: "Don't say everything twice." But this I can say at least twice without hesitation: thanks to Professor Fairbank, my own life became happily Chinabound. I hope he knew how grateful I am.

ANDREW J. NATHAN
*Columbia University*

John's style could be impersonal—perhaps especially to younger cohorts of students who were more distant from him in age—but he was a personal force in many lives.

It may seem self-centered to speak of him in relation to my own life, except that his impact on individual careers was so much the essence of what he was, both as a person and as a professional. He was a builder whose constructions ranged from the architectonics of large institutions to the detail work of individual careers that make up such institutions.

I first encountered John as a 17-year-old in 1960, at the opening lecture for that year's "Rice Paddies" (Soc. Sci. 111). He seemed the stereotypical New England professor, balding, tall, elegant, dry. He could have been an actor on a movie screen. I was safely invisible in the audience—so I thought.

What engaged me in his subject, in contrast to a course I was taking at the time on medieval history, was his harping on the unanswered questions, the frontiers of the field, the research that needed to be done. He conveyed that we in the class might be the ones to do this work. The great two-volume textbook was on reserve in the library in what was called "ditto" format. The field was open.

Openness was part of John's personality. He did not try to control people, but he was persistently there as a resource. He had a vision of each student's potentialities that the student could not have had. To the extent that one cooperated he molded one's career to this vision. When I declared my major in modern Chinese history, he told me, "Of course you'll want to take intensive Chinese." After I had floundered a while looking for a senior thesis topic, he suggested one, edited the result, and had it published. When I threatened to stray into another subject, he arranged a traveling fellowship to Hong Kong where the hook of China got stuck too deeply to dislodge. When I returned to graduate school, he said, "There are enough people in history. Why don't you go into political science?"

Legend among his late-sleeping graduate students were John's 8 a. m. phone calls with a tip about an academic event or a source for a seminar paper in progress. One morning he delivered his critique of a seminar paper, while we walked from Winthrop Street to 1737 Cambridge Street, using a portable electric razor with his free hand. Each of his many students received personal though efficient attention. Job recommendations, publications, and fellowships are the building blocks of an academic career. John was a practical man. He was swift with necessary help to the last months of his life.

This was not patronage. No loyalty was expected in return. It was not quite mentoring either, because John did not seek to create workers in his own image or tell you how to run your life. What he constructed was not a clique but a field. The health of China studies—its diversity, breadth, pluralism, and vigor, which perhaps exceed those of any other area studies field in American academia—is a reflection of its builder's qualities of mind and character. For

John, the subject was really the subject. For scholars fascinated with China, it was John who provided a model of what being fascinated meant.

John was an idea man. He took criticism not only without rancor but with pleasure. He gave thoughtful responses to manuscripts and proposals, written with the same gnomic wit as his published writings and equally stimulating to reread years later. He circulated his manuscripts for comment, was alert for new ideas, welcomed them, and enjoyed them with visible pleasure. His last book is a tribute to the new ideas of his students, his students' students, and, without prejudice, of scholars who had nothing particularly to do with him. The new ideas in the field have developed the insights he taught in Soc. Sci. 111, but to my eyes have not superseded them.

John was always ready for a student to grow into a colleague. Very early the letters started to come with the signature "John." Eventually I came to feel the appropriateness of addressing him in the same way. Although when I first met him he was only a little older than I am now, he never seemed to change physically. He was still the image of a New England professor, still something of a movie star.

I now appreciate how much work it took to do the infinite things that he did for me, multiplied by scores and hundreds of others. John built his monument not only in scholarship and institutions but in lives. Like a Taoist carpenter, he built with no waste motion and to last.

## Fred Drake

*University of Massachusetts, Amherst*

John Fairbank changed my life. *The United States and China*, which I read as an undergraduate, introduced me to a new world and persuaded me to begin studying Chinese history. Later, when we met at the Inter-University Center in Taiwan, he invited me to study modern Chinese history at Harvard. By 1964 the gravitational attraction of this grand historian pulled me, like some wandering asteroid, into the community of students and scholars that orbited around him.

I was drawn to a teacher who personified many of the best traits of the cultural tradition he studied, yet who remained quintessentially American. He never lost his understated, midwestern style and self-reflective humor that prompted him to reply to the accolades on his 60th birthday party, "Shucks, fellahs, it was easy! Just get in on the ground floor between the world's greatest revolution and the world's greatest university—it's a pianola!"

He had discovered that the concept of *chi-mi* ("loose-rein"), used by nineteenth-century Chinese experts to govern unruly foreigners, worked even better with American graduate students. "Have you considered looking into this question?" or, "Have you looked at that documentation?" he would query, an inscrutable smile masking his real intent. Those seemingly innocent questions typically launched research endeavors that consumed our lives; before too many years passed, a book would appear on the topic, written by a disciple but conceived and molded by the master.

He also took the Chinese ideal of *hsien-sheng*—teacher—to heart. Long after any institutional obligation to his students had ceased, he regularly summoned us to his home, ostensibly for tea, where we (sometimes sheepishly) reported the progress of on-going projects. During the 27 years that I knew him, he always made time to listen, encourage, and advise, regardless of the state of his health or the demands of his own work. This devotion to his students reflected his belief that research should have practical effects. We were the agents charged with promoting his liberal, pragmatic vision of an America less provincial and better prepared to understand East Asia.

What attracted us to him was not just his intellectual vigor and achievement, or his studied understatement and dry wit. He consistently demonstrated, in ways fully known to no one (but certainly best to Wilma), that however careful he was in its expression, he sincerely cared about us. Still, the warmth of this elegant, impeccably casual man was not immediately obvious. Eminently fair, Fairbank's criticisms in a seminar could be sharp and painful, not just for the student receiving the thrust, but also for the rest who thought "there but for the grace." So in my third semester at Harvard, I was surprised to receive a late-evening telephone call, "John Fairbank here," expressing concern and consoling me after my father died suddenly. The private, unrelenting taskmaster, whom I faced in weekly seminars with some trepidation, told me of his own difficulty in overcoming the grief of his father's death and suggested postponing my exams.

In the end, it was his deep concern for the people who surrounded him that distinguished this humane, gentle man, John Fairbank, and made him my hero.

GAIL LEE BERNSTEIN
*University of Arizona*

In the nineteen-sixties, when I was a young graduate student in East Asian history at Harvard University, John Fairbank's middle name aptly conveyed my impression of him: cool and aloof, he presided over the East Asian Research Center like a monarch. A tall man, he seemed to float through the Center's dining room, solemnly nodding to the right and left as he greeted each diner by name and then exited, the slightest hint of a smile on his face. Many careers rested on his largesse, and students understandably worried about his opinion of them. But John was unfathomable and, frankly, intimidating. It was only years later, when I was myself a professional historian, that I could begin to appreciate how he had carefully managed his time and energy in order to focus on promoting the study of China, to the benefit of countless numbers of students and scholars from around the world.

John had a large office in Widener Library where he allowed graduate students to study, giving them access to his vast personal collection—a library within a library. The only rule, as I recall, was that we put the books back on the shelf exactly where we had found them. Overwhelmed by the daunting task of mastering a portion of that collection for my minor field in modern Chinese history, I took these generous arrangements for granted. Today, remembering

John's generosity, I invite even my undergraduates to browse through my considerably more modest personal library and allow them to borrow books as well. When they ask incredulously, "Are all these books yours? Have you read them all?" I nod, the slightest hint of a smile on my face.

John was a master of the terse memo. He could say more in one sentence spoken or written, than most people can say in two pages. His first message to me came after I had completed one year as "head sectionman" for the Far Eastern civilization course, known to everyone as Rice Paddies. He had entrusted me with the task of filing his slides after he showed them in class. The large glass slides were stored in boxes kept outside the Common Room at the Harvard-Yenching Institute, and John sent me a two-line note, written in speedwriting on a small piece of yellow paper, thanking me for taking good care of them. I kept this slip of paper for years among my few memorabilia. Now I wonder how he had found the time for such thoughtfulness in the midst of his extraordinarily productive career.

The thoughtful notes continued for the next twenty-five years. One arrived after I had won the John King Fairbank prize of the American Historical Association in 1977 for my first book, and, thereafter, he sent me notes for every publication I sent him. Prompt and brief, they said just enough to convince me that he had indeed read my work, and were complimentary in such a precise way that I knew he had understood what I had been trying to say perhaps better than I had—the mark of the good editor that he was.

The last note, typed while he was putting the final touches on his last book, arrived one week before his death, and like all the others, I kept it. In two sentences, he thanked me for sending him a copy of my most recent book and crisply assessed its significance for women's history. Wilma also wrote and revealed, ominously, that due to John's poor health, they would not take their annual winter vacation in Tucson.

Friends who knew John on the East Coast recognized that he had never really retired. Those of us who came to look forward to the Fairbanks' Arizona visits knew that he never really vacationed either. When in Tucson, John and Wilma stayed with Jeannette and

Osborne Elliott, whose gracious guesthouse, set against the Catalina Mountains, provided welcome relief from the New England cold. Despite the swimming pool and the nearby golf course, however, the Fairbanks were not typical winter visitors. They came with manuscripts and worked faithfully on them, stopping only to hike, nap, and socialize with East Asian scholars in the area.

China was always on his mind. The Fairbanks' book-filled home in New Hampshire served as a summer work retreat, and a nearby shed became John's study—a small room with desk, chair, tape-recorder, and cot. I do not think he was ever without a writing project, and he was eager to try out his ideas on others as well as to hear what they were doing. Wearing a plaid flannel shirt and leaning against the refrigerator, John once expounded on the place of Mao Zedong in Chinese history to my husband, a political scientist, who was cooking the breakfast sausage. On another occasion in the last year of his life, fatigued after a long day, he had stretched out on a bed shortly before dinner at our house, and I wondered whether he would be able to get through the evening, but as soon as historian Michael Schaller arrived and launched into a lively description of his year in Beijing, John popped back up and spent the rest of the evening in animated discussion, as though the very mention of China had cancelled his weariness.

The only time I ever saw John intellectually defeated was when he tried to talk about modern dance with his daughter, Holly, herself a dancer. He had boned up by reading a book on the subject as he sprawled out on a chair in front of the fireplace. That night at dinner, when the topic of conversation came around to modern dance, he ventured a comment about "that fellow, what's his name? Baryshnikov? Isn't he supposed to be good?"

"Oh daddy!" Holly groaned.

Yet, in the woods outside their New Hampshire house, John and Wilma had built for Holly a perfect dance studio, with wood floor, mirrors, large windows, a barre, a loft, and a dressing room. The dance studio, like John's many workplaces—his office at the East Asian Research Center (with a cot for naps), his library at Widener, the Elliotts' guesthouse in Tucson and the shed converted into a study in New Hampshire—all capture for me the essence of a man for whom living and work were inseparable.

RANBIR VOHRA
*Trinity College*

When I came to Harvard Graduate School in 1964, I had to make two major adjustments: I had to adapt myself to life in America—I had never been to the West and the only time I had spent outside India was in China where I studied at Beijing University for three years—and I had to re-learn the art of being a student—I had been with the Government of India for 18 years and had just resigned my job to come to Harvard. As an older foreign graduate student who was shifting careers at the age of 36, I was not always comfortable with my new environment.

The adjustment, however, came with relative ease because, within a year, the Fairbanks had adopted my wife and me as honorary, but close, members of their family. As the years passed, the sense of intimacy and friendship grew and John's departure has indeed left a void in our personal lives.

John was not a gregarious person and definitely incapable of engaging in small talk. He also gave the impression of being withdrawn. But you had only to mention a problem that you were facing in your research to have him open up; suddenly he was a different person who had all the time in the world to talk to you about books that you needed to look at and scholars around the world who were working on your subject and whom you should get in touch with.

In the course of time I realized that there was a very human heart that throbbed behind the impenetrable facade John had raised around himself. In fact it is my conviction that he was very sensitive to the personal lives of his students though he did not always care to reveal his feelings; it is this reticence of his that tended to create the impression that he was an inscrutable and unfeeling tyrant whose only interest lay in training ruthlessly and relentlessly his herd of graduate students to pursue with a single-minded devotion the painfully rugged path of Chinese studies. I have a story to tell which proves my point—a story I have so far told no more than two or three persons.

A few years after our arrival, John one day called me to his office and in a tone of voice that was nearly gentle spoke to me about life in general and then remarked that he had been worried about Meena (my wife); Meena had a cheerful disposition but John sensed that deep inside her she was rather unhappy. He thought this was due to the fact that we had no children and since Meena could not bear any it was John's advice that we adopt a child. "Do you know that our daughters Laura and Holly are both adopted?" Not only did we not know that his children were adopted (we always thought that Laura took after Wilma and Holly after her father!) but I would never have imagined that John could be so personal, so humane, and so compassionately understanding. And, of course, he was absolutely right in his analysis although we had never shared with him this particularly private concern of ours (try to picture a graduate student discussing such a personal subject with John!). I don't think that I ever thanked him fully for his interest in our welfare and for his advice. We did adopt a child later and our lives did change for the better for having done so.

It is not necessary for me to dwell on the subject of what John did for me as my mentor because his contribution to the scholarly and academic life of all his students was equally great. With his unique skill, which many of us did not quite recognize or fully appreciate at the time, he unobtrusively guided me to choose my thesis topic. He made me feel that it was my choice, whereas all the time it was he who knew the gaps that needed to be filled in our knowledge of China and it was he who decided who among us would best fill which gap. Later John helped me polish the thesis and publish it.

As with much else we were not always sure of John's designs for us—they showed up in most unexpected ways. During my last year as a graduate student I was the Head Teaching Fellow in "Rice Paddies" and was prompted by John to contribute two lectures to the course. On the day I gave the second lecture I was startled to see

John, Ben Schwartz and Ed Reischauer sitting in the last row of the auditorium at 2 Divinity Avenue. I managed to get through the lecture but I do believe that the wobbling of my knees kept me from concentrating on what I was saying. A few mornings later the telephone in my apartment rang at the unearthly hour of 7 and when I picked it up the voice at the other end announced "God here." I practically jumped out of bed—it was John. He told me that I had been given a faculty appointment and that I should go see the Chair of the History Department.

At John's memorial service one of the speakers referred to John as "Emperor"—I think "God" would be more appropriate: in his own sly way John knew that we all looked upon him with a tremendous feeling of awe and it was his distinctive sense of wry and ironic humor that allowed him to use the term for himself.

ERIC WIDMER
*Brown University*

The unresolved question of American recognition of China may have hung heavily over the decade of the 1960s, but for those of us who were John Fairbank's students at the time it was wonderful. It was why many of us found our work exciting, or why we were in the China field in the first place, or why we had fellowship support from the National Defense Education Act. Since no one could actually get to China we could all very rapidly become experts on the country—chips off of John's block and (with him standing somewhere behind us) bravely ready to twit politicians and journalists who were slower to ascend to our level of knowing.

We decided to have a conference. With some money from the National Committee on U. S.-China Relations, we were going to have a conference for journalists. And we were going to trot out Fairbank as our keynote speaker, to tell them a thing or two for their columns.

By the mid-sixties John had become a truly Delphic figure, and he did not disappoint us that evening. His speech was vintage Fairbank, punctuated with many examples of his enigmatic style. This was all fine, but the moment of truth had now arrived. The issue, after all, was what our journalists were supposed to do about American policy toward China. "What is needed for people to understand?" asked the obliging first questioner. As his student-priests stood ready to hear and help translate the answer of the Great Oracle, Fairbank replied after a moment's reflection: "What we need is a new history of the Ming Dynasty."

In a few words John had not only answered the question in his marvelously quizzical way; he had also put us in our place by reminding us of what we were supposed to be doing in graduate school.

Throughout our professional lives many of us have stuck together, bonded by the special distinction—if not chauvinism—of having been Fairbank's students. As aging priests ourselves we continue to translate Fairbank, in our ways, to our audiences. Now and then we would visit him, to be rejuvenated by his own example of immortality, or to catch up on the gossip and report back to one another. This was the provenance of a story which I did not figure in myself but shall tell lest the principals involved consider it too silly to mention. It shows the quintessential Fairbank, certainly—but now also someone who in his wry old age had apparently introduced some punning into his pronouncements.

In the summer of 1990 Ranbir and Meena Vohra had been invited to the Fairbank's place in Franklin for the weekend. Wilma was there when the Vohras arrived, and John was due later, in time for dinner. When he got there he immediately took Ranbir into his study and, with some excitement, showed him five or six letters from Robert Hart to his fiancée in England. The letters had just been discovered in Hong Kong and would help to resolve a problem about Hart that John had been working out in his book on the Inspector General, which was very much engaging him at that time. Only after the book was discussed would dinner be served.

Somewhat later that summer another one of John's former students, Don Price, was visiting the East Coast. As was his custom on such visits, he dropped in on the Vohras in Connecticut. Price told Vohra that he was very worried about John's health. Vohra replied that he was quite surprised to hear that, for after all he had just seen Fairbank, who seemed quite fit and was working as hard as always. "Well," Don answered, "I attempted but was unable to call upon John, who said something about having a heart problem."

"My dear Don," Vohra said, "I know that John is concerned about his heart, but the problem is rather with Sir Robert Hart, for which everything, including my dinner and your visit, must wait."

CHARLES W. HAYFORD
*Evanston, Illinois*

John Fairbank was not a father figure for me—I already had a perfectly good father—but he certainly was a figure. As an undergraduate I was a virtual theater major: in those medieval days of the early 1960s, Harvard offered no theater courses (and certainly no field of concentration in the "lower manual arts"). We just put all our time into it. It was not Fairbank who enticed me from the stage. The acolytic Mark Mancall, Akira Iriye, and Ezra Vogel saw to that. But he did finger me: the lights of the old Brattle Theater came up after the movie my senior year exam period—was it *Casablanca*?—and there were John and Wilma making their way up the aisle. He spotted me, and without a pause or a wink gave the high sign. He'd read my History 183 bluebook and I was o.k. An A. I set off for the world and Taiwan equipped with his standard issue letter at level No. 1. Three sentences, on Harvard's creamy, bullet-proof-thick stationery, warranted my existence and thanked whom it might concern for any assistance to which I was entitled.

Back to Cambridge after Taiwan. Let the record show that I was the first to get the Ph. D. in History and *East Asian* Languages: earlier degrees were in Orientalist-tainted History and *Far Eastern* Languages. Fairbank kindly advised us there was no need to be apprehensive about our general exams: "it might be a big event in *your* lives, but not in *mine*." Just before I took those generals, Andy

Nathan took his. JKF asked when Tseng Kuo-fan was born. Andy said "1820?" JKF said, "Good guess. I don't know either." Phil West, Ranbir Vohra, and I quickly swotted up the b. and d. of every nineteenth- or twentieth-century figure in the book. That year, while John and Wilma were off on a world tour, Betty and I stayed with Holly and Laddie at 41 Winthrop. Holly did fine, Laddie bit the mailman. Our eagerness to have children owed something to Holly, but we have had nothing but cats.

Meanwhile ARFEP (Americans for a Reappraisal of Far Eastern Policy—remember?), the League of Women Voters, JKF, I, and a few others were engaged in making the world safe for Red China (Mao was engaged in making China unsafe for the world). While Fairbank covered Congress and the White House, Betty and I drove down to address the North Barnstable World Federalist League. The town paper reported that "Mr. Hayford said that the Chinese Revolution neither was nor was not caused by the Russians," and I smugly concluded that my Fairbankian style was nearing perfection.

At JKF's suggestion, I took up James Yen and village China, not exactly a hot topic then, for it suggested that Mao was not all of modern China or even all of the Revolution. Neither of us knew whether Yen was still alive; drawing on my Sinological training, I found him listed in the Manhattan phone book. We wrote to Pearl Buck, she wrote a letter of introduction to Yen, and I was off.

Betty and I missed the searing polarization of Cambridge by being in Taiwan during 1968-1969 when Vietnam hit the fan and University Hall turned into Pork Chop Hill. Cambodia. Kent State. Jackson State. JKF in CCAS. JKF vs. CCAS. JKF warns Richard Bernstein to be careful in writing polemics about areas where you "don't know if it's a reference to a man or a bridge." I was lured off to Oberlin, where I found Bill Byrd, Tom Gold, Gail Henderson, Dan Kelliher, Charlie Mehl, Jean Robinson, Heidi Ross, Buzzy Teiser, all of whom are now in the AAS Membership Directory, though not listed as the honorary grand-progeny of JKF that they are. We found a *mistake* in *United States and China* (1971), which states on p. 313 that in the mid-1940s prices "doubled" (should read "increased") 67 times. The Oberlin Society for the Detection and Correction of Error informed JKF that $2^{67}$ had been too big to be calculated on the college mainframe computer, but could be expressed as 1,152,921,504,606,846,967 times 64. The next edition of *US and China* omitted the sentence entirely. Shortly after, Oberlin decided that my position didn't really exist.

In Hong Kong, having gone over to Yale, or at least Yale-China, with the timely introduction of Jim Thomson, as Associate Director of the International Asian Studies Program, of which JKF was a long-term international adviser, I found that he and Eugene Wu wanted me to shake down Harvard alumni of Hong Kong for millions of dollars. No such luck, but I did have an awfully nice dinner with John, Wilma, and the Fung family.

I last saw John last summer. I dropped by the Center to say hello and good-bye to his assistant Joan Hill, but found JKF and Muffy Henderson Coolidge huddled over John's ms., trying to decide whether to call it "The" or "A" history. For fifteen or twenty minutes we argued whether there were "peasants" or "farmers" in China. Probably I didn't convince him that they were farmers—I'll wait to see the book—but it was fun trying.

VIPAN CHANDRA
*Wheaton College*

Since my college days in India when Socrates and the Upanishads together weaned me away from the conventionally sacred, the only thing really sacred for me has been free inquiry. Consequently, I have been a grouch ever since. I have griped endlessly, for example, about the irrationality and destructiveness of political ideologies, or what some scholars call the "grand organizing ideas" of history. Having lately run out of such targets, thanks to the demise of the Cold War, I have started ranting against the decline of good manners in our society—the reluctance to say "please" or to express gratitude, the failure to return calls or respond to letters, the readiness to hurl epithets as a substitute for reason, and the tendency to blame everything and everyone but oneself for one's setbacks or disappointments. You get my drift: The collapse of our civilization is imminent.

My friends tell me such irritability is a consequence of my having recently turned fifty. I tell them, no, it is all the fault of John Fairbank and Ed Reischauer. JKF and EOR? How come? I answer by saying that JKF and EOR spoiled me by unwittingly raising my expectations of human behavior to what to them were ordinary, decent levels but no doubt are considered abnormal today. I will confine myself here to JKF.

As a graduate student in the early 1970s, I came to know JKF well, particularly during my stints as chief section-man in the popular "Rice Paddies" courses. Like countless others, I learned much about all aspects of Chinese history from this intellectual kin of Ssu-ma Ch'ien. The sweeping range of JKF's knowledge and his sense of the interconnectedness of all things certainly remind one of the other Grand Historian. All this is well known. What I saw of JKF as a mentor and friend is something else.

I must confess that at first I found him somewhat difficult to approach as a person. He wasn't stern or forbidding but he struck me as a little too earnest and a little too businesslike. At a superficial glance he could have easily passed for an inspiring personification of the proverbial Protestant Ethic. He was of course that but as I was to find out gradually, there was far more to JKF than just that.

Through my weekly conferences with him and through our exchange of notes and phone calls I discovered a side of JKF that was nothing less than the welcome glow of dawn. He was not given to elaborate verbal expressions of warmth and support for his students but his actions were quintessentially warm and supportive. No written query from me or anyone else was ever too trivial to evoke a response from this busy man, and no phone call was ever left unreturned. All responses were prompt and invariably conveyed considered, not casual, answers. Encouragement, advice, praise were all given judiciously and were often couched in the understated, amiable sarcasm that was a hallmark of the JKF style.

What was special about this pattern was that it was not special. JKF took this kind of interest in all his students. Sustained communication was his unique way of showing he cared—and cared deeply—about the intellectual and personal growth of those under his wings. And I am sure I am not the only one to testify that if you felt like keeping in touch with him long after you had left Cambridge, you would find JKF equally responsive. Your letters would get the same courteous and prompt attention, except now he would sign off as John.

Something in this experience tells me that JKF understood very deeply how all of us are interconnected and how important it is to keep life in holistic perspective. Often our dreams and plans flower and bear fruit or wither and die because a word from a valued mentor speeds us on or its absence kills our enthusiasm and prevents us from taking the next step. JKF knew that he was a vital link in this human chain and he understood very well that we valued this connection. From all I can tell, he was a closet Taoist.

JKF did a great deal of this kind of nurturing, although I suspect that the word itself does not sit well with his style. One incident that particularly epitomizes this aspect of his personality has remained with me to this day. It shows that JKF had an uncanny ability to peer into the souls of people close to him. If he suspected that they were troubled he would spring into action without waiting to be asked. One day in 1976, a year before obtaining my Ph. D., I casually mentioned to him the difficulty I was having in finding a teaching position. Underneath my usual stoical expression perhaps lurked some feeling of despair, which he must have noticed. The next day—yes, the next day—I found at my desk a packet of twelve letters complete with envelopes, all individually written and addressed to JKF's well-placed friends around the country inquiring if they could be of any help to me. Attached to the packet was a note asking me to mail each letter forthwith and send along a copy of my latest *vitae*. Needless to say, I was overwhelmed by this act of spontaneous magnanimity. I know from others that such generosity was typical of this extraordinary man.

JKF was an old-fashioned teacher par excellence. He did not merely instruct us brilliantly in an academic discipline but also taught us, through personal acts, large and small, much about life itself. A thoroughly nonideological truth-seeker himself, he also strengthened my personal skepticism about grand, single-factor explanations and "overarching" theories. So I guess I will soon find some new dogmatic mumbo jumbo as a target for my darts. Something else is certain as well: The next time I predict the downfall of our civilization due to declining manners I will have clearer memories of men like JKF and EOR to reassure me that there is hope of recovery.

ALBERT FEUERWERKER
*University of Michigan*

Among all the memories of John that run through my mind, allow me to attempt to share two. The first is of a summer 1972 visit to Wilma and John in New Hampshire by Yi-tsi and me and our children, Alison and Paul. We had a fine time, stayed overnight, and in the morning the four of us accompanied John, bearing axe and saw, to the hillside outside the house. Paul (age 9) was thrilled that John let him "help" with what looked like the Sisyphean task of clearing the underbrush and low trees that perennially threatened to block the magnificent view of the mountains in the distance. More important, neither he nor Alison have ever forgotten their image that day of John tirelessly sawing and hacking away at the thicket. Whenever we have subsequently complained of difficulties, aches, or aging, we have inevitably been greeted with "remember John Fairbank clearing the hillside in New Hampshire!" This archetype (and lesson) of persistent and optimistic effort in face of each goal and every obstacle—large and small, very personal and more distantly professional—is one that we have cherished since that time, even when we have been short of the remarkable Fairbankian will and ability to follow it.

My second selected memory is of one of the conventions (alas, always held between Christmas and New Years so as to get favorable hotel rates) of the American Historical Association. While we China types were now in some degree integrated into the AHA and into its annual program as well (in large part of course this too was John's accomplishment), perhaps more than a proportional share of the

Asia panels were still scheduled for the afternoon of the very last day of the meetings. I recall vividly a much too large room and a much too small audience devoted to a session on Chinese history, the panel participants including two of John's former students who were presenting papers and one who was to be a commentator. As the afternoon waned the numbers in the room dwindled—airplanes were to be caught—until only the panelists and perhaps a half-dozen others remained. But John stayed until the very end, with legal pad and pencil registering the reports and discussions of the panelists. All of them surely felt deeply grateful that their teacher had stayed on to hear them out, and to participate himself with a question or comment. No one who has been John's student can ever forget his genuine and persisting interest in their work, in their careers, in their views and ideas. We could always freely turn to him for support and assistance—and later, when we had begun to make small academic contributions of our own, he generously honored us by asking our assistance and cooperation in some of his scholarly projects.

It was a glorious life, and John Fairbank was a magnificent man.

HAROLD L. KAHN
*Stanford University*

Early in the spring of 1966, a young lecturer in Chinese history from the University of London appeared at the Harvard Yenching Institute in Cambridge (Massachusetts) to give a lecture. He fancied himself a cut above the Tweeds and Herringbones in a hand-tailored suit and City shirt. He was to be introduced by Professor Fairbank, his teacher. Professor Fairbank was never late. That day he was. Tweeds and Herringbones grew restive, City shirt sweat through. Finally, at that delicate point between hysteria and resignation, in swept an apparition in academic regalia, resplendent in the reds and blues of the Oxford D. Phil. cap and gown. The place broke up. John Fairbank, his timing impeccable, then proceeded in a boffo introduction to trace the young lecturer's retreat from the modernist agenda to the history of eighteenth-century emperors, a trajectory of discovery and false starts and as yet unfulfilled promise. It was kind and funny, knowledgeable, flattering, silly and learned. I know, because I was that lecturer.

John Fairbank understood how hard Chinese history is. There is too much of it, inscribed in a language always ready to bushwack the unwary or overconfident, embattled as often in ideological disputes as in historiographical debate. Knowing that, he fairly insisted on comic relief. Playfulness became a requirement of erudition. His wacky doggerel verses, strewn with shards of half-forgotten languages, celebrated colleagues' accomplishments and his own. His multi-colored handwritten notes to beleaguered thesis writers, or to their spouses, urging closure, threatening theft of unfinished drafts, cheering aperçus, were collected and passed from hand to hand: comic *samisdat* to be shared in the darker hours of scholarship. His rules for frisbee on the front lawn were inscrutable and hilarious. His carefully juxtaposed photos of Himself in the Empress Dowager's court punctured the solemnity of a profession that often took itself too seriously. He brought us through, laughing and thinking—a generation taught to believe that if there was room in our field for an article called "The Banana in Chinese Literature," there was room for the banana peel as well. We were trained to take pratfalls on the way to the faculty club. I like to think there's no better way to go.

# *Encouragement of Scholars and Scholarship*

BEATRICE S. BARTLETT
*Yale University*

My earliest views of John Fairbank were shaped by my first dissertation director, Mary Wright, who admired John's intellectual power and described him as a tolerant being who welcomed the give-and-take of discussion. I was soon to learn this for myself. Direct contact came when I was toiling on distant research frontiers in the Taipei Palace Museum and somehow my first article in the Museum *Bulletin* found its way to John's hand. Out of the blue he sent me a brief typed note of appreciation. I felt as if I had received an imperial vermilion rescript from the Emperor of Chinese Studies himself.

Of course I wrote back. Thus was inaugurated a correspondence that lasted, off and on, until the last note arrived, dated only ten days before his death. Somehow during those years he saw and even read just about everything I wrote and he always responded with encouragement and specificity. Unlike so many longer letters of this genre his were written on a solid basis of having read not only my own pieces but everything else as well—his replies frequently contained helpful references to the works of others.

Other missives prodded me to greater productivity: "What MS is now in press and why is it not?" came a pointed question at the end of one letter. On another occasion he sounded a more positive note: "I want to see you have public credit as a pioneer and I think your publications would also greatly advance the Ch'ing documents field. Can you tell me what the present situation is and also of some way that I could assist in expediting publication?"

I knew of course that numerous other one- and two-liners were going out to other scholars scattered all over the world. Nevertheless

I treasured mine and have them still. Like everyone else, I marveled at the energy that John mobilized for this enterprise, which was, after all, only one of his countless projects.

Correspondence was in abeyance once I arrived at Cambridge as a post-doctoral fellow (1981-83), but delightful substitutes followed now in the form of imperial audiences—weekend invitations to the Fairbanks' house in Franklin, New Hampshire. There I enjoyed munificent hospitality and good conversations with both Wilma and John. On one occasion John himself cooked the dinner.

The first visit took place in a February thaw. At my first morning conference with John I was invited to draw up a list—for his perusal—of all the topics in the field of archives and communications that I could think worth writing on. By lunch time I had concocted about fifty possibilities—a wonderfully efficient way, I later reflected, for a busy scholar to find out what I might have to tell him that he wanted to know. In the afternoon we discussed the list as he led me on a tramp around Franklin, not always sticking to the roads but instead marching through slush and briars and an occasional backwoods trail. As my feet and ears grew colder, John persevered, apparently impervious to the elements, combining exercise and intellectual intake, a tower of energy ahead on a path of his own devising.

That is how I shall remember him: a tower of energy ahead of us all, on a path of his own devising.

JONATHAN SPENCE
*Yale University*

Mr. Fairbank was someone I knew from almost the first moment I came to America to study Chinese history in 1959. When I arrived at Yale that summer, I was introduced to him by Arthur and Mary Wright, who headed the program here. Mary Wright had been a very special student of his, so when I became her Ph. D. student Mr. Fairbank felt it was almost like a grandson-grandfather relationship. And he took an amazing interest in my work, which astonished me, knowing that I wasn't even one of his students. I felt the respect for him you feel for somebody very senior who notices you when you're just beginning. And I never lost that admiration for him and his energy.

Some years ago, after I'd started teaching, there was a get-together at his home with students and professors. There was supper, with some wine. While it wasn't uproarious, the conversation was quite animated. Later, papers were to be delivered about nine o'clock. After supper Mr. Fairbank got up. I was a bit puzzled by this; it was *his* party. So I said, "Oh, you're going?" He looked around the table and said, "Nothing's going to happen till nine, so I'll get an hour's work done." Nobody really minded, because it was understood that that was his block of time to seize. I wonder sometimes, with both admiration and sadness, about what such determination must have cost him.

## Robert B. Oxnam
*The Asia Society*

I remember well Mary Wright referring to Professor Fairbank with substantial filiality in her voice when she introduced him to History 45B as a guest lecturer in 1964. As I heard him lecture on the familiar topic of nineteenth-century treaty ports, crisp points interspersed with wry humor, the world of China studies suddenly seemed to take on a family-like order. Fairbank was a genial grandfather, Wright a caring though somewhat overwrought mother, and we were all sansei. I still think of it that way.

I also recall the fluttering in my stomach in 1977 when I summoned the courage to call "Professor Fairbank" by the name "John." It wasn't inappropriate since I had known him for over a decade and since we were working together fairly closely in the Asia Society's China Council of which he was chairman. He was quite relaxed about the matter and appeared not even to notice the change in address. But for me it seemed a coming of age—the chance to call the Dean of Sinology by first name was a big deal. Even now, after his passing, it seems right to remember him as "John King Fairbank" with the emphasis on the middle name.

A year or so later, I recall, John was involved in an inaugural meeting of the Committee of Concerned Asian Scholars. We sat on the stage together before an audience of several hundred students and scholars all of whom shared a general sense that the Vietnam War demanded more public response from Asia experts (even Asia experts, junior grade, like myself). He had the conviction to attend the meeting and to speak fervently on how concepts of "national interest" had caused so many problems in American perceptions and policies. But he also seemed slightly uncomfortable in the role, as if offering his insights before a cheering, and sometimes jeering, throng was not his proper milieu. Indeed that may have been a problem later in life when his always dignified, sometimes patrician style could convey the impression that he lacked passion and commitment.

I don't mean this to be disrespectful, but I find it easier to deal with John's passing than I thought it would be. Perhaps it's partly that he lived to a good age, survived earlier health problems, and even spoke with eloquence at some of his students' memorial services (I know he found those of Mary Wright and Teddy White particularly difficult). But I think it's more that he truly lives on in the enormous number of people he nurtured in the China field around the globe. The extended intellectual family of John King Fairbank and Wilma Fairbank is extraordinary in its numbers and its devotion. Not too long ago, an acquaintance described me as his "intellectual grandfather" (meaning I taught the person who taught him about China)—which means that there may be as many as five intellectual generations in the Fairbank tree of scholarship (since John is my "intellectual grandfather").

I do remember my first visit to a Harvard China seminar after starting to teach. "You're going to get a lot out of this," he offered, gesturing to his protégés in the room, "they're the cream of the China field." I'm still a bit perplexed about how he meant the remark, but this barbarian (i.e. Yalie, then without doctorate) knew he had entered the Gu Gong of the field.

He was indeed John King Fairbank. Wan Sui.

Stuart R. Schram
*Harvard University*

John K. Fairbank was, with Mary Wright, one of the two people who played decisive roles in drawing me into the China field. After undergraduate work at Minnesota in mathematical physics, I had switched to political science for my doctorate at Columbia. While in residence there, I had studied Soviet affairs, but not China, except for one course with Nat Peffer on foreign policy. In the early 1950s, I developed an interest in Chinese history and culture, and started learning Chinese. Subsequently, while working at the Fondation Nationale des Sciences Politiques in Paris, in the section devoted to Soviet affairs, I began casting around for a research topic which would involve China as well, and hit upon the idea of studying the thought of that odd-ball Chinese Leninist, Mao Zedong.

In order to lay a foundation for such work, I wished to spend some time at a major American center. Two friends, Marshall Shulman, who had been a classmate at Columbia, and Herbert Marcuse, whom I had met through my thesis supervisor, Franz Neumann, kindly undertook in 1960 to wait upon the Directors of the Russian and East Asian Research Centers, and persuaded them to contribute one month's stipend each, so that I could spend a period as a visitor at the two centers, in October and November 1960. Merle Fainsod I had met when I gave a talk at the Russian Research Center in 1957; John Fairbank I did not know at all.

During these two months, I became acquainted both with John's generous and enthusiastic side, and with the rigor he imposed on himself and others. One of my first and wisest decisions was to attend his Qing seminar, at which I gave a paper on the 1911 revolution in Hunan as seen by Mao, and as recorded in the documents. On my last day in Dunster Street (the former home of both the East Asian and Russian Research Centers), John came over to where I was lunching with Merle Fainsod, and made a brief speech to the effect that he had known nothing about me when he had agreed to my visit, and had let himself be persuaded by Marshall and Herbert, but had in the end been pleased by what he had seen. I could read Chinese, he said, even Qing documents, and he had liked my seminar paper. In short, he was glad I had turned up. A few months later, however, when after missing the deadline for revision, I wrote to ask whether he was still interested in my piece for the Harvard *Papers on China*, he replied firmly that the date was past, and as far as he knew my contribution had not been received. Although I subsequently drew on the substance, and even on the wording, of this seminar paper in the introduction to my Mao biography, so that it was not entirely wasted, I was left with an abiding regret at having failed John in this way. That, I think, is what he wanted me to feel.

While at Harvard in the fall of 1960, I went briefly to Yale to visit Arthur and Mary Wright, whom I had met at Stanford in 1957. During a long evening at their home, which John called "the castle," I discussed with Mary in particular the question of whether or not, given that I was in my mid-thirties and had begun the study of Chinese at the age of 28, there was any point in even trying to do serious work on Chinese politics, or whether I should stick to Soviet affairs. She encouraged me very warmly, arguing that there were only degrees of ignorance on the part of Westerners trying to understand China, so I might as well get into the act too. Her words, and John Fairbank's approval during this first visit to Harvard, were the two crucial factors in my decision henceforth to concentrate my research on China, instead of treating it merely as a hobby.

From these beginnings flowed most of my subsequent career. In 1962-1963, I was able to return to Dunster Street (this time to the East Asian Research Center alone), on a Rockefeller Foundation fellowship which John had actively supported me in obtaining. While there I completed work on *The Political Thought of Mao Tse-tung*, in which John took a very lively interest. Every time I came up with a passage which underscored the links between Mao's interpretation of Marxism and Chinese thought, he was, not surprisingly, enthusiastic, and he greeted the appearance of the book with generous praise.

Of the many memories which have accumulated during the thirty years since these experiences of the early 1960s, I would like here to single out only a few, which illustrate the point I made at the beginning about John as an editor and organizer. He could, and did, provide both guidance and inspiration; but at the same time, he was not a man to be trifled with. I recall one conversation I had with him shortly after I became Head of the Contemporary China Institute at SOAS in 1968. He began by urging me to face up to my responsibilities. "You have been used to looking up to others," he said, "but now there's nobody up there but us directors, so look to yourself." He then went on to speak of a scholar who had spent a year at the East Asian Research Center, but had failed to produce the promised book, then or subsequently. "There are these ghosts floating around," said John. "Every now and then you will spy one, and you will point your finger at him, and he will quiver with fright, and go 'boing!'." Those who failed in their obligations were not likely to be allowed to forget it. He pointed his finger at them, not out of any personal malice, but out of a sense of his responsibilities to the field, and to those who had financed the work.

For the past decade and a half, it was in his capacity as editor of the *Cambridge History of China* that John continued to impose discipline and deadlines upon us. My chapter on Mao's post-1949 thought for Volume 15 he left largely to Rod MacFarquhar, but that for Volume 13 on the earlier period he read very meticulously himself. The ten single-spaced pages he sent me in 1981 combined incisive comments with high comedy. The opening sentences set the tone: "I am spending these days with your revised chapter and enjoying it very much. You have distilled an essence through time. It is like the young W. B. Cannon watching peristalsis in his laboratory goose, except that what comes out of the process is not goose droppings but a gargantuan revolution."

In one of several passages underscoring the importance of citing a variety of different views on controversial issues, John wrote: "My experience suggests that the longer-lived historian is he who speaks through the words of others. His lips move, his pen writes, but always the words of others, who thereby become attached to his chariot. This is what turns us fellahs into HISTORY."

Throughout the ensuing decade, his presence, though slightly less in the foreground, was constantly with us, urging us on. In October 1988, he began a letter demanding my bibliographic essay and glossary cards for Volume 15: "I occasionally descend from the hills to stir up the town for a few days and then enjoy getting back to our rocks and trees. On my current foray I have shot up the *CHOC* vol. 15 project and Rod says he will press on faster." To my promise to send them shortly, he replied: "It would help if you could kindly send these cards and your bibliographic essay *last week* so as to arrive here not later than ***today***."

The man is no longer here to shoot us up, but the sense of purpose which he incarnated will not soon vanish from the collective memory of those who knew him. I end with a parallel which might have pleased neither of the persons concerned. No doubt there would have been a revolution in China in the mid-twentieth century even if Mao Zedong had never existed, but it would almost certainly not have taken the same form without him. Similarly, the realities of world politics after 1945 made it inevitable that Americans would take a more serious interest in China than hitherto, and that the academic field devoted to China would be expanded. Without John Fairbank, however, it would hardly have been the broad-based, dynamic, and entertaining arena which it has become.

Daniel H. Bays
*University of Kansas*

My memories of John Fairbank center on his warm and generous treatment of me as a young scholar despite the fact that I had never been one of his students and indeed had no connection with Harvard. But John had a view for the field which was ecumenical, encompassing the products of all universities, and an impulse to encourage younger people which was several generations deep—helping the students of his former students, and even some of their students, yea unto the fourth generation.

The natural initial awe in which I held John when as a beginning graduate student I first heard him lecture in Ann Arbor was supplanted by appreciation of his work as an academic manager during the Congress of Orientalists in Ann Arbor in 1967, when I was part of the local team of Al Feuerwerker's students who assisted with the Congress. Later, as a young assistant professor I saw, at two extended research conferences held at Harvard in the 1970s, how he treated as peers and equals our cadre of scholars just getting established in the field.

Finally, while I was on a Fulbright in Taiwan in 1984, I was surprised to receive from John a letter which was also a bequest. Having failed to put together an organized study program for one of the areas that he believed to be both important and understudied in modern China—missions and the role of Christianity—he passed it all on to me, because my research had moved into that area. He included a suggestion to create a more modest project than he had originally envisioned, for a finite number of years and with a single director. But he gave no further directions, only enthusiastic encouragement. He did not meddle or try to shape the final proposal, even when I moved the project away from a focus on foreign missions and more towards the role of Christianity in China on Chinese terms and as part of Chinese issues. Thus part of John's legacy is the History of Christianity in China Project, funded by the Henry Luce Foundation, which ran from 1985 to 1992. John served conscientiously and with his characteristic wit as one of the Advisory Board members for the first three years of the project, participating in meetings by memo. When the research results supported by the project come into print, they will constitute yet another monument to John's seminal role in our field.

MAN-HOUNG LIN
*Institute of Modern History, Academia Sinica*

I had contact with Professor Fairbank in his final stage of life. My last letter from him was dated February 20, 1991. Between September 1988 and March 1989, we communicated about ten times concerning H. B. Morse and the circuit intendants in relation to the Chinese Maritime Customs. His last letter to me was about my Harvard dissertation.

Such contact with him impressed me in three ways:

(1) I think the recent description of Professor Fairbank as representing the school of "the Western impact on China" is not a

fair one. I have been studying trade and late imperial China's societal change for about fifteen years. If I were asked to write the histories of H. B. Morse and the Chinese Maritime Customs, I would think of using Western sources. But he used Chinese sources to trace how H. B. Morse and the Chinese Maritime Customs fit into the Chinese bureaucracy and played their role in China. He also used Ch'ing documents and the perspective of China's traditional foreign relations to study the unequal treaties.

(2) He was a thoughtful and considerate person. I wrote him several letters to which I didn't expect any response, yet I always received one. In addition to some book reviews he wrote for the *New York Review of Books*, once I received a letter from him saying, "there are many books in the USA that you cannot now peruse, but if you accumulate some of them (especially in paperback) they can be of use in future. Hence my enclosure." What was enclosed was a $105 book certificate from Wordsworth Bookstore.

(3) He was a strong supporter of the efforts of younger generations. The most unexpected letter from him came in February 1991. He gave me suggestions on conveying my ideas more effectively to Western readers. He also suggested several related topics to investigate. In addition, he thanked me for my introductory remarks about *Papers on China* in our institute's newsletter. (They were written at Director Chang Yu-fa's suggestion.)

As a graduate of the Ph. D. Committee on History and East Asian Languages in 1989, I was fortunate to have had such contact with Professor Fairbank. His energetic and enthusiastic spirit, as revealed to me in his eighty-fourth year, will remain an inspiration for life. That he took time out of his retirement to advise me, a student of his student, reminds me of a senior colleague's comment: "Professor Fairbank is a founder of a school rather than a teacher."

Stephen Hay
*University of California, Santa Barbara*

We who have served at the court of King John
Know well how he helped us on,
Showering us with grants and letters of rec,
Hospitality and laughter a peck.

John, John, we follow you still,
For our days, too, will end.
But not until we've written our fill,
Like you, great scholar and friend.

# *Field Building*

Henry Rosovsky*
*Harvard University*

Whenever a person of John Fairbank's stature dies, the somewhat trite expression "end of an era" quickly comes to mind. But for our University, there was never a better moment to contemplate the true meaning of this phrase. Both fathers of East Asian Studies at Harvard—Ed Reischauer and John—have now passed away. They have left us—their many children—a great treasure. We will surely be judged in terms of how we make use of this inheritance.

I did not have the privilege to study with John. Of course, that was not his fault because he tried to recruit nearly everyone he knew (even quite casually) into the field of Chinese studies. That someone might prefer the study of another country was always difficult for him to understand. I think that he consoled himself by thinking of a large part of the world as really belonging to the Chinese culture area, with Japan representing a mildly amusing mutation.

Although never a student of John's—at least in the classroom sense—I want to say a few words from the perspective of the University. There is not enough time to mention the many contributions of one of Harvard's genuine giants: the course nicknamed Rice Paddies, the East Asian Research Center, the many dissertations, FAS and university committees, Kirkland House . . . and so much more.

The best way to understand John's institutional contributions is to think briefly of the present state of East Asian studies at Harvard. Hundreds of undergraduates studying languages; a full complement of professors in nearly all appropriate departments; thriving research

* This memoir, in slightly different form, was delivered at the memorial service for Fairbank, held at Harvard University on October 21, 1991.

centers and excellent Ph. D. training; a student body and even a faculty that accepts China, Japan, Korea and Vietnam on their own terms as being intellectually challenging and of vital importance in our future—all that has much to do with John's presence in our midst. Of course in the last 55 years, a lot of it would have happened anyway but there would have been much less quantity and above all less quality, and it also would have been far less fun. This is true because John was both a lover of institutions and one of our great intellectual missionaries. In fact, I can think of no one else in modern Harvard history who rivaled him in this regard. The combination of love for Harvard and zeal for his subject has left an indelible imprint on the University. Some may have thought of him as a "Chinese Firster," but I always believed that that represented excessive non-Chinese paranoia. He cared deeply about the entire field and deplored the splitting of our research centers into separate units, even if named Fairbank and Reischauer.

When I became dean in 1973, John was the only person to lodge a vigorous face to face protest with President Bok. This was not because—as you might think—he was especially familiar with some of the base sides of my character. Not at all: he objected strongly to a Japan specialist wasting long years of expensive training on trivial administrative pursuits. But I have to add that once the die was cast, he appeared regularly in University Hall, urging more resources, new chairs, more books—in short, more of everything East Asian. At that point he even appeared pleased by my possession of the FAS checkbook.

In very recent times, a number of people have raised questions concerning professorial citizenship. Are we sufficiently conscientious teachers? Are we mentors of graduate students? Are we in Cambridge at the service of our students or too frequently jetting across one or another ocean? Do our outside interests dominate university obligations? There are no easy answers; not everything is getting worse. But if we seek a model of university citizenship—a yardstick with which to measure our own standards—I can think of no one more appropriate than our recently departed colleague and friend.

Eugene Wu
*Harvard University*

I knew John Fairbank only by name until 1964, when I came to Harvard for an interview about the Librarian's position at the Harvard-Yenching Library. He was not on the search committee appointed by the Harvard-Yenching Institute (the Library was still a part of the Institute at that time), but he was one of the people I was scheduled to meet. I found him to be a person of great charm and civility, and also of many insights into the problems of developing a research collection on modern and contemporary China. He also showed a deep interest in providing better intellectual access to research materials through bibliographical research. His enthusiasm about the prospects of the Harvard-Yenching Library was as obvious as it was contagious. I went away from our meeting quite impressed. Later that year, I came back to Cambridge for a return visit, and this time the Harvard-Yenching Institute also invited my wife, Nadine. We knew we were to be met at Logan airport by Gordon Bechanan, the personnel officer of the Harvard College Library, but we were totally surprised to see John Fairbank there as well. In the characteristic Fairbank fashion, John took immediate charge of things, and before we had a chance to check into the Dana Palmer House, where we were going to stay, we were whisked to 41 Winthrop Street. At the Fairbanks' residence, John had arranged a reception for us. There we were introduced to a large group of Harvard faculty, visiting scholars at the East Asian Research Center, and some graduate students. For two days, John acted as our escort. Nadine still remembers her difficulty in keeping up with John's stride, and her fears about his total disregard for traffic lights while crossing Cambridge streets!

After taking up my position at the Harvard-Yenching Library in the fall of 1965, I began to learn more about John's involvement with the Library. As early as 1945, when he was posted in Chungking with the USIS, John was already sending books back to the Library as a volunteer service to his Alma Mater. In his annual report that year, Dr. A. Kaiming Chiu, my predecessor, acknowledged that the more than 1,400 volumes of Chinese books received that year were "new publications published in Chungking and other interior cities during the war years. We are much indebted to Professor John K. Fairbank for his services in purchasing these books, and for his efforts in securing gifts from the National Central Library and other Chinese cultural institutions." Following his return to Harvard in 1946, John continued to offer his assistance to the Library. He introduced book dealers as well as friends in China and Hong Kong to Dr. Chiu, and also arranged an exchange with the Hoover Institution whereby the Harvard-Yenching Library would receive many duplicates of Chinese Communist publications which Mary C. Wright had earlier acquired in Communist-controlled areas in China for the newly established Chinese Collection at Hoover.

In addition to securing books, John also used his good offices to secure financial support for the Library over the years. He obtained funds from the Harvard College Library for the purchase of Chinese-language publications on modern and contemporary China for the East Asian Regional Studies Program, funding which lasted for a number of years. In Harvard's application for government funding of East Asian studies under the National Defense and Education Act (NDEA) in the late 1950s, library support was listed as a priority need. Because of his initial effort, the Library has been a beneficiary of that program ever since. During his tenure as director of the East Asian Research Center, John provided the seed money for the publication of the Harvard-Yenching Library Bibliographical Series. The proceeds from the sales of the three titles already published—one an index to Chinese periodicals, one the Library's Korean catalog, and one an annotated bibliography of the Chen Cheng Collection on the Kiangsi Soviet Republic—have made possible the establishment of a revolving fund for future publications in the series. When the Library began its fund drive in the mid-1970s, John lent his full support to the campaign. He arranged with the University Library Visiting Committee and the East Asian Visiting Committee to form a Joint Subcommittee on the Harvard-Yenching Library, and took an active part in the drafting of a campaign brochure and in planning sessions. We took a number of trips together to visit prospective donors in the country. His message was always simple and to the point. As he wrote in the brochure, "Scholarship cannot be maintained if a library ceases to function . . . . As the American people turn toward East Asia in the hope of peace and stable relations, their need for books and knowledge will steadily increase. The maintenance of faculty members and of fellowships for students will be of no avail if the library withers and decays. Harvard has a first-rate faculty because it has a first-rate library and the two must sink or swim together." The donation which made possible the naming of the Library's main reading room in honor of Chinn Ho, and the gift of the Joseph Buttinger papers on Vietnam to the Library were the direct result of John's efforts.

John Fairbank was a true friend to the Harvard-Yenching Library. I shall miss him as an advocate for the Library, a personal friend, and a respected colleague.

## Jerome Alan Cohen
*New York, New York*

"Fairbank as farsighted catalyst" must inevitably be a major theme of this volume. By 1961, when my wife Joan and I first met him and Wilma at the home of Rosemary and Joe Levenson in Berkeley, John was already well known for his ability to extend the study of China to new subjects. He would see the need for another groundbreaking effort and then help turn possibility into actuality. If in the process Harvard proved to be the beneficiary, so much the better, for no one was more aware than John of its legitimating role. Harvard's imprimatur stimulated competing universities to undertake similar programs that might otherwise have been deemed visionary, if not quixotic.

Law proved to be a classic case for the Fairbank formula. Unlike some China specialists, John understood law's importance as a discipline for analyzing both traditional Chinese society and its modern transformation. After he became Director of Harvard's East Asian Research Center, John and his dynamic Associate Director, John Lindbeck, made several attempts during the 1950s to entice promising Harvard Law School graduates into the China field. Each time prospects for success seemed bright, however, the allure of Wall Street or the threat of disinheritance frustrated their plan.

Thus, when Fairbank learned from Levenson that I had recently begun the study of China's law and language while teaching at Berkeley's Law School, Boalt Hall, he lost no time in contacting Milton Katz, then Director of International Legal Studies at Harvard Law School, and his colleague Arthur Von Mehren, professor of comparative law. Von Mehren, with the cooperation of Harvard's leading Sinologist, L. S. Yang, was actually in the midst of teaching an experimental seminar on Chinese law.

In short order, Harvard Law School Dean Erwin Griswold invited me to come to Cambridge as a visiting professor for the academic year 1964-65. To make sure this was an offer a young man could not refuse, Fairbank asked whether there was a scholar of Chinese law anywhere in the world I might welcome as a collaborator for the year, and this resulted in the East Asian Research Center's support for the visit of M. H. Van der Valk of Leiden.

This evidence of Fairbank's organizational vigor was impressive. Yet, as I was to learn, it was only a specific manifestation of his model for developing new academic enterprises. Even before arriving in Cambridge, I was lucky enough to be present at one of the rare occasions when he explicitly acknowledged the outlook that motivated him. John was being lionized by the Royal Asiatic Society of Hong Kong in early 1964 during one of his periodic swings through the Far East. Before launching into his announced lecture, he responded to the accolades of the chairman's introduction by attributing to Harvard rather than to himself most of the credit for his having become the "dean of Chinese studies in the United States," a cliché he later came to abhor as the premature obituaries of retirement accumulated. The secret, he said, was to have the good fortune to be at a place with some of the world's best libraries, professors and graduate students in the China field; any scholar who found himself in such circumstances would be a sinner if he failed to harness the available resources to maximize their yield.

Of course, John's gracious exercise in Chinese modesty fooled no one in the audience, which was sophisticated enough to suspect how much he had done to put Harvard in that favored position. Yet what shone through most clearly was the earnestness, bordering on religious faith, of John's commitment to the study of modern China.

During the next fifteen years I had ample opportunity to test that commitment, as I frequently sought the Master's counsel about how to apply his model to the development of East Asian Legal Studies at Harvard Law School. John's advice was invariably practical and statesmanlike. I will never forget his answer when I once asked about the wisdom of soliciting a donation to our program from a possibly dubious foreign source. "Don't worry," he said. "Harvard sanitizes money by accepting it!"

In addition, John always made himself available for bag lunch talks, guest lectures, symposia and social occasions. He seemed pleased that the program of law teaching and research that he had done much to spawn had managed to take root, and he endorsed its East Asian, rather than exclusively Chinese, focus. He was also gratified that EALS, as the students like to call it, itself became a model for similar programs at other major law schools, in large part thanks to the efforts of Harvard alumni who themselves had benefited from the Fairbank formula.

DWIGHT PERKINS
*Harvard University*

Some people are students of the institutions of modern society. Others are builders of those institutions. John Fairbank was both.

As anyone who worked with John knows, he had a broad and quite detailed conception of where the "China field" was at any given point of time and where it ought to be heading in the future. While John's mornings were usually spent in writing and study, his afternoons and many evenings were devoted to moving the field from where it was to where it ought to be.

Knight Biggerstaff, a friend of John's, had gotten me started on the study of China at Cornell and it was Knight who said I should go see John Fairbank when I started graduate school at Harvard. So the day of class registration in the fall of 1958 I went to see John to seek advice on which Chinese language courses I should mix in with my study for a Ph. D. in economics. John, after looking at my four Chinese courses at Cornell and my two years of using Chinese in the Navy, stated forcefully and unequivocally that I shouldn't spend any more time for the present in studying Chinese. My job was to prove to the economists in the Department of Economics that I was one of them. I followed this advice even though I was on a Foreign Area Training Fellowship at the time and my interest in economics derived from my commitment to studying China rather than vice versa. Not surprisingly I soon ran afoul of an administrator at the Ford Foundation which was still directly managing the Foreign Area Training Fellowships in 1958-59. When the administrator put pressure on me to take China-related courses, I went again to John Fairbank for advice. A forceful letter from John to Ford suggested that Ford should leave advice to students to those better suited to provide it. For the next four years the checks kept coming but without even the hint of a suggestion that I should do anything to be worthy of this support.

John, from early on, had seen economics as an essential component of a well-rounded China program, but getting cooperation from departments of economics was not proving to be easy. Before my arrival at Harvard John, perhaps with others, had persuaded the Ford Foundation to give the University a professorship for someone studying the economy of China. But the Economics Department had refused to accept the chair on the grounds that economics departments did not approve of chairs tied to any particular field, and especially not to area studies. By 1960 the Economics Department had finally decided to accept the professorship and I had passed my oral exams. Writing in the middle of the 1991 recession and a decade and more of poor job opportunities in academia, it is difficult to understand how different the job market was in 1960. Anyone who could breathe and write three consecutive grammatical sentences could get a teaching job. I did not even have a dissertation topic when I received my first assistant professorship offer from a west coast university and, as always, I went to John Fairbank for advice as to what to do. John got Arthur Smithies to offer me an instructorship at Harvard as soon as I finished my dissertation which, it turned out, was three years later. John soon thereafter armed me with numerous letters of introduction in Japan, Taiwan, and Hong Kong and off I went to Asia as a 26-year-old prospective holder of a Harvard position.

I worked with John for a good many years after I finished my dissertation as a member and later Associate Director of what is now the Fairbank Center. We were on seven history Ph. D. committees together, usually at his initiative, we spoke at numerous East Asian functions, and I was the Center's representative to the fund drive that he and Ed Reischauer led. But it is these earlier years in which he nurtured a young graduate student and maneuvered Harvard into a China economics chair that best illustrate to me how John Fairbank built the China field. He knew what he wanted and how to make the system work for him and he was decisive when decisions were required.

John Fairbank also had the integrity to say what he believed whether or not the view expressed was currently in favor. That this got him into trouble in the McCarthy era is well known. As I learned from personal experience, it also occasionally got him in trouble with the Chinese. At the invitation of Zhou Enlai, John and Wilma had gone to China in 1972 and John wanted to use his new-found close ties with Zhou to help the East Asian Research Center's faculty get to China. So in 1973 John set up a meeting at the Chinese Liaison Office in Beijing for Ben Schwartz and myself. In due course the Center received an invitation to send a delegation to Beijing. Two days before we were to leave the U.S. in July, we received word that the trip was being "postponed" but with no further explanation.

It was not until the next summer at a dinner at the Chinese Liaison Office prior to my accompanying Senator Henry M. Jackson to China that I learned the reason. Because the Chinese wanted the Jackson trip to go well, they thought they owed me an explanation of the earlier debacle. For some reason they also decided to make the explanation in Chinese, which, given the quality of my spoken Chinese, meant they couldn't be subtle. It turns out our trip was canceled because John had written a review of a book titled *Prisoner of Mao* for I believe the *New York Review of Books*. The Chinese had not liked the review or even the fact that John Fairbank would review such a book. If John Fairbank wanted favors from China, still then under the influence of the Cultural Revolution, he would have to be more careful about the positions he took on issues affecting China. But if John Fairbank ever trimmed his views to fit the "requirements of the times" either before that time or after, I am unaware of it.

## Rulan Chao Pian
*Harvard University*

I had heard my parents mention the name "John Fairbank" long before we came to this country and made our home here. I became acquainted with John personally in 1947, when I began to teach modern Chinese at Harvard in the Far Eastern Department, first by assisting Francis Cleaves, and later on my own.

To be sure, I was already involved in Chinese language teaching in connection with the Army Special Training Program at Harvard as far back as 1943, when I was still an undergraduate at Radcliffe. But I believe that the firm establishment of the requirement at Harvard for all students in the Chinese field to gain an active command of the language in speaking and in writing began with the Regional Studies Program established by John. This was not only an obvious training procedure for students of modern Chinese history, it has proven to be a wise policy for future scholars in all aspects of Chinese language and civilization.

Ezra Vogel
*Harvard University*

When I became John Fairbank's deputy director for the East Asian Research Center in 1967, John (as I could unflinchingly call him since I had never been his student) explained the basic rules of the Harvard East Asian Empire: "Communication within the office (Fairbank, Ginny Briggs, and Vogel) is to be by memos. The director and associate director will keep each other informed by sending duplicates of all outgoing correspondence."

Having been part of the Center for several years, I was under no illusion that the Empire was run by consensus. I also knew that the written word had great meaning in Chinese culture and that Fairbank had mastered the art of dictating elegant and lean prose that hung together without the need for further editing. For Fairbank the short memo avoided lengthy unnecessary idle chitchat.

But even more important, notes and correspondence were available for the record. Of course, having had his national loyalty unfairly questioned during the heyday of Senator Joseph McCarthy, John was acutely aware of the need to keep a record that he could happily show to anyone who raised questions. In reading Fairbank's outgoing correspondence day by day it became clear that his letters reflected a perspective that transcended daily business. As a historian who had begun his career reading records of officials, Fairbank seemed to be thinking as he wrote each letter how a historian going through his correspondence might someday view his work. His correspondence was peppered with wry comments on the era, with frequent analogies to Chinese history. His correspondence had a touch of grandeur that would have been hard for anyone to achieve unless he were a historian working on a society that thought in terms of centuries.

The Harvard East Asian Studies Empire, like the Chinese Empire, had its hierarchy, and entrance to the status of respected scholar was determined by merit, as measured by quality of written work. Talented students were admitted into the M. A. program, and the M. A. candidates were tested by a term paper. Those who failed to write what Fairbank regarded as outstanding M. A. papers were not admitted into the Ph. D. program, sometimes much to their dismay, but the successful candidates were then given the careful Fairbank tutelage: guidance in how to select a topic, make use of sources, read documents, and above all how to write a good thesis that could eventually be made into a book. Each successful candidate carved out an important hitherto neglected topic, and when the thesis was done, the candidate moved toward a higher stage of scholardom, a year fellowship needed to round out whatever necessary travel, extra source material, and editing were needed to make the thesis a good book. The book of course was published in one of the Harvard East Asian series.

I have no doubt that once his program was in full swing, Fairbank believed that within the world of East Asian studies, Harvard was the central kingdom. As much as others may have respected Harvard's efforts, in the era of popular democracy, Fairbank was seen as an elitist, a ready target of attack that intensified in the aftermath of the Vietnam War and China's Cultural Revolution when it was popular to attack "those in positions of authority."

The Harvard East Asian Empire's "World Order" rested on relationships with all serious institutions of East Asian studies around the world. As director of the East Asian Research Center, Fairbank kept a list of outstanding scholars in each major country of the world. He traveled abroad to maintain contact with all these major institutions, a task that by the end of his reign had grown to exceed his span of control.

Fairbank received visitors from around the world and treated them with his own style of diplomacy. Discussion centered around the big issues in Chinese studies. Wit was not only allowed but encouraged; only small talk was out of bounds. Visitors were allowed to view the series of volumes published in the East Asian series displayed in his office and were invited to his weekly tea. He sometimes greeted Chinese visitors with a few words of Chinese, but he never tried conversing with them in Chinese. I suspect that he gave up on conversational Chinese because he had high standards for the language a person in his position ought to use. Rather than go below his standards in Chinese, he spoke his own elegant English. His identification with Harvard and its East Asian Empire was so great that borders became blurred, but he never fuzzed the line of national identity. Fairbank admired much of Chinese high culture, but he was more Oxford than Qinghua; in China, Fairbank was unmistakably the foreigner, his wit that of the bemused observer.

Among visitors, Fairbank distinguished between the general visitor, to whom he was polite and gracious, and the serious young person who he thought might be able to produce a good study. Even if a person happened to get his training outside Harvard, Fairbank was always on the look-out for the talented scholar. Of course, the most desirable solution was for the scholar to spend a year at Harvard working on the book that would then be published in the Harvard series. But even if the volume was never part of the Harvard series, the talented young scholar was cultivated for his potential contributions to putting in place one of the important building blocks for East Asian studies. If necessary, the young scholar's superior would be invited for a visit, with all the diplomatic niceties, but Fairbank's purpose was to get the superior's permission so that the underling would then be allowed to come for a year of research.

I must confess that when I succeeded John Fairbank as Director of the East Asian Research Center in 1973, I did not find it an easy task. The field was in disorder, badly divided in the wake of the Vietnam War, and the fifteen glorious years of foundation support for the building of China studies had already tapered off. How could one maintain a coherent vital kingdom? Furthermore, I found myself wondering how the second emperor of a Chinese dynasty would have felt if he had assumed office while the powerful dynastic founder were still alive and vigorous. With modern bureaucracy and rules of retirement, Fairbank gave up the position, but it was not easy to give up the notion that quite naturally he was the spokesman and the decision-maker for the Empire.

But in truth there was no second emperor in the East Asian Studies Dynasty that Fairbank founded. Fairbank worked with Edwin Reischauer when Chinese and Japanese cooperation was required and with Benjamin Schwartz on intellectual issues. But in running the Chinese sphere at Harvard, Fairbank was the great initiator and institution builder. His successor was not an individual but a group of scholars. We scholars who remain here on duty are basically peers of similar age, working in different disciplines, with different groups of students. I for one see great advantage in our diversified collegiality, decision-making by consensus, and our broad intellectual scope. But we could not be thriving as we are today had there not been a self-assured driven warrior who conquered the wilderness and founded our East Asian Dynasty.

Betty B. Burch
*Harvard University*

John and Wilma were friends for a long time before I turned to the China field. When I first knew them, they were commuting weekly to Washington, D.C. where John was defending himself against leftist charges. They were deeply concerned because their lawyer who accompanied them charged $50 an hour, and hearings were constantly being delayed so that the lawyer's fee was eating into their relatively meager resources.

I fall into the category of those whose academic careers became focused on China because of John's ingenious strategies to involve scholars. He used all conceivable ways to do so, none too small to escape his attention. I succumbed to at least three approaches. One was the Fairbank weekly teas with their welcome but unvarying cucumber sandwiches and brownies. John presided and, as usual with John, conversation rarely strayed from China. The teas were interesting. They enabled China students to come together, and they were enlivened by visiting specialists like Owen Lattimore.

Another means used by John to strengthen interest in China was the now famous China table. When the Center moved from Dunster Street to 1737 Cambridge Street, John and other planners realized that eating together was a natural and effective way to encourage communication between areas and disciplines. Provision was made to reserve a small room for lunch, magnificently catered by Mrs. Black, for the Russian, Chinese and Japanese centers. John anticipated a mutual exchange between them and the broadening of horizons by so doing. But this was not to be: China scholars immediately congregated all at one table, and under no circumstances would they go to another. Occasionally a Japanese or Russian specialist strayed to the China table because they didn't form tables of their own, but not often. For while not excluded, they did not feel comfortable. (Exceptions were Ed Reischauer and Al Craig.) The China table immediately developed a custom followed to the present. If the table was full, chairs were added to corners and corners of corners so that no China person would have to go elsewhere. When Coolidge Hall was renovated, a regular dining room open to all was established on the first floor, and again China people congregated at the same table. As usual conversation is 80% on China, and again chairs are added to corners to accommodate the group. John's original goal of cross-fertilization among areas failed, but he was correct that eating together daily forms a particularly deep and productive bond for those within the area.

Another of John's moves to widen the field was to procure in 1958 a grant from the Ford Foundation to encourage already established professors, who were not in the China field, to come to Harvard for a year of studying China. He had a particular goal in mind which in fact was ingenious. He knew that it took many years for teachers to become proficient in Chinese, but he wanted to fill university courses with classes on China as rapidly as possible. Therefore, the grant paid the salaries of six professors from other universities and various disciplines (history, political science, art, etc.) to come to Harvard for a year with no strings attached and with only a tacit understanding that their studies would center on Asia. I, personally, fell hook, line and sinker for the study of China and thereafter always taught several courses a year on this area at Tufts University and the Radcliffe Seminars. I was, I believe, the only one for whom China became the major focus of interest. The others injected aspects of China in whatever course they could. On the whole, therefore, John achieved his goal. It did, however, leave me with a basic flaw: I could teach about China but I could not do adequate research because I didn't know the Chinese language. John at one point said to go ahead anyway, but it was a crippling defect.

Upon retiring from Tufts in 1972, I became a Research Associate (now Associate in Research) at what was to become the Fairbank Center for East Asian Research. In the last few years of his life John occupied an office directly across from mine. Gradually, he became solely involved in producing his two or three books a year. He came in for an hour or so, but few except his assistant Joan Hill dared to enter to talk. He was clearly not to be disturbed. Very occasionally he would stop by to ask me how I was doing, and several times to murmur chidingly "always reading, reading, reading!" to indicate that only words written on the page counted. I am deeply grateful to John for encouraging me to enter one of the richest aspects of my life.

P.S. It took me years to learn to leave off the "s" in Fairbank. Now it will take years to get the "s" back on Fairbanks, Alaska. So powerful a man was he.

LUCIAN W. PYE*
*Massachusetts Institute of Technology*

John Fairbank's creativity in advancing the study of China extended far beyond Harvard University. It was John's shepherding that made China and East Asia programs the flagship among all area studies programs in American colleges and universities. In building the China field nationally he was the quintessential American inventor, visionary but pragmatic, patient with others but demanding of himself, with no apparent need for rest.

More than any one else he had the vision that transformed what had been a Europe-based Sinology into a modern American social science. While still a graduate student, during four years of soaking up the nuances of Chinese life in Peking, he became the acknowledged leader of a remarkable group of young American scholars who had decided that the study of China should lead them not first to Paris and Berlin but to China itself. This band of scholars in time populated

* This memoir, in slightly different form, was originally delivered at the memorial service for Fairbank, held at Harvard University on October 21, 1991.

social science departments across America: Martin Wilbur at Columbia; Derk Bodde, Pennsylvania; Knight Biggerstaff, Cornell; George Taylor, University of Washington; Herrlee Creel, Chicago; Harold Isaacs, M.I.T.; Michael Lindsay, American University; and Owen Lattimore, Johns Hopkins.

John Fairbank's vision for China studies had its practical side: Early on he realized that the training universities would soon run into trouble if there was no market for their graduates. Combining idealism and wiliness, John helped implant the idea that no self-respecting college could be without instruction in Chinese affairs. Furthermore he established as academic orthodoxy that, whereas teaching about other cultures might be done by intelligent generalists, China was special, requiring arcane knowledge, and therefore there must be trained China specialists on every campus.

To achieve his goal of diffusing the study of China, John was not content to let nature take its course; he had a compelling need to organize China scholars on a nationwide basis. Whether it was his experiences in government during World War II or just his innate spirit of activism is not clear, but in any case, right after the war, and just after he had received tenure at Harvard, John spearheaded the move to break away from the American Oriental Society and establish the Far Eastern Association. The founding meeting of the new organization took place at Columbia University, and it was there, as a graduate student from Yale, that I first saw John in action. With his distinctive style of hurried dignity and kindly arm-twisting, John was everywhere, talking up his vision for the Association, inspiring Bill Lockwood among others to spread the missionary message, while also getting down to brass tacks on the details of a constitution with Earl Pritchard.

The next year at the first annual meeting held in New Haven, John was again the center of attention with his unique combination of a commanding presence but a totally approachable personality. As he greeted old and new acquaintances he was both courtly yet down to earth, reserved but warm and friendly; and above all, he was still ahead of everybody in both the expansiveness of his ambitions for the organization, and the specificity of his plans. Indeed, no sooner was the Far Eastern Association established than John was raising funds from the Rockefeller Foundation for his next brainchild, the Association's Committee on Chinese Thought, which he got Arthur Wright to chair.

Over the next decade his vision repeatedly outran the possible. In 1957, as president of the Far Eastern Association, John's expansive spirit seemed to go against the grain of his China-centered world, for he took the lead in transforming the organization into the Association for Asian Studies, which appeared to dilute the Confucian cultural focus by adding the countries of South and Southeast Asia. He probably unconsciously classified them as countries which had, or should have, paid tribute to the suzerain Celestial Kingdom, vassal entities in a China-centered world.

The change in name and scope did not, however, blind John to the organization's inherent weaknesses and so, in an effort to give it a stronger fulcrum for lifting Asian studies to new heights, he came up with the idea for an Advisory Committee on Research and Development. As a subsequent chairman of that committee I was acutely aware that, lacking a permanent staff, it could never perform the key function which John envisioned for it, that of serving as a conduit for passing on foundation funds to individual scholars.

It seemed for a time that John's building efforts had reached their limits. But he was not to be stopped. Without any slackening of purpose he quietly built upon the proposals of others, graciously seeing to it that others received the credits and the honors. This all came out in the 1959 Gould House meeting to which John had gathered China specialists from across the country to deliberate on how best to create a national mechanism for funding research. In riding the train up to Dobbs Ferry he confided to me that he still hoped that we could house it in the AAS, but after the meeting he accepted the suggestion of others that it would be sounder to turn to the SSRC and the ACLS and the combined skills of Pendleton Herring and Frederick Burkhardt. The result was the Joint Committee on Contemporary China which came as close to realizing John's dreams for national research on China as was possible in an imperfect world.

John's ambitions in building national institutions might have aroused unfriendly criticism that he was, in the spirit of either Han chauvinism or Harvard elitism, engaged in personal empire-building. But John's personality precluded any such thoughts, for he always took great interest in the concerns and interests of other scholars. John never came across a book about China, especially one by a young author, in which he could not find some merit—a proclivity which publishers discovered and exploited to get dustjacket blurbs.

John's accomplishments in building national institutions were all the more remarkable because they came in the midst of chaotic times when the field of China studies was contentiously divided; it often seemed that the center might not hold. He, however, maintained a quality of profound serenity which I believe was sustained by his faith in what he was doing and in an unworldly belief in the fairness of others.

Workaholic that he was, he was not a dour person but was always the optimist—indeed, an irrepressibly fun-loving man. Even when engaged in his most worthy efforts, John could not rid himself of the aura of still being a slightly mischievous boy enjoying a prank. He could not mask the fact that he relished the idea that he possessed master skills in stealthily getting others to accomplish good things. Yet, while pretending to be invisible, John was, much like stage hands in Chinese and Japanese theater, just awkward enough to be eye-catching, and so it was never hard to see through what he was up to.

John could not have been our great national leader in organizing scholarship on China if he had not also been universally acknowledged as a preeminent historian and teacher. Happily for John, he saw no contradictions between scholarship and the world of action. While still a graduate student in China, he wrote to one of his cohorts of future China scholars, saying: "In the present state of the world, scholarship appears to be one of the better means of approach to action—partly because the complexity of modern life demands knowledge before action, partly because education and research, like banking or diplomacy, are an international field in which opportunities are increasing and action is possible on a wide scale."*

* Paul M. Evans, *John Fairbank and the American Understanding of Modern China* (New York: Basil Blackwell, 1988), p. 41.

John Fairbank's vision and ceaseless efforts benefited not just the community of China specialists but our country as a whole, for he taught Americans that China is important, regardless of whether the China of the moment was a "good" China or a "bad" China. He was always building platforms on which to raise other people to greater visibility. There are many of us who were not Harvard products but who feel deeply indebted to John Fairbank. John was a great scholar and leader; he was also a dear person.

WM. THEODORE DE BARY
*Columbia University*

When I first went to Harvard in the fall of 1941, it was in the expectation that I would study modern Chinese history with John Fairbank, at the suggestion of the Western cultural historian at Columbia, Carlton Hayes. Like many aspiring graduate students since then, when I arrived on the scene I found that my prospective mentor was away on leave. This proved to be less of a hardship when I found that my time could be well spent with Edwin Reischauer (as I have related in my preface to the Reischauer Lectures*). It meant, however, that well before I became involved with John in the American Council of Learned Societies' Chinese Thought conferences of the 1950s, my view of Chinese history was already an East Asian one, shaped by exposure to the perspectives of Ryusaku Tsunoda at Columbia and Edwin Reischauer, both of them influenced or affected by the great Japanese Sinologues, and especially Naito Konan.

John's autobiography, *Chinabound*, in the double entendre of its title, suggests his later self-awareness of being a very China-centered historian. This is certainly the way his early views, particularly on the issue of Confucianism and the Chinese dynastic state, appeared to me. He was given to equating the two as fused in a "Confucian state," and in many ways he seemed to hold

* *East Asian Civilizations: A Dialogue in Five Stages* (Cambridge, Mass.: Harvard University Press, 1989).

Confucianism responsible for most of the ills of modern China that were in need of radical remediation. My view, by the time we first met, differed in that I saw Confucianism as subject to greater variation in different East Asian contexts, and not to be so exclusively identified with Chinese dynastic regimes.

At the first ACLS conference on Chinese thought, mostly arranged by John and Arthur Wright, I raised the question whether it was appropriate to see Confucianism as so wholly a reactionary force in China, and so largely responsible for China's failure to modernize, since it had had no such inhibiting or disabling effect on Meiji-period Japanese leaders who, though Confucian-educated, were eminently successful in most areas of modernization. John, as I recall, was taken aback by this question, and so far as I can judge he never really accepted the further implication that Confucianism could have had a far more ambiguous relation to state and society than he had allowed and could even be seen, to some degree, as a countervailing tradition vis-à-vis the dynastic state. Perhaps I am wrong in this, however, and will find out differently when I see his final views as set forth in his posthumous *China: A New History*.

The real point of these remarks, however, is not to prolong an old argument, but rather to emphasize that despite rather fundamental differences in outlook between us (only one aspect of which I have cited here), John, as a leader in the field of Chinese studies, did not allow these differences to affect his judgment with respect to the broad development of the field, to which he gave such powerful encouragement on many fronts, and not alone in respect to the continuing series of ACLS-sponsored conferences on Chinese civilization, to which I have referred.

Let me cite just one example of John's superlative efforts on behalf of the development of the field that I happen to know about firsthand. In the discussions we held in the ACLS Committee on Chinese Studies, the proposal emerged for a project to produce a biographical reference work for the Ming comparable to *Eminent Chinese of the Ch'ing Period*, edited by Arthur Hummel. John became a strong proponent of this idea, which he referred to initially as the Ming History Project in order to emphasize its larger potential significance for the study of Ming China and Chinese history as a whole. As it turned out, because of the availability of L. Carrington Goodrich to conduct the project at Columbia, the work was done there, and given Goodrich's greater circumspection and more cautious approach to things, the resultant volumes were more modestly entitled *Dictionary of Ming Biography*. But there can be no doubt that, though many scholars contributed to the success of the project, John's bolder and more expansive approach to Chinese history was crucial to its initial promotion and in its gaining sustained support for the ten-year-long effort. Again and again it was John's persuasive powers that convinced dubious foundation officials that this seemingly specialized and rather arcane research (at least in the eyes of persons primarily concerned with contemporary political issues) could represent a major contribution to our understanding of China and deserved their support. John may have been "Chinabound" but he was certainly capable of seeing, presenting and eloquently articulating the "big picture."

No doubt in retrospecting the political vicissitudes of Chinese studies, the stormy years of the fifties will come to mind and much will be said about highly charged atmospheres and the intense personal conflicts among leading scholars. I was one of perhaps not too many persons who managed to carry on a friendship with both John and Karl August Wittfogel over the years, if only because I was not that closely identified with either of them. In any case, when I last saw Wittfogel a year or so before his death, it happened that I was about to visit Harvard for several days and when we parted K. A. made a special point of asking me to convey his greetings to the Fairbanks. He spoke especially of his feelings for Wilma, whom he remembered as a warm, gracious and generous-minded person. Somehow—and perhaps it was only my own imagination since I think of John as sharing these qualities too—I sensed that in a roundabout way, Wittfogel was extending an olive branch to John as well. As it turned out, I did have a chance to convey the message to Wilma, and trust that it got through to John. After all, notwithstanding the dim view that John took of Confucianism, he had in his large-minded, generous manner, gentlemanly ways, and a sense of leadership responsibility, many of the attributes of the Confucian noble man (*chün-tzu*).

## A. Doak Barnett
*Johns Hopkins University*

I never was formally a student of John's, that is, I never took a course under him. (At times, I have had the feeling that this puts me in a small minority in the China field.) Yet, I have always looked upon him as my teacher. Some of his books, and perhaps most of all *The United States and China*, helped define, early in my own search for understanding of China— before I had even started an academic career myself—some of the most important ways of looking at and studying China. Part of John's genius was his ability to synthesize knowledge and communicate it with skill in ways that reached far beyond his peers in the field of Chinese history. His view that scholars have an obligation not only to add to knowledge but to educate the public and affect public policy also was one I deeply admired and shared.

I first met John—or, I should say, Professor Fairbank, because he had already become an impressive icon—soon after I returned from reporting on the revolutionary changes in China during 1947-1949. The way that he encouraged me highlights another of his characteristics. I was young, had no real academic credentials, and in fact had no intention at that time to become an academic specialist on China. Yet John made it clear to me that he took my interest in China seriously, and genuinely wished to know my views; he also strongly encouraged me to become an active member of the field. The number of people he encouraged and supported and counseled unquestionably numbered in the thousands. My impression is that he was genuinely interested in all of them and thought that they all were important because they might be able, somehow, to contribute to a greater understanding of China. There was nothing contrived or phony about his passionate interest in everyone and everything related to China, and the genuineness of that interest was one of the reasons his influence reached so far.

I first began to get to know John well in the late 1950s after I had joined the staff of the Ford Foundation, to spend a period of time as their China specialist. The foundation decided at that time to provide major support to China programs at several universities and to help the field to build a variety of new national institutions to expand research as well as teaching on China. It soon became clear to me—and, I think, to most others concerned about developing China studies—that John had a very special sense about what strategies were required to develop the field, both at individual universities and nationally. I believe it is fair to say that no one made a more crucial contribution to the rapid development of both teaching and research on China in the United States from the late 1950s on.

I was greatly impressed by John's supreme self-confidence about the leading role that he believed Harvard should play, yet at the same time I was impressed by his ability to look beyond Harvard's parochial interests and do all he could to support China studies at other institutions and nationally. I remember well when he visited the Ford Foundation together with McGeorge Bundy —then dean at Harvard—to make a comprehensive presentation of the funds Harvard wished to request from the foundation to support China studies. It was a superb presentation, but everyone at the foundation was bowled over by the size of their request and pointed out that the amount they wished to ask for almost equalled the total of the foundation's initial estimate of what it should give to four major universities for its initial grants. Undaunted, John and Mac Bundy, responded by saying, in effect, that in that case the foundation's problem, obviously, was to expand its budget for support of China studies (which it ultimately did), not to give Harvard less than it needed. Whether one labels this attitude self-confidence or arrogance—and I suppose one could call it both—it revealed the kind of commitment and determination that made John the most effective academic entrepreneur (in the best sense) in the China field. Yet, at the same time, more than any of his peers at that time, John seemed to be able, in my judgment, to address national needs, rise above parochialism, bridge differences (the aftermath of McCarthysim was still divisive), and infuse a sense of cooperation and common purpose into the field.

My admiration for John's special talent for nurturing the institutions necessary to develop both teaching and research in the China field rose even higher when, in the 1960s, I myself became an academic and assumed responsibilities for developing a contemporary China program at Columbia University and joined the group of scholars (then still fairly small) most actively involved in developing new national institutions. I do not know that at the time I looked on John, in any clear-cut or self-conscious way, as providing a model for what I was trying to do, but in retrospect it is apparent to me that I did in fact look on him as a model, and I believe that this was true of virtually everyone else who followed his footsteps in trying to develop either national China programs or programs at particular universities.

Having, with due—probably undue—solemnity, acknowledged a few of the ways in which I am indebted to John Fairbank as a teacher and model, I must say that I will remember him, and miss him, most for other reasons and other qualities—for his humanity and warmth as a person, for his one-track determination to educate us all about the importance of history, for his ability to bring history alive, for his wry wit and sense of humor, and for his friendship. I should say, also, that I always have thought of John as part of the remarkable team of John and Wilma. The humanistic interests and skills of John and Wilma complemented and reinforced each other, it seemed to me (her artistic talent was a more important part of the mix than many realized), and any tribute to either of them should be a tribute to both.

WARREN I. COHEN
*Michigan State University*
*University of Maryland, Baltimore County*

John had a little trouble taking seriously those of us who didn't study at Harvard—but he did try.

I gave my first paper at the AHA in 1967, at Toronto, something out of my dissertation on the American revisionist historians and intervention in World War I. Afterward, I was sitting in the bar with friends when John, president-elect of the AHA, whom I had never met and who couldn't have been less interested in my subject, came over to congratulate me. Why had he bothered to attend my session?

Why had he taken the trouble to seek me out and bestow his blessing? The answer was Dorothy Borg and the "new" field of American-East Asian relations. She had learned that I had spent 1964-1966 on Taiwan reading Chinese documents for a study of Chinese Communist policy toward the United States. She had delegated John to take my measure.

Dorothy Borg, whose 1964 volume on the Far Eastern Crisis, 1933-38 had won the Bancroft Prize, was not only the leading scholar in the field of American-East Asian relations, but also passionately committed to developing the field, to recruiting and training young scholars. She wanted us all to be steeped in the culture and history of China and Japan, as well as that of the United States, and competent in at least one Asian language. She was prepared to devote her energies and her not inconsiderable financial resources to promoting the field. Dorothy was a great scholar—but she had *no* entrepreneurial talent. One cannot imagine her selling anything or writing a grant proposal. On the other hand she was an excellent judge of other people's skills, a superb manipulator, and a close personal friend of John Fairbank, probably the academy's most gifted promoter.

Together John and Dorothy created the Committee on American-East Asian Relations, packed its letterhead with relatives and friends—Arthur Schlesinger, Jr., Oscar Handlin, Richard Leopold, and Ernest May—attached it to the American Historical Association and went after outside funding. John had been instrumental in interesting the Ford Foundation in financing the development of Asian studies in the United States in the 1950s and 1960s. Now he persuaded Ford to fund the new committee, to be housed at Harvard and chaired by May. Immediately the committee began promoting language training, research, conferences, and historiographic studies. In 1968, John devoted his presidential address to the AHA to declaring the study of American-East Asian relations to be our "Assignment for the '70s."

Launching the new field did not conclude John's activities in support of it. One of his rare failures was his initial effort to create a chair in American-East Asian relations at Harvard. Eventually, Akira Iriye returned to fulfill that desire. But John succeeded, in the difficult economic times of the 1970s, in persuading the Harvard University Press to accept a new series of books on American-East Asian relations, beginning with the first survey of the field, May and Jim Thomson's volume of essays published in 1972. And, as time permitted, he reached out in reviews, essays, and public addresses, continuing to promote the field, serving on the AEAR committee in an advisory capacity until his death. Whenever he could be useful, John was willing to lend his name, to make a phone call, or write a letter to help the work of the successor generation flourish.

I was not one of John's protégés, but he retained an interest in my work to the end. He read some of it in manuscript and I have dozens of his handwritten notes in my files. Most recently I had asked for Wilma's critique of a book I was writing on East Asian art, and got John's as well. My greatest regret is that the last time he invited me over for lunch, Wilma wasn't there. His hot dogs were execrable.

AKIRA IRIYE
*Harvard University*

In June 1960 John and Wilma Fairbank were in Tokyo, a stopping point in their travels around the world. I had studied with John as a graduate student and was then working on my dissertation. He had always insisted on my studying the Chinese language; I was able to read the characters, but he felt I needed to pick up spoken Chinese as well. As I was spending the summer in Tokyo, he thought I should seize the opportunity and go to Taiwan for language study, if only for a few weeks. At that time there were still foreign exchange restrictions in Japan, making it very difficult to obtain hard currency with which to purchase tickets for going abroad. John realized this, and one day, when he and Wilma visited us in my parents' home, he took out a checkbook and wrote a check for $200, telling me I should use it to buy a roundtrip ticket between Tokyo and Taipei.

I was, naturally, astounded by the offer and most grateful for his generosity, but hesitated for a moment to accept the gift; I had just gotten married, and the thought of leaving my wife for a month's language study in Taiwan didn't quite appeal to me. John immediately recognized what was on my mind, tore up the check he had just handed me, and wrote a new check, this time for $400, saying, "The two of you can now go to Taipei." What could I do but accept and proceed to Taiwan with Mitsuko? We did enjoy our trip, but, unfortunately, we made little progress in conversational Chinese as we were together all the time. Four years later, John arranged for an SSRC-ACLS Joint Committee fellowship, and told me that this time I was to go to Taiwan alone. I did, and was more successful in acquiring conversational Chinese.

I recall these events whenever I think of John Fairbank's unparalleled concern for younger scholars and their work. From the very first time that I met him—in 1956, when I was a college senior hoping to come to Harvard to pursue graduate study—he took a personal interest in my professional development, as he did in the programs and careers of hundreds of other students and junior colleagues. The examples cited above will not come as a surprise to anyone who has been his student and benefited from his generosity.

John's generosity was more than personal kindness; it had a purpose. He was eager to develop a corps of specialists who would advance the field of modern Chinese history as an integral part of the study of history. Others more qualified than I can speak about this, so I would like to pay tribute to John Fairbank as a founding father of another field of study, the history of American-East Asian relations.

Fairbank became interested in U. S.-East Asian relations as a result of his wartime and postwar experiences in China. His writings then showed a strong commitment to liberal reform in China patterned after the American example. After 1949, however, he became equally concerned about U. S. policy in Asia, which, it seemed to him, had brought about the tragic confrontation with China in Korea and elsewhere. He was fascinated, and dismayed, by shifting American images of China, fluctuating from idealistic descriptions of the Chinese as heroic freedom-fighters to negative characterizations of them as mindless and fanatical mobs doing their communist masters' bidding.

In 1957 Fairbank published an important essay in the *American Historical Review*, calling on historians to undertake "historical sociology," the study of the sources of historical knowledge and imagination. Though he did not use such fashionable terms as epistemology, sociology of knowledge, and semiotics, he raised the same types of questions that others would through these categories. He wanted to know what lay behind knowledge and how ideas were formed. He clearly had in mind American-Asian relations in which superficial mutual images seemed to conceal historical conditions that made it extremely difficult for different peoples to come to understand one another.

It was in the same year that Harvard University's History Department established a new graduate program in what was initially called "American Far Eastern Policy Study." The program was headed by Oscar Handlin, and the committee included William L. Langer, Arthur Schlesinger, Jr., and John K. Fairbank. (Dorothy Borg, affiliated with Columbia University, was a major inspirer and benefactor of the program.) The idea was to train graduate students in both American and East Asian history so that they would be able to bridge two cultures. Gunther Barth (now teaching at Berkeley) and I were fortunate to be selected as the first students to enroll in the program. (We were joined in 1958 by Marilyn Blatt [Young] and Harvey Pressman.) Under the committee's auspices, a lecture course and a graduate seminar in U. S.-East Asian relations were established, initially taught by visiting scholars such as Robert Schwantes and Harold Vinacke.

John was the mainstay of the program, deeply committed to its progress and always eager to recruit students to the field. He and Ernest May, who became the program's chairman in 1959, even invited the four of us (Barth, Blatt, Pressman, and myself) to teach jointly the lecture course in the spring of 1961 even though we were still graduate students. Since then, the course has been taught by many others, including John Fairbank himself as well as Edwin O. Reischauer, Peter Stanley, Bradford Lee, and James Thomson. Over the years hundreds of students have enrolled in the course, some of them eventually becoming leading scholars in the field.

But Fairbank did not limit his activities on behalf of the new field to the Harvard campus alone. With Borg, May, Schlesinger, and others, he helped create a nationwide committee on American-East Asian relations. First affiliated with the American Historical Association and, since 1979, with the Society for Historians of American Foreign Relations, the committee organized scholarly symposia and funded a graduate fellowship program to train young historians in the field. It also established connections with scholars in East Asia, especially with those in the People's Republic of China after the reestablishment of diplomatic relations between Washington and Beijing. The field made such impressive progress that Warren Cohen, one of its leaders today, felt justified in asserting, in his presidential address before the Society for Historians of American Foreign Relations in 1984, that American-East Asian relations were at the cutting-edge of the historical discipline. Those of us who have worked in the field feel John's leadership in this area was as important as his contribution to modern Chinese history.

In January 1991, some of us met to discuss the feasibility of establishing a new journal devoted to the field. We felt the time was opportune to create a medium for intellectual exchange between scholars of North America and East Asia (broadly defined to include all areas in the Pacific region). The *Journal of American-East Asian Relations* is due to start publication in the spring of 1992. I wanted to tell John about this and ask him to contribute an essay for the first issue, although I learned that he had heard about the journal and expressed his pleasure at the enterprise. It would have been fitting for the first issue to include an article by him. Even in its absence, however, the journal will stand as a monument to a pioneering scholar's tireless, selfless dedication to establish and develop a new area of inquiry.

HARRISON E. SALISBURY
*Taconic, Connecticut*

In the spring of 1972 John and Wilma Fairbank returned to China after an absence of 27 years. My wife Charlotte and I chanced to be there at the same time and with the Fairbanks (and several other Americans) were guests of Zhou Enlai at a memorable dinner in the Anhui room of the Great Hall of the People on the evening of June 16, 1972.

John sat at Zhou's right, the guest of honor, with Wilma beside him and beside Wilma, Nancy Tang, the interpreter extraordinary who went from Radcliffe to Beijing and on to a precipitous fall with the Gang of Four. The rest of us, Jerry Cohen, Jeremy Stone, Dick Dudman of the *St. Louis Post-Dispatch*, Helen Dudman and the Chinese including Qiao Guanhua, the brilliant Vice Foreign Minister (also to fall with the Gang), arranged ourselves around the table.

It was John and Wilma's evening. Zhou Enlai opened the conversation by asking John how long he had been absent from China. He replied that he had left in 1946 and reminded Zhou of their last dinner in Chongqing. Marshal Ye Jianying had been of their company. Zhou and Ye had sung military songs, songs of the Long March and the anti-Japanese war, Zhou keeping time by pounding on the wooden table. John and Wilma hadn't known any contemporary songs so they filled in with "The Battle Hymn of the Republic" and "Tenting on the Old Camp Ground." Zhou laughed. He couldn't remember the evening in detail and confessed that he didn't sing very often himself.

John had a not very secret agenda for the evening and had mentioned it when we dined at the Beijing Hotel a night or two earlier. The Chinese, he had deduced after a fortnight's travel and talk in the wake of the Nixon visit, were more interested in an amorphous "friendship," ceremonial gestures and words rather than meaningful interchange. Nonetheless, he had determined to lay the basis, if he could, for the beginning of academic exchanges. He wanted to get Harvard in on the ground floor.

The Zhou Enlai dinner gave him an excellent opening. Zhou was in good form. The nostalgia of the Yanan days and the Dixie Mission was in the air. Zhou embarked on what the communiqué called "a wide-ranging conversation." He tilted with Jeremy Stone about cigarette smoking, gave himself a rather emotional self-criticism about failing to realize the U. S. would not abide by the 1954 Geneva agreements on Vietnam and picked up some ideas from Dudman and myself which he said he would use on Henry Kissinger who was arriving the next day.

John took little part in these preliminaries but when the feast began of winter greens soup, Peking duck, crispy rice scraped from the sides of the pot, he "seized the hour," in the words of Chairman Mao. He opened with a seemingly innocent question: did Zhou believe it would be possible to control the new drive for industrialization or would it inevitably lead to mass demands—bicycle riders, for instance, insisting on having small cars? Zhou was certain China could control the demand. This led him on a long detour but John eventually got him back to the question of relations between China and America.

Zhou responded by offering a toast to the friendship of the two peoples and for the exchange of "some" scientists, educators, cultural figures and (he paused for quite an interval) journalists. Now John had the opening he wanted. He told Zhou he believed there was great need for Chinese to come to the USA for study and research and hoped they could come "by their own choice" and "not be confined to official delegations."

Zhou began to throw up obstacles. There had been no exchanges for so long. It would take time to prepare. There was the question of interpreters. Fairbank suggested that Zhou send some Chinese who could freshen up American interpreters on contemporary usage and at the same time pursue their own studies.

But Zhou found another obstacle. Because of lack of diplomatic relations they could only send interpreters to the United Nations. John replied that Harvard was not part of the U. S. Government. Another objection came into Zhou's mind. Didn't Harvard have students from Taiwan? Wouldn't dispute and demonstrations arise between backers of Taiwan and the mainland? Fairbank firmly responded that Harvard had its own principles. "We do not mix politics with scholarship," he said. Zhou was not satisfied. He turned to Jerry Cohen who supported Fairbank's argument.

Zhou was somewhat mollified but said: "To be honest, you can talk of your academic things but I will keep to my political thoughts." But he gradually backtracked and accepted the principle of mutual exchanges and insisted he was not against Taiwan students coming to American universities. Jeremy Stone assured Zhou there was not any reason why his objections could not be overcome. "There are many ways of skinning a cat," he observed.

The cat phrase brought the discussion to an end. Nancy Tang could not produce a Chinese equivalent. All the Chinese speakers at the dinner chimed in. Finally Zhou Enlai got the idea and agreed. In principle he accepted Fairbank's proposal—to begin academic interchanges, step-by-step. With Harvard, of course. Once again Fairbank's diplomacy had won out.

Franz Schurmann
*University of California, Berkeley*

I never had a course with Fairbank and always knew him from the outside in. His student and to some extent protégé Joe Levenson and I were close friends until his death in April 1969. That too is a long time ago. I got to know Fairbank a little bit when I was a Fulbright/Ford grantee in Japan, in 1954 or 1955, I think it was. Arthur and Mary Wright, who were close friends of his (Mary was a protégée of his too), were also there, and I was close to both of them. So an indirect bond linked me to him. I remember one evening when we were all at dinner together at Fairbank's house that the conversation was spirited until I ventured to change the subject away from China. JKF abruptly left and Wilma explained that he always went to bed early.

It took me a while to realize that Fairbank was really an American Confucian with the spirit of a late Ch'ing reformer. He radiated a deep conviction that China had a destiny and America had a destiny and that both were interlocked and that individuals pushed along by some moral force like himself and his students would make that intertwined destiny real. I have changed my earlier views on Confucianism and dimly come to realize its enormous power. JKF sensed that power and managed to use it, in a good sense, to create his own concentric circles of power.

Fairbank was a giant on the American scene. As I look at the world today, the one part of it that seems to have it together, value-wise, is East Asia. Nowadays the value they all agree on is "make money." The bottom line of these reflections is that Fairbank may have been right, that somehow the destinies of the U. S. and China (more broadly East Asia) are historically linked.

# *Impact on Scholarship Abroad*

OLGA MOREL-BASANOFF
*Paris, France*

Others who pursued their careers in Chinese history will speak of the great historian John Fairbank, of the indefatigable entrepreneur, of the creator of a vast empire of China hands. I was fortunate, myself, however fleetingly, as a young graduate student in the mid-sixties, discovering America, Harvard and Qing documents all at once, in benefiting from his teaching and from his inordinate ability to extract the most out of one.

Certainly, he taught me a great deal about how to find one's way in the vast ocean of material that exists about China, and about how to extract from it, creatively, a segment, however minute, of new knowledge, new understanding, new comprehension of such an enormous subject. (In my case, it was research on a forgotten episode of relations between Russia and China: the sending away by a ritualistic Mongol Prince and official of a pompous Russian embassy in a nonglorious year of Jiaqing's reign. It may have been, in many ways, an ideologically mimetic exercise but it was part of a legitimate effort at understanding mutual perceptions.)

It was in fact my knowledge of Russian that aroused John Fairbank's interest in me and made a floating graduate student into one of his tribe. He felt, as he wrote in *Chinabound*, that the Russian experience in China had been neglected. He regretted it because, as he wrote, "Russians appeared on the Ch'ing dynasty's horizon from its inception in the early seventeenth century, 150 years before Americans reached Canton in 1784," and "in Peking's strategic concerns, Russia bulked larger than America." He hoped I would follow in Mark Mancall and Eric Widmer's footsteps. However instrumental his first interest in me had been, he accepted it when I followed another path.

Whatever knowledge and understanding I acquired was certainly of direct use to me, whether in Peking, where I was posted from 1968 to 1970, or at the Quai d'Orsay (the French Foreign Ministry) in Paris, where I was in charge of the "Extrême Orient" in the early eighties, or in present research on the Chinese period of a great French poet-diplomat and Nobel laureate, Saint-John Perse.

But during a two-year stay in Cambridge with John Fairbank and a 25-year correspondence, I learned many other things. I learned the humility of a man who was better equipped than any to understand the history and politics of China and had an immense influence in shaping general knowledge and perceptions of that land, yet who knew how elusive historical or any reality is. The official pundit was, at heart, an anti-pundit.

When I was posted in Peking, he wrote to me, in 1968: "I think the China specialists in the USA, except for those that are stupid, are all really completely baffled by current events. We have no esoteric insights and our solemn statements to the public are pretty hollow." In the same vein, he wrote from Cambridge (England) in October 1973 after his return to China: "For a time, all my usual generalizations were stopped by *Reality*, but now that I am at a distance, they are resuming again, backed by the fact that I was there. (Where? Asleep and eating half the time in the Peking Hotel.)"

I think the intellectual distance he maintained contributed to a truth that he knew to be elusive, and I wonder whether it helped him (whatever the wounds) when he was exposed to fanaticism or dogmatism, whether in the McCarthy period or in the radical sixties. "The senior professors were berated for various shortcomings in a polite way," he wrote to me in Peking in 1968, telling of the debate on the role of East Asian scholars in policy formation and in relations with the U. S. government. In both cases, the intellectual distance was accompanied by a pragmatic resilience.

Radical illusions about Maoist China were still very vivid when I briefly returned to Harvard from Peking in 1970. And to one who had seen and dared express what the Cultural Revolution looked like on the streets of Peking and had done to China, the disbelief was a painful cultural shock.

What I also learned was John Fairbank's generosity, his capacity to enter into your life and change it. When he believed in you, you believed in yourself. He encouraged me to write what I saw and felt in Peking in 1968-70. He sent me books in Hungary. He mused (after he had abandoned the hope that I would become a scholar): "It is a most dramatic-romantic question what will happen to you."

I suppose that dealing with non-academics, and foreign ones at that, he savored the rare holidays we provided in a life so totally devoted to the pursuit of modern Chinese history. In Paris, I would take him to the cinema (we thus saw "India Song", a Marguerite Duras film that perplexed him—and me). In Moscow, where he stayed at my place in the diplomatic compound on Kutuzovski Avenue in 1977, in addition to his meetings with Soviet Sinologists and officials, we went to see Bulgakov's "Master and Margarita" at the Taganka and attended a concert of eighteenth-century military music! He remembered the whole stay as a holiday, and it was a holiday indeed, despite the failures he encountered in what was the main purpose of his visit: establishing research links with Soviet scholars and institutions.

Professor Fairbank liked to evoke his first stay in France at age five, where he stayed with his beautiful mother. He was, certainly, much more oriented towards Britain, which had nurtured him as a Rhodes scholar, but he was also interested in France and hospitable to its scholars. He was proud of the reverse flow from Europe to America. He had joined the Chinese studies field when the French school of Sinology was dominant and noted with pleasure a French interest in a field, modern Chinese history, that he had done so much to create and expand (I think I was his first French graduate student). Jean Chesneaux, Marie-Claire Bergère, Lucien Bianco, and Marianne Bastid all found warm hospitality at Harvard. In a letter (from Guatemala) in 1977, he wrote: "I am increasingly impressed with the degree to which France is part of the American world, much more than Germany and Italy, quite similar to Britain." And he specified: "I don't mean imperialistically. It is simply that the USA is indebted to France for so many things all the time."

I wish I had more space to tell of the exquisite memories about his life in China with Wilma in the forties that some of my letters evoked, especially his encounters with Chinese whom I met 20 or 30 years later: when I mentioned to Qiao Guanhua in Peking in 1969 that I had been a student of John Fairbank, it created a bond and abolished the distance of decades and continents.

I hope others will tell what it was like to have access to Widener 745, his study, or go to Thursday teas at 41 Winthrop Street (Wilma's cucumber sandwiches and brownies were the "petites madeleines" of those two beautiful years in Cambridge ) or to stay at Franklin, New Hampshire, and take a shower filled from huge and beautiful water bottles lined on shelves (I hope they are still there).

I hoped John Fairbank would live to be 105, like his mother, that somehow I could resume the study of Chinese history, that that door would not close because he would still be there. But it did close when I heard on the radio in a car in Paris that John Fairbank, a great China historian, had died.

MARIE-CLAIRE BERGÈRE
*Institut National des Langues et Civilisations Orientales*

The passing of John K. Fairbank is a great loss not only for American Sinologists but for French ones as well. Very few among us have been his students but we are all indebted to him for his vigorous and successful promotion of modern China studies. In France, where the great tradition of classical Sinology was deeply rooted, it was difficult to establish modern China studies as a respectable research field. In our efforts to do so, we relied heavily on the precedent established by Fairbank, following the path that he had opened.

The first time I met John was in August 1965 at Wentworth-by-the-Sea, Portsmouth, New Hampshire, during the conference on the 1911 Revolution. By this time many French colleagues had been welcomed by John in Cambridge. During these visits we were caught up in the dynamics of the East Asian Research Center. JKF provided us with intellectual as well as material support. He gave us access to sources and documents, including papers by his own students, which were kept in his quiet study in Widener Library.

John's efficiency as an academic entrepreneur was widely admired. But among all his good qualities, his intellectual generosity was the one which most attracted me. I remember the talks when John attentively listened to my arguments or my projects, asking the right questions, and compelling me to search for adequate answers. John had the very special talent of instilling enthusiasm at the moment he was suggesting new efforts toward better results.

However severe, his criticism was never discouraging. Just the opposite. Many students and colleagues have experienced the alchemy of these interviews. In my case, I still wondered how it worked. I came from a different cultural background, had been trained by Marxist professors, had no special interest in nineteenth-century China, certainly not in missionary work or in Sino-American relations. But the signals sent by this intelligent, generous and strong individual could be heard across the cultural and ideological divide.

In fact, just observing John's work habits taught me much. During a brief visit to Paris in the summer of 1975, John, suddenly feeling idle, asked for my thesis manuscript, and began reading and editing it "as an experiment," as he said. Of the first thirty pages, about twenty lines survived. For me it came as a real shock and the best lesson in writing and editing that I have ever had.

John enjoyed walking fast. He set the pace and to keep up with him we had to walk fast too. Now, thinking of him, let us not slow down.

Lucien Bianco
*Paris, France*

"The dean of Chinese studies in the U. S." has also been, and permanently remained, our dean here in Europe. Speaking for myself, I began to understand what modern China was all about only after reading *The United States and China*, then in its second edition (1958). That discovery was soon followed by the discovery of the man behind the author, when I had the good fortune to spend a year at Harvard in 1964-65. Under Fairbank's guidance, I learned more in one year at the EARC than ever before. Every morning or almost, John Fairbank wrote in his study (room 745 in Widener Library). Every afternoon, while teaching or directing the EARC, he opened his study for the use of his students. After 27 years, I still remember the emotion that overwhelmed me when I was given access, without further ceremony, to the magical realm. Emotion was soon overtaken by excitement, as we dug into the treasure of unpublished papers and well-organized files which were generously, although in a very matter-of-fact way, made available to us.

If I can mention yet another personal reminiscence, I shall refer to the very next year, when John Fairbank visited Paris during the summer of 1966. On our way to the French Foreign Ministry Archives, as we were striding along Boulevard Saint-Germain, I could not repress the question that was haunting me at the time: what sense did JKF make out of the strange events that had just taken place in Peking? The sharp, unhesitating answer came abruptly and to me shockingly: "struggle for power." By the time Philip Bridgham's article on Mao's Cultural Revolution was published early in 1967 in the *China Quarterly* (No. 29), I had sufficiently ruminated upon Fairbank's reply to be ready to absorb its content.

Sarasin Viraphol
*Ministry of Foreign Affairs of Thailand*

Thailand and China have historically been very close since the times of tributary relations. One significant factor has been the migration of large numbers of Chinese from China's southeastern coastal provinces to Thailand, particularly at the turn of the century. Notwithstanding the Cold War, Thailand and China have had few problems with each other.

Twenty years ago, in search of an intellectual understanding of China, I went to Harvard to study under Professor Fairbank. During my four-year sojourn, Professor Fairbank was not only my teacher, he was also my source of inspiration. In essence, he was my mentor. I was probably one of the first Thai students of Chinese history he had. As such, Professor Fairbank encouraged me to do research on Thai-Chinese relations. A concrete manifestation of his encouragement was my Ph. D. dissertation on Sino-Siamese tributary relations of the Qing period, which was subsequently published as a book by the East Asian Research Center (now the John King Fairbank Center for East Asian Research) at Harvard.

I followed Professor Fairbank's advice and taught Chinese studies at Chulalongkorn University upon my return to Bangkok. With the establishment of diplomatic relations between Bangkok and Beijing in 1975, an opportunity arose for a student of Chinese history like myself to serve in our newly opened mission in China as a political observer. Professor Fairbank was supportive of the idea. He and Mrs. Fairbank eventually visited Beijing during my three-year assignment there. Our reunion in the Middle Kingdom was a memorable one: between a professor who was visiting in Beijing, his old "haunt," for the first time under Communist rule and his former Thai student, now stationed in China as a diplomatic representative of his country. We were also able to meet with Professor Fairbank's former Chinese associates and noted Chinese scholars whose works he had introduced to us while at Harvard, among whom was noted sociologist Professor Fei Xiaotong. During my tour of duty in Beijing, I was always proud to tell colleagues and friends that I had studied under Professor Fairbank.

Upon my return to Thailand in 1979, I continued to serve in the Thai Foreign Ministry's division dealing with Chinese affairs. This continued right up to early 1990 when I was appointed ambassador to the Philippines. I was able to put what I learned at Harvard under Professor Fairbank to good practical use in the Foreign Ministry. At the same time, I managed to teach and write about modern Chinese history—what I had learned from Professor Fairbank—which was then regarded as pioneer work in Thai educational and intellectual circles.

I shall forever be indebted to Professor Fairbank, not only for the knowledge of Chinese history which he imparted to me, but also for the personal warmth and consideration he had for me and all his students. I remember those weekly get-togethers at the Fairbank residence on Winthrop Street where students really met with the great teacher. I also recall those one-on-one sessions in his office during the four years I spent in Cambridge, where I benefited immensely from his wise counsel. Professor Fairbank was my *laoshi* in every sense of the word.

As a tribute to Professor Fairbank's lifetime dedication and commitment to the propagation of understanding and appreciation of China and her rich historical heritage, I am resolved to continue my effort to contribute to Chinese studies in Thailand. This is particularly relevant for someone like myself, who possesses a sense of kinship with China though he may identify himself first and foremost as a Thai. The valuable contribution Professor Fairbank made was to instill in me a greater awareness of my ancestral Chinese identity which in turn reinforces my sense of belonging to my country, Thailand.

MICHAEL LOEWE
*Cambridge University*

Opportunities to meet John Fairbank were not all that frequent for those of us who have been domiciled in Europe and whose professional interests have lain in the earlier rather than the later stages of China's growth. And the situations when such opportunities presented themselves were not always conducive to develop a professional relationship or to engage in personal exchanges. For all the world would attend those major conferences on Chinese studies, and some of us were reluctant to push ourselves forward at times when John clearly had his own business on hand or his own contacts to maintain.

But, rare as they were, such opportunities were memorable, fruitful and delightful. Very quickly it became possible to talk at ease, for one of John's gifts was that of dispensing with formality without delay and concentrating on matters of interest that he shared with those around him. The awe that filled some of us when first meeting him was soon dissipated when we realized that the path to friendship lay open, and the respect that we brought with us met an immediate and warm appreciation of where our own efforts were leading. Instead of keeping a careful watch on our words, we heard ourselves speaking freely without inhibition; for John also possessed the rare gift of treating juniors as if they were equals, with no trace whatsoever that a conscious effort was needed to do so.

We learnt many things from him: how to chair a meeting so as to ensure that it would reach an intellectual conclusion; how history should be written with an eye to clarity and purpose; how to edit other scholars' writings with a minimum of change and a maximum of deference. The encouragement that John gave to younger scholars was priceless, and it brought him its own just reward. For he could witness the success achieved by later generations in following the guidelines that he set, in contributing to the critical appreciation of China's past, and in ensuring that Chinese studies would deserve the recognition as a major division of the humanities that they received in his lifetime. That that recognition was largely due to his own work constitutes his most fitting memorial. Personal recollections include a sunny afternoon on the banks of a swimming pool at Dedham; a brisk walk through Harvard yard of which he was so proud; a warm welcome to the comforts of his own home.

HAROLD Z. SCHIFFRIN
*The Hebrew University of Jerusalem*

Thirty-five years ago I wrote to John Fairbank from Jerusalem, where I was a graduate student at the Hebrew University. I was thinking about doing research on Sun Yat-sen and sought his advice. He did not know me and I had no credentials or accomplishments other than a year at the Army's China program at Berkeley during World War II. To my amazement, I received a long letter in return offering encouragement and practical advice. He recommended Berkeley where, he informed me, his former student, Bob Scalapino, was also interested in Sun Yat-sen. He also sent me a copy of Joe Levenson's book on Liang Ch'i-ch'ao to give me an idea of the kind of work that was needed in modern Chinese history. I was thus introduced to John's role as a one-man "Society for the Promotion of Chinese Studies."

A few years later another facet of his personality was revealed to me—his scholarly integrity and generosity. As it happened, the first thing that I wrote on Sun Yat-sen was an interpretation of his land policy that differed from that which had appeared in *China's Response to the West.* I submitted it to *JAS*, and the editor, Don Shively, suggested that I send the article to John before it was published. Rather than taking offense at what could have been considered a novice's presumption to challenge a senior scholar, John welcomed my contribution.

We finally met in 1960 when he and his family visited Israel. Even here, Chinese studies remained uppermost in his mind, and his discussions with senior faculty provided a strong impetus for the development of the field at the Hebrew University. He later sent us a number of books, including items from Hong Kong that I needed for my research. Two years later, he invited me to Harvard, where I began my work on my book, which was eventually published, thanks to his moral and practical support.

John had a strong penchant for practical action. Someone who had lost his job told me that whereas others had merely voiced sympathy, John was the one who made sure that he was not left without income until another post became available. The urge to act also extended to his sense of justice. When I told him that some years previously a distinguished American scholar whom we wanted to invite as a Fulbright Fellow at the Hebrew University had been rejected in Washington because of his vocal opposition to the Vietnam War, John's immediate response was, "Let's do something about it." The urge to do something without wasting words was the hallmark of his style.

S. Tikhvinskii
*Moscow, Russia*

In June 1985 I got a notice from the head of the Special Book Deposit of the Institute of Information in the field of Social Sciences of the USSR Academy of Sciences informing me that they had in their custody "a book of restricted circulation by J. K. Fairbank published in Madrid in 1982" and that I might read this book on the premises of the Special Book Deposit daily from 9 till 18 o'clock.

The book was *Chinabound: A Fifty-Year Memoir* with the author's dedication on the front page: "For Professor S. Tikhvinskii with cordial regards and best wishes John King Fairbank 1982."

A few years later, with the acceleration of the democratization process in the Soviet Union, the system of restrictions imposed since Stalin's times on books by "suspicious authors" was abolished (as well as the Special Book Deposits in all libraries) and I received in my own possession this precious book. Now everyone has free access to all books in public libraries—exactly the procedure on which Professor Fairbank so vigorously insisted in 1960 during the International Congress of Oriental Studies in Moscow, which he attended. So in a way, Professor Fairbank had contributed to the "perestroika" in the Soviet Union that had started only in the middle of the 1980s.

I had heard about Professor Fairbank's popularity amongst the foreign and Chinese communities in Chongqing, China's wartime capital, when I arrived there at the end of 1943 as a young Second Secretary of the USSR Embassy. But at that time Professor Fairbank had already left his post as USIS Bureau Director in Chongqing and returned home.

The first time I met him was in early spring of 1946 in Beiping when he and his wife Wilma visited their young American colleagues and former students Mary and Arthur Wright. I was then deeply impressed by his personality, his profound knowledge of Chinese history and present-day politics, his openness and frank expression of his views, his humor and wit, the spirit of camaraderie in his relations with his younger colleagues. Later we met each other on several occasions at conferences on Chinese and Oriental studies. Once, when I was in the States, I visited the Fairbanks at their home at Harvard.

Notwithstanding his criticism in *Chinabound* of Soviet policy towards China, the state of Chinese studies in Russia, and my personal performance of my administrative functions at the Oriental Congress of 1960, we always remained on friendly terms and to the very end continued to exchange our publications and books. On two occasions he invited me to lecture at Harvard but my bureaucratic functions prevented me from accepting.

In his books and articles the dean of American Sinology expressed many profound and far-reaching ideas about Chinese history, China's place in the world, the process of modernization during the nineteenth century, American policy towards China and Chinese-American relations, the destiny of mankind.

He openly denounced the then 35-year-long Soviet-American rivalry and called the arms race between the USA and USSR "probably the most wasteful enterprise in all history." Professor Fairbank stressed the importance of profound study of the history of Chinese-Russian relations dating over three centuries and recommended that Russian be added to the list of working languages of a student of Chinese history.

I highly appreciate Professor Fairbank's humanistic approach to Chinese and world history and share his views on the necessity of active scholarly cooperation between American and Russian Sinologists, especially between representatives of the younger generation of scholars, free from the impact of the "Cold War syndrome" that had so strongly influenced many of us during the period from the 1950s through the 1970s.

In my lectures I frequently quote the following words of Professor Fairbank about the future of relations between American and Russian specialists on Chinese history and culture: ". . . in our history in Asia we have more in common than we realize . . . . Since we share a uniquely overwhelming concern—survival—we must keep on dealing with each other as best we can."

In Russia we will always remember this outstanding authority on Chinese history and American-Chinese relations, a man of great scholarly achievements who represented the best democratic and humanistic traditions of American scholarship.

MIN TU-KI
*Seoul National University*

One day in October 1965, I received a letter from the late Professor Mary Wright in which she stated that she had learned from Professor Fairbank that I was interested in late Qing local self-government. She kindly introduced me to some American and Taiwanese scholars who were also interested in this topic. Professor Wright also put me in touch with the Chinese Materials Center, headed by Dr. Robert Irick, as a source of materials that I might need. Through contacts with the Chinese Materials Center, China historians in Korea, including myself, who had been almost completely cut off from international channels of scholarly information, were able to gain access to source materials published or reprinted in Taiwan. I wrote two successive pieces in 1972 and in 1973 thanks to the materials I had obtained from Taiwan. Those two pieces were finally translated into English to be included in my book put out in 1989 by the Harvard Council on East Asian Studies.

Some time later, the editors of *Ch'ing-shih wen-t'i* forwarded the latest issues to me without mentioning how they had obtained my address. From that time on, *Ch'ing-shih wen-t'i* became another vehicle for scholarly communication between Korean scholars and American and Taiwanese colleagues. When I visited Professor Fairbank's house near Harvard Square, the first time in 1979 with my friend Phil Kuhn, Professor Fairbank made no mention of the *Ch'ing-shih wen-t'i* mailing list. I still believe, however, that he was the person who gave the editors my address. Professors Fairbank and Mary Wright probably would not be able to imagine the degree to which their kindnesses were rewarded by the development of historical studies of China in Korea.

In late 1966, USIS in Seoul asked Professor Chun Hae-jong and me to translate *East Asia: The Modern Transformation* into Korean.

We accepted the offer and the Korean version of this text came out in April 1969. It was welcomed not only by students of East Asian history, but also by general readers because no readable general history of East Asia had yet been written in Korean at that time. *The Modern Transformation* was regarded for some time after as a "standard" source of historical knowledge on China. Together with *East Asia: The Great Tradition*, which had been translated by others and published a year earlier, it acquainted Korean readers, possibly for the first time, with an interpretative approach to history, in contrast to the histories of China in Chinese or in Japanese they had previously encountered, which involved the simple juxtaposition of facts. Recently, Korean scholars, newly armed with a diversity of approaches to the history of China and with abundant source materials, have started writing a general history of China in Korean with the "ambition" to replace *The Great Tradition* and *The Modern Transformation*. Such is the influence that the Fairbank volumes have exerted.

Tatsuo Arima*
*Prime Minister's Office*
*Tokyo, Japan*

Professor Maruyama Masao, a close friend of Professor Fairbank, helped me to select the following passage. It is taken from *Dojikyo* (The lesson for children), a textbook on morals widely used from the late Kamakura to the early Meiji period. The oldest text dates back to 1377. It is presumed to be the work of Buddhist priests. A free translation goes like this:

> We respect and remember anyone who can be our teacher, even only for a day; how much more do we respect and remember the teacher of our lifetime. Friendship is a bond of a lifetime. Our ties with our

* This memoir, in slightly different form, was originally delivered at the memorial service for Fairbank, held at Harvard University on October 21, 1991.

> teacher are woven into our karma, into our life before, now, and after. Keep a respectful distance from your teacher as you should not step on his shadow.

Early this morning [October 21, 1991] I went for a stroll through the Yard for the first time in almost 30 years. As I passed Boylston Hall, which used to house the Harvard-Yenching Institute, and went by the back of Widener Library, where Professor Fairbank had his study-like office, I could clearly recall the time when such professors as Ichiko Chuzo and the late Banno Masataka were here as visiting scholars. This was an important time for Japanese scholarship on modern China.

Almost singlehandedly, Professor Fairbank took the initiative—for example, by publishing with Professor Banno an annotated bibliography of Japanese studies of modern China—to open up an intense interchange between American and Japanese historians, enabling them to gain in mutual respect and appreciation. Perhaps unwittingly, he also helped Japanese scholars regain the confidence they had lost after the war by giving due recognition to their work in the United States. At the same time Professors Banno, Ichiko, Eto Shinkichi and others began to introduce the writings of Fairbank, Benjamin Schwartz and the Wrights to Japan. Many scholars on both sides of the Pacific have since benefited from this cross-fertilization started by Professor Fairbank.

As a Harvard undergraduate and graduate student I was flattered to be allowed to assist Professor Fairbank in this cross-fertilization process, though in a small way and only in response to his request. I supplied him with summaries and partial translations of Japanese monographs and articles and went over the texts together with him to help him with his spoken Japanese. We became close friends and he sometimes would step around the corner to watch me wrestle.

Last July when I was passing through Boston, I heard that the Fairbanks were due home from New Hampshire. I waited on their Winthrop Street doorstep for nearly an hour. As the dusk deepened, I had to return to my hotel to host a dinner. Just as I stepped into my room, the phone rang. It was first Wilma, then John Fairbank. "Hi Tatsuo, how are you?" he said, and I replied, "I'm fine, John." With a sense of discomfort, I realized that I had addressed him by his first name for the first time. I felt as if I had almost stepped on his shadow. At once I reverted to my former ways and said, "Sensei, ogenki de rasshaimasuka?" (Teacher, how are you?)

If I had known he was to pass away so soon, I certainly would have waited on the doorstep much longer. Today as I mourn the passing of the teacher of my lifetime, a consoling thought is that, if the old passage I cited is to be believed, my ties with Professor Fairbank may go beyond the present.

Shinkichi Eto
*Asia University, Tokyo*

An old dark blue book is on my desk: the Fairbank-Banno bibliography presented to me by the authors. Looking through the book page by page, many pleasant memories of John come to mind. Among them, I will write of two anecdotes.

It was early in the summer of 1951 when I first met John in Professor Toshio Ueda's office at the Institute of Oriental Culture, University of Tokyo. I still remember the first impression I had of him. Unlike many Americans, he was quiet and seemed to be a man of few words. Several months later, he began to work in Ueda's office with Banno-sensei on Japanese books on modern China. John commuted to Ueda's office four times a week and Banno-sensei was busy bringing in dozens of books and then returning them to the library. John first wrote annotations, Banno-sensei rewrote and then John edited.

John did not use a typewriter like most Americans; rather he used pencils. What we Japanese envied was his lunch: a generous portion of roast beef, lettuce, smoked ham, with plenty of butter on pieces of bread. It was an embodiment of the affluent United States. John shared the sandwiches he brought with Banno-sensei, and we envied Banno-sensei, too. One day I had an urgent errand during lunch hour and I hurried to see Banno-sensei. He and John were just biting into their sandwiches. The Japanese were starving then, as it was six years after Japan's surrender, and I was really hungry.

John's words, "Shin, why don't you join us—I have some more sandwiches," sounded like a voice from paradise. I still remember that the sandwich tasted too good for this world.

John worked very efficiently for half a year at the Institute of Oriental Culture and left for the U. S. after he had finished the first draft of the annotated bibliography of *Japanese Studies of Modern China* that was later published in 1955. It was and still is an indispensable bibliographical guide to Japanese studies of modern China.

Before John's stay in Tokyo, Professor Marius B. Jansen worked with us at the Institute for Oriental Culture in 1951 for a short period. Japan was still occupied by the allied military forces. Rumors went around. "Who is this *gaijin* (foreigner)?" "Could be a SCAP (Supreme Commander of the Allied Powers) spy." "He is *hen-na-gaijin* (strange foreigner), speaks fluent Japanese and understands our conversations." "Be careful. Better not chat beside him." "His smile is too charming for him to be a serious scholar." However, Marius was so friendly that suspicions faded quickly. Similarly, when John came to the University of Tokyo, rumors surfaced again. "Jansen-san was a good guy, but this *Feabankusu* could be a bad guy." (Some people continued to attach an "s" after John's family name because Douglas Fairbanks, a prewar Hollywood movie star, was well known among the older generation in Japan.) There were a few in the Institute who were suspicious of John. Banno-sensei tried hard to ease their suspicions. "Professor Fairbank is a liberal," he explained. "He is suspected by the McCarthy Committee. That means he is not a reactionary American. It is not possible that a liberal like Professor Fairbank could be a spy for the SCAP." Of course, John's serious and scrutinizing work impressed the Japanese scholars there and they soon began to respect him.

Sixteen years after his work at the University of Tokyo, John celebrated his sixtieth birthday in Cambridge. Professor Kenichiro Hirano was his student then and participated in the party there. Hirano sent me a long letter with detailed descriptions of the party and one of John's poems was enclosed. Hirano wrote that after toasts were given by professors, researchers, students, staff and friends, a picture of John's face set in a large photograph of a standing Mao

Zedong was hung on the wall. John stood up and began to read his poem, a mixture of English, French, German, Chinese and Japanese. The poem started as follows:

> Im neunzehnhundert und sieben Jahre
> There appeared like another Avalokitesvara
> Ein Shina-tsu on this famous date
> In Minami Dakota, the Sunshine State.

And ended with:

> They pick up the spoor of History.
> The droppings it leaves, as a mystery,
> Examining each with consummate care
> And then pronouncing what used to be there.
> The files, when examined, will demonstrate
> That this "Fairbank" so-called was a syndicate
> Who were busy writing memos and in other ways
> During Benjamin Schwartz's earlier phase.

I immediately collected dictionaries of English and French and laughed, grinned and smiled while I was reading his poem. I tried to translate it into Japanese but did not succeed in doing so. John's humorous implications disappeared in Japanese translation.

Much time has gone by, but many good memories of John still remain in my heart.

CHANG P'ENG-YUAN
*Institute of Modern History, Academia Sinica*

Thinking of John King Fairbank brings back memories of the farewell party at the end of Mary Wright's 1911 Revolution conference in New Hampshire in 1965. That evening John came to me and said: "You're to have another year in the States, it will be good to have you with us at Harvard for a semester." "That I must do," I happily replied. It was an invitation too good to be missed. That was to be the second part of my visit to America under the support of the Ford Foundation; I had spent the first half at Columbia.

The morning I arrived at Harvard and paid my courtesy visit to John, he was buried in work as usual. In the middle of everything, he managed to raise his head and noted my presence. "P'eng-yuan, it's good you're here. Your office is ready for you. The secretary will show you the way. Let's have lunch together at our Center's cafeteria later." That was all he said before he lowered his head and went on with his work. That noon, we each bought our lunch for ninety-nine cents, and sat down face to face with our roast beef platter (made by Mrs. Black). When he finished telling me everything I needed to know about my stay at Harvard, I sensed the beginning of a new phase of my American experience. In addition to Widener and the Center's seminars, I also joined John in the "Ch'ing documents" class. I will never forget the day he walked me to the classroom (concerned that I might get lost). I fell behind him passing through the Harvard yard. His legs were so long I could not keep up. That year, John was fifty-nine and I a mere "young fellow" some twenty years his junior.

When in the fall my time at Harvard was up and I went in to bid him farewell, John had another quiz for me: "Where have you been in your two years in America?" "Well, three big cities, New York, Boston, and D. C.," I told him. The next day, his secretary told me that John wanted me to draw up a tour plan of all the major academic centers away from the east coast. He wanted me to see the States before I returned to Taiwan. That thoughtful idea led me to six famous campuses (Ann Arbor, Chicago, Washington University in St. Louis, Berkeley, Stanford, and the University of Washington) with his recommendations in an envelope and financed by Harvard and Columbia. Needless to say, it was a trip that greatly broadened my view of the United States and deepened my understanding of Chinese studies in America.

John Fairbank's last visit to Taipei was in September of 1977, a time when rumors of the severing of relations between the United States and the Republic of China were already circulating. John favored extending formal recognition to the Chinese Communist regime in Peking. The authorities in Taipei were quite concerned that his views would aggravate the already tense relations with Washington. He thus appeared as an unwelcome guest, though it was not acknowledged publicly. There was no official reception and many old friends avoided contact with him. On September 16,

William Speidel (then director of the Stanford Language Center in Taipei) invited people to meet with him. Only three Chinese scholars showed up, Ma Han-pao, Chen Chieh-hsien, and myself. On September 19, I asked the Harvard visiting scholars in Taiwan to host a dinner for John; again only three appeared (including myself). At the party, we consciously or unconsciously steered the conversation away from politics. Knowing that I then was heading the graduate institute of history at the National Normal University, he pointed out four principles: develop faculty-student and student-student relations, promote training in the social sciences, facilitate the publication of student writing, and maintain good contacts with the outside.

The sound of John's voice brought back memories of our luncheon together in Cambridge and of the many walks I had taken with him both at Harvard and in Nankang. I remembered the time when we took him on a hike up the small hill behind Academia Sinica. He always moved fast, too fast for most of us to keep up. But I still count myself a fortunate person to have had the privilege to follow the steps of his long legs in front.

CHANG YU-FA
*Institute of Modern History, Academia Sinica*

In July 1970, I visited Harvard and had a chance to talk with John Fairbank, then Director of the East Asian Research Center. At that time, I was planning an academic tour of the United States. Fairbank told me what institutions I should visit. Twelve years later, I visited Harvard again and saw Fairbank at home. This time, he was already retired, but still working hard on a new book. We talked about his *Chinabound*. During the decades of 1950-1980, Fairbank came to the Institute of Modern History, Academia Sinica several times. Since he was quite busy, I had no chance to talk with him alone.

Frankly speaking, I do not feel that I can be taken as Fairbank's friend. I knew Fairbank really more from his writings than from direct personal contacts with him. In the past six years, however, as the Director of the Institute of Modern History, I received several letters from him. In some of the letters, he suggested that the Fairbank Center and the Institute of Modern History should consider coauthoring a mutual history of scholarly exchanges.

In the period from 1950 to 1980, the exchange contact between the Institute of Modern History and the East Asian Research Center, in fact, raised deep suspicions among many people in Taiwan, who expressed their indignation to Fairbank whenever he visited the island. The main reason, I think, was that they considered both his political and his academic points of view as unfriendly to Taiwan, even though, ironically, those same views did not please the Mainland China authorities either. However, I and my colleagues in the Institute of Modern History still regarded Fairbank as a great scholar. Indeed, our confidence in Fairbank grew over the years.

As a historian of modern China, Fairbank contributed a great deal to both the historiography and history of Sino-American relations as well as other fields. We need not share all of his academic views, but his research and his help in promoting academic institutions as well as individuals in their study of modern Chinese history will never be forgotten by historians and social scientists in the field of Sinology the world over.

LÜ SHIH-CH'IANG
*Institute of Modern History, Academia Sinica*

On suddenly learning of the death from illness of Professor John King Fairbank, I was deeply shocked and grieved. He had always been hale and hearty and exercised regularly in an unremitting effort to maintain his strength. Why, before reaching his 85th year, had he suddenly passed away? I am mindful of the fact that he suffered from a longstanding heart condition and that he had been critically ill more than ten years before; thirty years ago Director Hu Shih of the Academia Sinica had a sudden heart attack and fell to the ground never to rise. So, I know it really isn't something to be surprised at. Human life doesn't extend beyond a hundred years, and if during one's allotted span one fulfills one's ideals and aspirations, there should be no cause for regret.

I remember Professor Fairbank as a tall man, dignified in appearance and erect in bearing, who never stopped learning and writing, teaching students and opening the minds of colleagues. The tirelessness of his learning and his unwearying instruction of others stemmed from a natural gift. As a teacher and as a person, not only did he reach the point where he could "dispel confusion, determine the truth, and pass it on," but also, "being so dedicated to his work that he neglected to take his meals, finding such enjoyment in life that he forgot his cares, he paid no notice to advancing age." Although his physical life has come to an end, his sagely wisdom and spiritual example will live on permanently. His disciples, emulating his learning and moral character, will bring illumination throughout the world, and outstanding talents will arise in the future, who will pattern themselves after him, so that his enlightenment will extend far and wide and all will honor and cherish him for a long, long time.

TAO WENZHAO

*Institute of Modern History, Chinese Academy of Social Sciences*

In August 1990 the Tianjin Publishing House asked me to edit *John King Fairbank's Selected Works*. I thought this would be a meaningful contribution and agreed to do it. I gathered all the books I could find written or coauthored, edited or coedited by Professor Fairbank, scanned them, and made a selection of articles and book chapters to be included. I wrote a letter to Professor Fairbank in which I introduced myself and asked for his assistance. As I happened to be in the United States in October 1990, I wrote him from Washington, D. C. on October 22.

Professor Fairbank did not keep me waiting very long. He replied on November 7. He began his long letter by saying, "I am enthusiastic about your project to translate and publish a selection of my writings. I hope we can work out the details to our mutual satisfaction." He expressed his consent to the inclusion of most of the items I had selected in the *Works*, and disapproved of only a few. Instead of simply saying yes or no, he listed the items one by one, reviewed all of them, and explained why he agreed or disagreed. For instance, he voted against including some chapters on the Chinese revolution from *China: Tradition and Transformation* for two reasons: one, it would preempt much of the space, the other, and more important, "as a widely used textbook, much of it would be general knowledge rather than represent me as an individual historian. Selected writings do not. . .generally include textbooks." Needless to say, Professor Fairbank was right. He agreed to include "Assignment for the '70s" because "it was my presidential address to the American Historical Association in 1968. It launched a movement for a national training program in 'American-East Asian Relations' which created a committee and has got results." He also pointed out that the missionary movement having been generally disregarded both in the American and Chinese academic worlds, it would be well to include "The Many Faces of Protestant Missions in China and the United States" and "The Place of Protestant Writings in China's Cultural History" under the heading "Promoting the New Field of American-East Asian Relations." Reading his letter, I did not feel the gap between us in age and academic position, but felt that he was exchanging views with me as a friend. Instead of imposing his authority on a younger researcher, he asked for my response, whether positive or negative. He concluded, "Since you initiated the project, you should have a veto power while as author I also have a veto power. I see no problem in our working out a contents agreeable to both of us." With regard to the publishing arrangements Professor Fairbank stated two views: "first I do not seek payments to me but second I do think China should join the international world. So therefore I would favor some nominal royalty to me, even as low as 1 percent, just to establish the principle."

Professor Fairbank's letter was a great source of encouragement to me. I accepted most of his suggestions about the items to be included in the *Works*, and proposed to incorporate several book reviews from *China Watch*, as it seemed to me that many of his book reviews were concise and penetrating. He willingly agreed to this. With reference to the "1 percent royalty," I told him that the publishing house had no objection, that the problem was to devise a means of payment, as remuneration Chinese authors received for their writings was rather low, and, furthermore, the publishing house had no foreign currency.

In his reply of January 11, 1991. Professor Fairbank made a new suggestion concerning the royalty matter. He said, "In place of royalties I wonder if you could ship me 50 copies of the book, in due time." This request was reasonable and practicable, and the Tianjin Publishing House gladly agreed to it. Professor Fairbank enclosed a draft of the Foreword to the *Works* and stressed that it was "for your comments." He asked: "What to add or reduce?"

I was moved by this. Being the author, Professor Fairbank was entitled to write as he liked without soliciting the editor's opinions. Moreover, he was such an authority in the East Asian studies field. But I knew that his request was sincere, not just a show of politeness. So after carefully reading the draft I did make some comments. There were many impressive ideas in it. For instance, he brilliantly elaborated on the point that, although there would always be a cultural gap between peoples, they could still understand each other and cooperate, that "we can survive roughly in proportion as all peoples can cooperate." But I still thought that some points did not seem quite necessary and appropriate. I wrote him bluntly on January 25 and said, "I am not sure how correct my opinions are. You can simply ignore them. But since you asked me to comment, I think I'd better be frank and honest." In spite of his seniority, Professor Fairbank was very open-minded and ready to accept the criticism and advice of younger and junior scholars. He wrote in his letter of February 22, 1991, "I appreciated your January 25 comments on my Foreword and have modified it accordingly."

In translating his selected writings my colleagues and I encountered various kinds of difficulties. In order to avoid mistakes and make the translation more accurate, I turned to Professor Fairbank again for help. I felt sorry to trouble him again and again. But he showed no impatience. In his letter of June 28, 1991, he gave the

Chinese characters for the names of the seven Chinese-American historians I had asked about and supplied satisfactory answers to all my questions, sometimes with detailed explanations. This was of course another valuable help to my work. This was his last letter to me, just two and a half months before his heart attack. It is extremely regrettable that he died before the publication of the *Selected Works* for he especially appreciated this opportunity to reach readers in China.

In Professor Fairbank's "Foreword" to the *Selected Works* he expressed a hope that American and Chinese scholars will study each other's histories as never before to promote mutual understanding. We will do this. And I think it is the best way to commemorate this pioneer of East Asian studies in the United States.

CHEN XIAFEI*

*Institute of Modern History, Chinese Academy of Social Sciences*

Professor John K. Fairbank, the renowned Sinologist, of Harvard University, died in Cambridge on September 14 at the age of 84. The news hit Chinese academic circles hard: the irremediable loss was immediately and deeply felt. It was especially devastating to me because only 40 days before I received a letter from him saying how interested he was in the publication of *The Archives of China's Imperial Maritime Customs*, which I had recently compiled.

My first contact with Professor Fairbank was quite by chance. In 1982, I undertook research into the Chinese Maritime Customs Service, a project funded by the Chinese Society of Maritime Customs and the Chinese Academy of Social Sciences. The work focused largely on the letters and telegraphs that passed between Robert Hart, a Briton who served as Inspector-General of the Chinese Maritime Customs for nearly half a century during the late

* This piece is drawn, with some modifications, from an article originally published in *China Daily* (Beijing), October 16, 1991.

Qing Dynasty (1644-1911), and James D. Campbell, director of the London Office of Maritime Customs.

My task was to rescue those valuable documents, translate them into Chinese, and publish the original scripts for the study of historians abroad. It turned out that before I and my colleagues had begun the project, Professor Fairbank had already published a book . . . which used a lot of letters written by Hart. In the foreword, he expressed some ideas [about China's modernization] which we found hard to accept. So we made clear our point of view in the preface of *The Archives of China's Imperial Maritime Customs*, saying that since the time of H. B. Morse, a former commissioner of Chinese Customs early this century, and author of many books on China, Western scholars had studied the modern history of China from a lopsided perspective, and that the professor's assessment of Robert Hart remained much the same as Morse's. . . .

In July 1990, the Second International Seminar on China's Maritime Customs was held in Xiamen, Fujian Province. We sent the professor an English version of Volume 1 of *The Archives of China's Imperial Maritime Customs*. Soon after we got his first letter, in which he said we "may be correct" that he had used the word "modernization" inappropriately, because the word has a rather broad meaning. His modesty made me uneasy because I had realized by then that it was boorish of us to criticize his ideas. So I wrote to him expressing my admiration for his noble modesty and told him that other volumes would soon be published. I did not expect an 84-year-old scholar would pay further attention to my work, but I got another letter from him early in September, saying he would like to write a review as soon as he got all four volumes. He said: "This work would set an example of hands-across-the-sea bi-lateral co-operation in scholarship."

This was too complimentary to me because all I had done was to sort out and chronicle the dated letters and to publish them for international researchers. But Professor Fairbank's early book contained only the letters written by Robert Hart. He said that without the letters from Campbell, many things Hart had talked about would be unintelligible.

Instead of imposing authority on younger researchers, the professor was very open-minded and fond of academic challenges. He impressed me as a dedicated scholar, always attentive to minute details and tireless in his research.

His departure deprived us of a good opportunity for academic exchanges. But he left us a firm conviction that an objective evaluation of China's modern history can be obtained through the finding of more historical documents and the effort to shake off traditional bias.

LIU ZUNQI
*Beijing, China*

Recently I was grieved to learn the news of Professor John King Fairbank's death and saddened at the loss of another old friend.

Professor Fairbank wrote many books during his lifetime. He always spoke the truth. In his writings he used plain language, so that everyone could understand his meaning. His lifelong goal was, through a continuous flow of simple and factually based writing, to ensure that the bridge linking China and America would remain open. This was the central theme of his study of modern Chinese history.

WANG GUNGWU*
*The University of Hong Kong*

My admiration for John was largely from afar. We corresponded and met from time to time at conferences. He offered encouragement and advice, but mostly encouragement that helped

* This memoir, in slightly different form, was delivered at the memorial service for Fairbank, held at Harvard University on October 21, 1991.

me in my professional career. I never told him so directly, but I think he knew that I had much to thank him for.

We first met during my visit to Harvard some 30 years ago. I recall that meeting clearly. Having read his books and used them as teaching materials, I regretted I had done little research in modern Chinese history and told him so. He kindly set me to thinking afresh about how to understand modern and contemporary China and within minutes had me excited about what he was doing for long-term research. He outlined what was to be his life work and introduced me to the state of Chinese studies in the United States and its future potential. Years later, I realized that what he had shown me was his vision of what should happen. He had then set about to make it happen. Over the next two decades, I saw much of that vision fulfilled. You can imagine how that added to my admiration of him.

We had other things in common, most of all a conviction that friendly relations between China and the United States would be good for the world. Making that possible in the face of antagonism and misunderstanding during the two decades after the Chinese Communist Party's victory in 1949 seemed well-nigh impossible, but John was never discouraged. A few years after our first meeting, he invited me to join him in a forum held during the Orientalists Congress in Ann Arbor in 1967. This forum aroused a great deal of interest, having as its central theme the importance of resuming normal diplomatic relations between the two great countries. There, close up, I saw the strength of commitment and the steel in the man. It was an unforgettable experience for me.

John will be remembered by many people for many things. Let me remember him as the teacher who led several generations of young Americans to study the modern history of China. What a marvellous adventure that has been.

John always said that he had come to China studies almost by accident. As a young historian, he looked at China's attempts to confront and deal with a modern world it could not reconcile itself with, and could not resist asking how it had all begun. Arriving in Peking as he did in the early 1930s, he was in the right place at the right time to join the Chinese scholars who were also asking the same question. No one was to know then that he was also the right person and that Harvard, to which he returned to teach, was also the right place for what he wanted to do. With the Harvard-Yenching Institute and a superb History Department in support, the University was the magnet for the bright young scholars and colleagues with whom John was able to launch the most systematic and sustained training of the professional modern historian of China anywhere in the world.

John set an agenda which began with China's relations with the West but soon reached into the interior of China and across to the northern and western borders. Each new class of his students, Westerners and Chinese alike, pushed farther and deeper into the field with excitement and curiosity. With China and its modern archives divided and other sources dispersed on four continents, the search for accuracy and perspective was a daunting one. John's example and inspiration firmly guided that difficult search.

So successfully was this done that the Chinese themselves were challenged to find new post-imperial, post-Confucian, ways to explain the past century and a half of their own history. Writing history in times of great turbulence opens the historian to controversy. John did not escape that, nor would he have wished to do so. He had important things to say. Even his critics had to grant him that. And from the way he wrote and spoke, they would have had to acknowledge two qualities he had in plenty: his passionate advocacy of good teaching and research and his leadership in the field of modern Chinese history.

This is how I shall remember him: the patriotic American who loved China, who embodied something of both the Harvard tradition of engagement and the Chinese literati tradition of loyal service and fearless advice. Let me end on a personal note as someone who now works in Hong Kong.

John was always China-bound and saw the country largely from its northern capital. But he traced its modern beginnings to the opening of the Treaty Ports, to the trade and diplomacy that had failed to bring peace to the China coast. Hong Kong therefore appeared early in his sights from the island's cession to Britain in 1842. He would have been interested to see what will happen to Hong Kong after it reverts to China in 1997. John was an orderly and methodical historian and the return of Hong Kong to China would neatly symbolize the end of that period of Western influence that he himself worked on. But he would have gone further. He would have seen the return of Hong Kong to China not as a concluding chapter. I expect he would have seen it as a new start whose history his successors would take up in the spirit he had begun sixty years ago.

*Writer, Editor, Collaborator*

Richard J. Smith
*Rice University*

There are many ways to remember Professor Fairbank and none to forget him. I recall, for example, the acknowledgments of his guidance that grace the pages of so many seminal works on Chinese history (Harold Kahn's *Monarchy in the Emperor's Eyes* springs immediately to mind) and would have loved to put these tributes together into some sort of order; but to do it right would have required entirely too much space. So I content myself here with a few personal reminiscences.

The first of these dates from the early 1970s, when John came to Houston for a public lecture (and, predictably, a private visit with local Harvard alums). As his host at Rice, and new to the history profession myself, I eagerly invited him to the Smith apartment for a chat on the afternoon of his arrival. We talked shop for about an hour, after which he decided to take what I came to discover was his "ritual nap." Realizing that I had not yet made the bed upstairs—and knowing that my wife, Lisa, would be mortified to discover that the great Fairbank had dropped by and I had not done my daily chores—I asked him to sit down for a moment while I rushed off to tidy things up. When I returned he was elbow-deep in soap suds, doing the dishes. "We China types have to stick together," he explained.

Thereafter, John and I corresponded occasionally. He took a certain interest in my research on China's military modernization in the nineteenth century, and in fact kindly wrote a foreword to my first book, on the Ever-Victorious Army—although it was, I am sure, simply a personal and professional courtesy to my teacher, Kwang-Ching Liu, one of John's many gifted students.

I did not get to know Fairbank well until he, Katherine Bruner, and I began editing the journals of Robert Hart. In a relatively short time we became good friends—no mean feat in a long-term, long-distance collaborative venture. Our teamwork periodically involved John's visits to Houston, mine to Cambridge, and a couple of especially memorable trips to John and Wilma's summer home in New Hampshire. But mostly there was correspondence—reams of it.

Going through the huge pile of my letters from John, spanning well over a decade and culled from several different files, I am struck by a number of things. One is the sheer volume of his output—at least two hundred separate communications—from lengthy disquisitions on Chinese history and historiography to pithy nuggets of useful advice on writing and research. His wonderful, dry sense of humor appears everywhere. "I am taking this [pile of Hart's journal entries] to Guatemala for three weeks," he wrote in early 1987, "and hope to seem wise and helpful by the time I return."

John neither minced nor wasted words. When I seemed to be dragging my feet in the early stages of work on our second volume, he goaded me with a brief note beginning: "I was about to write and ask you in that friendly but actually coercive manner used by us professors, how your research [on Hart] is going." His ruminations on Hart's shift in emphasis in his journal from religious self-examination to customs affairs produced the following four-word paragraph: "What happens to God?" And after I had enthusiastically but indiscriminately deluged John and Katherine with written materials of great bulk but uncertain significance, he wrote a long memo, ostensibly to the two of us, which ended with the observation that: "Rich should think more and work less."

Despite his well-deserved reputation for self-confidence, John could also be self-effacing. In the early stages of putting together our second Hart volume, to which he of course contributed mightily, he asked me to "try to think of something useful that I can do to deserve if possible to be a co-author," adding parenthetically: "I don't believe in being a stuffed shirt, beyond a certain point." In fact, John readily acknowledged, both in his letters and in conversation, the virtues and contributions of others—including, naturally enough, Katherine, whom he often described as "the remarkable Kay." (She has never liked the nickname Kay, but she never told him.) After our first volume appeared in print, John wrote: "Florence [Trefethen] and Kay between them, with various kinds of assistance including you and me, have produced a book which is not only elegant in form but fascinating in content, easy to read and sure to find readers."

Above all, John appreciated Wilma—for her love, her tangible scholarly assistance and her unwavering moral support. He was not sentimental, however. I recall suggesting once that he, Katherine and I might dedicate our second volume to our respective families; but John brushed the suggestion aside, remarking that such a dedication was not only "too general," but also "quite unnecessary"—by which he meant, I think, that the people closest to us didn't need this sort of acknowledgment, that our affection and appreciation for them was obvious enough, and need not be a matter of public record.

Of all John's letters, the one that means the most to me was not, in fact, addressed to me. It was, instead, written to my son, Tyler, who in the fall of 1984, at the age of nine, was hospitalized for about a month with what the doctors finally diagnosed as osteomyelitis. When John first heard about Ty's painful and debilitating affliction (at the time they thought it was juvenile rheumatoid arthritis, and that he would probably be severely impaired for life), he wrote to me on October 17, 1984: "I am very much distressed at the news about Ty, and I can imagine how it has preempted the care and attention of you and Lisa. Of course anything you can do in drafting a chapter for the next Hart volume will be greatly appreciated [I had volunteered to make the effort], but we can hardly expect it to be a high priority. I enclose a letter to Ty."

The letter reads: "Dear Ty: I am very sorry to hear you have been laid up and I can imagine you find it takes a lot of adjustment. Nevertheless I think I know you well enough from our few meetings to know that you are quite thoughtful and will already have developed your own perspective on the situation. You will see that all our lives are precarious and yet in spite of all kinds of troubles many people are able to go right ahead as you are doing. In fact a few years from now you may find that you have gained a capacity to manage your life and daily activities so that you are well prepared for anything that may happen. Some of the people who have accomplished the most have done so in part because they quite early had to overcome unusual difficulties and learn how to manage themselves and get results in spite of everything."

Fairbank goes on to say, giving much-needed support to Lisa and me, as well as to Tyler: "Another thing I have noted is that you have particularly loving parents and therefore have a remarkable sense of self-confidence and are not fearful and this will enable you to overcome all sorts of obstacles as time goes on whenever you meet them. I hope we can get together next time I come your way. With best regards, John."

In this effort to relieve suffering, as in so many other important ways, Fairbank, who clearly identified with Hart in his professional life, exemplified the best of Mencius in his personal life. I miss John's humanity as well as his mind.

KATHERINE FROST BRUNER
*Lexington, Massachusetts*

I first came to John Fairbank's professional notice in the 1960s through my stock in trade, the making of indexes. With his typical efficiency and economy of time, he pursued the entire undertaking of our first such contact by brief written instructions handed to me by Libby Matheson (then Editor at the East Asian Research Center) along with the page proofs—I think they were for *The Chinese World Order*. He would like, he wrote, to see the index cards before they were typed up as a finished index, he preferred a rather full coverage; these were my instructions. In due time I submitted (again through Libby) a shoe box stuffed with 3 x 5 cards—a fairly normal index. Promptly they were returned with a courteous and appreciative note: this was an excellent beginning. Would I please continue along the same lines and approximately double the number of entries?

Shortly thereafter, L. K. Little, the last foreign Inspector General of the Chinese Maritime Customs Service, from his retirement in New Hampshire brought to John's notice his copies of the twenty typed volumes of Hart's letters to his London agent, James Duncan

Campbell, containing the record of the development of that vital aspect of China's foreign relations through the latter half of the nineteenth century. Thus began "the Hart industry." Recognizing immediately the significance of such voluminous and intimate data, John began preparations for the publication of what seven years later became the two volumes of *The I. G. in Peking*. But who could deal with such a mass of detail without some kind of working index?

Since at just that time I was deciding to change jobs, I mentioned the fact to Libby Matheson. "Look what's come on the market," she told John. "Hire her," he said. And thus began my share in "the Hart industry" and my insights into John Fairbank as a scholar, a rigorous researcher, an appreciative critic, and a friend.

To publish the letters in a way to make them intelligible to present-day readers would obviously require copious notes. The original plan was to farm out sections to appropriate scholars. When such a procedure began to look cumbersome, John recognized that many, perhaps most, of the needed notes could be dealt with adequately by anyone who could read—that is, who could locate appropriate sources of information and summarize what was relevant. Libby Matheson and I were assigned this part of the task. We began on the English aspects of the letters, referring back to John those matters which needed a background of Chinese history and politics. Libby, alas, died before the task was half done and I carried on alone. It was fascinating work. I not only haunted the depths of Widener Library, but corresponded with retired Customs commissioners in England and the few members of the Hart family whom I could still locate.

In the fall of 1971 when I was to visit my daughter in London, John arranged for me to include a stopover of several days in Belfast, to have a look at the Hart journals, which had just been deposited in the library of the Queen's University, Hart's alma mater, by his great-grandson. These were a fascinating few days. The turmoil that was to engulf Belfast had not yet reached the neighborhood of the university, though the streets were ominously deserted when I tried to go for a stroll in the evening. But on the eighth floor of the library, the tall modern building looming over the traditional Victorian structures, were the treasures, behind locked open-work steel doors, and among them the journals, and trunks that had never been opened since Hart left China in 1908, full of photographs of his life there. I had difficulty reading Hart's cramped writing but made out enough to take copious notes and to forget the cold autumnal temperature, which the hospitable staff tried to mitigate by bringing me frequent cups of tea.

In the evenings I wrote John voluminous letters from my boarding house. He shared my excitement, knowing much better than I the background of the events about which Hart was writing and the significance of his reporting. He made me feel a partner in what was to me an adventure, though one in which one must perpetually have an eye for scholarship, for the verifiable fact, for the world of the Tsungli Yamen and all that its members faced on their side of the proceedings. Because John made the project so intriguing, I ended by knowing far more about Hart, his family, Campbell, and their doings than I could possibly put in the notes. So at the end John suggested with his customary generosity that I write a book of family sketches, which he would send to his publisher's editor. Though I did write the book, and the editor wrote an appreciative letter, it was never published. But the fact of its existence was one more indication of John Fairbank's willingness to foster any promising increase in knowledge and the encouragement of fellow workers whenever and wherever he could. I went on to edit with him two other books about Sir Robert Hart, and to know John better as the great scholar he was, and a warm sensitive friend.

A great man, dependable, profound, unsparing in the search for knowledge, a purveyor of fresh insights into old facts, a man to be sorely missed.

Roderick MacFarquhar*
*Harvard University*

I first came under the wing of John Fairbank in the fifties as a student in the East Asia program. He was a constant and dominating presence. In an introductory talk, he told us how he had got drawn into the study of China, and observed that China had a way of taking one over. I remember thinking "Not me." It was not the last time that he was right and I was wrong.

Every Thursday, John and Wilma spread affection and built esprit de corps by hosting our small coterie to brownies, cucumber sandwiches and tea; the only time I ever detected a moment's chill was when I ignorantly polluted some fragrant Chinese brew with milk and sugar, Indian-style.

I departed after my M. A., but John never lost sight of his students, and always had a shrewd concern for their future. In the seventies when I was in politics he suggested I turn a published book into a thesis, and get a Ph. D. degree. Why? "You never know when you might need it," he said. Indeed.

Later still, when I was wrestling with the wrenching decision to leave England to come to Harvard, it was John's letters, full of understanding yet impregnated with a deadly persuasiveness, that helped to make up my mind.

I'd already had a taste of this when he convinced me to work with him on the last two volumes of the *Cambridge History of China*, after I'd vowed to do no more editing. Collaborating with JKF on a major project was too much of a privilege to forgo.

After I moved to Cambridge, I found that it was not just a privilege. It involved work. Sitting in my office with a student, I'd become aware of a tall shadow at the door, patient but persistent. I felt like some miserable grand secretary whom the Qianlong Emperor had decided to inspect. Was I not up-to-schedule on proof-reading? Perhaps I had failed to find some map—John was an aficionado of maps, especially railway maps.

* This memoir was delivered at the memorial service for Fairbank, held at Harvard University on October 21, 1991.

He was a meticulous editor with a piercing eye for detail. There was no task too menial for him to worry about. He dealt with authors with that wonderful combination of playful charm and blow-torch determination that characterized his work style.

Editing the *Cambridge History* spread over a quarter of a century of John's life. He recruited over 50 scholars in four continents; John always saw the study of China as an international enterprise.

As an effort in collective scholarship, the *Cambridge History* was in many ways the symbol of John's intellectual and organizational contribution to China studies. He had encouraged and published large numbers of monographs. This was an attempt to put it all together, to provide a benchmark.

John soon saw that the multi-volume compendia of more leisurely eras could not keep pace with the flood of scholarship in the late twentieth century. Yet he did not abandon the original enterprise; he supplemented it. His book *The Great Chinese Revolution: 1800-1985*, which was dedicated to the contributors of his six volumes of the *Cambridge History*, was an attempt to catch history on the wing, an enterprise which, as he said, only an emeritus professor careless of reputation could risk.

Typically, once his enthusiasm was engaged, he would not stop. His last completed project was even more ambitious, an attempt to sum up several millennia in one volume. *China: A New History*, as it is titled, harnesses a lifetime of reading and thinking, a culmination of his life mission to understand and to educate people about a great civilization.

In winter, John worked in Cambridge, in the research center which he set up 36 years ago and which now bears his name. That name inspires loyal alumni to donate time and money to help expand the center's activities, and we all benefit from the network of scholars it attracts. The most diligent and productive research associate of all was JKF himself. Come sleet or snow, he arrived at the office in his red hunting cap and his logger's shirt.

It was there, on the afternoon of Thursday September 12, that he was taken ill. He'd handed in his final manuscript that morning. He died two days later. It was as if he felt it was the right time and the right place to let go.

John had that sense of occasion. For his last lecture before retiring, he dressed up in his Oxford D. Phil. robes, which he described as "the sort of colorful gewgaw the Hudson's Bay Company might have run up to dazzle the Northwest Indians." His characteristic comment on that last hurrah: "If you have to ride off into the sunset, you might as well look like a sunset."

John's memorials will last, for he was the master builder. The China field has developed into a vast empire of scholars and administrators, of programs and centers, of joint committees and national associations. But ultimately it is an empire of the mind, the kind on which the sun never sets, and John will always be remembered as the first emperor.

YUNG-CHEN CHIANG
*DePauw University*

I had heard comments about Professor Fairbank as a great mentor and loyal supporter of his students ever since I became interested in modern Chinese history in Taiwan. Little did I know that I would be fortunate enough to have the opportunity to work with this Dean of Chinese studies in the United States.

I was Professor Fairbank's bibliographical assistant for his *Cambridge History of China* project from the early 1980s to 1986 when I completed my dissertation and left Cambridge. There were many memorable episodes from those years. I would like to single out two that I believe well illustrate Professor Fairbank as a person with a big heart and genuine concern for the well-being of the people under his charge.

It was Professor Fairbank's style to go over personally everything from the manuscript stage to the final product, including proofreading—which I, as the bibliographical assistant, was never asked to do. One day when we were working on Volume 12, I pointed out to him a tiny mistake in the name of the Association to which one contributing author referred.

"How do you know it is wrong?" he asked plainly.

"I happen to know something about this Association," I answered. To bolster my case, I added that I had a friend who wrote an M. A. thesis on this very Association.

"There could be two different Associations that used all the same but one characters for their names," he responded, unperturbed.

"It would be highly unlikely," I countered. "Same membership and founded around the same time . . . ."

"But she has a Ph. D.!" Slow but crisp was his retort.

I was dumbfounded, but could only remain silent, for I had only recently graduated to the Ph. D. candidate status.

Undaunted—and not without a self-righteous sense of the grave responsibility of a bibliographical assistant!—I headed for the Yenching Library.

A few days later when I went to Professor Fairbank's office, he was already busy at work. I cleared my throat and said: "I have done some research at Yenching, Professor Fairbank, and . . . ." He looked at me, with a gentle and warm smile, and slowly and softly said, "I have corrected it." I could see one of his eyes winking at me through his glasses.

It is perhaps only my imagination. But I had the distinct feeling that he never after this episode looked at me just as a regular bibliographical assistant. And this brings me to my second episode.

One afternoon sometime early in 1985, I ran into Professor Fairbank at the corner of Gund Hall, both on our way to his office. I forgot how the conversation turned to the subject of finance. But I told him that I had decided to concentrate on my thesis, meaning that I would stop being a Teaching Fellow. He became concerned and said, "But you have to eat." I explained to him that, as a foreign graduate student, I was not eligible for most scholarships.

He became silent. We walked without saying anything more to each other into Coolidge Hall, and up to the third-floor suite he shared with Ms. Joan Hill. Then I realized that all the time he had been thinking, for no sooner did he drop his attaché case on the couch than he signaled me to follow him. He was visibly agitated. Outside his office in the hallway, he changed his mind and said that I had better wait in his office.

When he returned, he sat down behind his desk with a pencil in his hand and jotted down something on a piece of paper. Then he announced to me that from then on I would be put on a half-time basis on his *Cambridge History of China* project. Previously I had been paid according to time put in. Now it became regularized. But I soon realized that this decision of Professor Fairbank's meant more than just an increase in my pay. He wanted, also, to enable me to concentrate more on my writing. My work load with the *Cambridge History* project was in fact reduced; Ms. Joan Hill—bless her heart —now took on the responsibility (previously mine) of checking on the dates, page numbers, and publishers that the contributing authors did not provide.

To a casual observer, Professor Fairbank may have appeared distant, cold, or even arrogant. But for those who were privileged to know him, this great academic entrepreneur was a loving teacher with a big heart.

NORIKO KAMACHI
*University of Michigan, Dearborn*

I met Professor Fairbank for the first time in Tokyo in the spring of 1964 when I was waiting for a notice of admission from Harvard Graduate School. By the time he left Japan, I knew that I was going to study at Harvard, but I was still quite oblivious of his authority and the nature of teacher-student relationships at Harvard University. I did not realize how lucky I was, not only to be acquainted with him but also to have had an opportunity to assist him while he was in Tokyo. I helped him in reading Japanese books and preparing lectures for Japanese audiences, and accompanied him to bookstores in Kanda. On some days I spent whole mornings or afternoons with him reading Japanese works in a house he was renting.

At the start of our first appointment, he told me that I was going to be his teacher and therefore I was duty-bound to be strict with him. He read aloud sentence by sentence. When he was stuck, he told me,

"Don't help me, don't help me." After trying hard to figure out how to read the sentence by himself, he would wink at me asking for my help. One day, after long hours of intensive reading, his blue eyes looked very exhausted and helpless. It seemed to me totally out of character for this great professor with the bald head, on top of which some remaining hairs stood against the flooding light of the setting sun. A silly little woman, I could not hold myself back and broke out laughing. We laughed together.

Only after coming to Cambridge did I come to realize that, for graduate students, professors were like gods on lofty Olympus. Nevertheless, from my second year, I had the privilege of assisting Professor Fairbank again. From time to time, I sat with him in his study (Room 745, Widener) reading Japanese books. In the study, I recognized some of the books he had purchased in Kanda. He said, "it is easy to buy books but difficult to find time to read them." At that time, I was amazed to see him buying many books even without checking the prices. Now, I am amazed that he kept finding time to read those books.

One day in February 1967, a year after I was admitted to the Ph. D. program, Professor Fairbank asked me to come over to his house. He took out a copy of *Japanese Studies of Modern China: A Bibliographical Guide to Historical and Social Science Research on the 19th and 20th Centuries* by Fairbank and Banno (later it was republished with the name of Sumiko Yamamoto added). He said that it had been over a decade since the publication of the volume and he wished to catch up with recent Japanese works. He gave me the copy and told me to start making summaries of works, an activity which would also be useful as preparation for my general examination. This is how I got involved in the compilation of the supplement to the Fairbank-Banno-Yamamoto volume (FBY).

To select the titles to be included in the supplementary volume, I went through all issues of the journals included in FBY and all new journals and books published since 1953, the cut-off year of the original bibliography. I wrote descriptions of each work on a cover sheet and my summary and comments on another sheet of yellow writing paper. I stuck the draft sheets in the books and the journals and put them on reserve in my stall at the Harvard-Yenching

Library. Professor Fairbank would then come by to check my drafts against the Japanese works. It was his principle not to include any book or article that he had not personally examined. He edited my drafts with red pen and made numerous corrections especially in my usage of English. I then examined the changes he made and took the drafts to his secretary who typed them up with a carbon copy. In those days xerox copying was not in regular use. On the typed sheets I wrote characters for the Japanese names and titles. Since Professor Fairbank could come to my stall only once in a while, the material kept piling up. Eventually, Mr. Potter, the Superintendent of Circulation, vacated an entire bookcase next to my stall for my use. In those days, when I ran into Professor Fairbank, he would say as the first thing, "I'll catch up with you soon."

In 1969, Professor Fairbank suggested that we include Professor Ichiko as a coauthor, and Ichiko agreed to review the manuscript. With two big names as coauthors, I thought that I would be lucky if my name were to be mentioned somewhere in the preface. I was greatly impressed when Professor Fairbank said that he would put the name of the author who had done the greatest amount of work first. The work continued even after I started to teach in Michigan. I kept coming back to Cambridge at every semester break.

Throughout this project, we developed a sense of camaraderie, attempting to overcome the daunting task. We also developed a kind of attachment to the manuscript which went back and forth between us so many times over so many years. When it was finally published, we had a "libation ceremony" for ritual burial of the manuscript. It took place in the late afternoon of July 17, 1975 in the garden of Florence Trefethen of the Publication Office who had undertaken the awesome task of preparing the manuscript for printing. The ceremony was inspired by Huang Tsun-hsien, a nineteenth-century Chinese poet, who had a stone tablet built for the "tomb" of his manuscript after the publication of his *Miscellaneous Poems on Japan*. Professor Fairbank was excited by the idea and telephoned Florence *very* early in the day, telling her that we should bury the editor's red pencil and glasses together with the manuscript. That afternoon, he came with two suitcases full of academic gowns and hoods of various universities and told all the participants to pick one out to wear. He officiated at the ceremony, chanting invocations in several foreign languages. We all had fun. The original yellow-sheet drafts with Professor Fairbank's writing in red pen were kept in his office until 1977, when he wrote to me asking if I wanted them. Since I could not possibly keep such a large box in my small place, I asked him to send me just some samples. He sent me a few of them with a covering letter saying: "Here are some random samples of the manuscript. I shall throw the rest of it away *in two weeks* if I don't hear from you further. It is a monument." The underlining was added in his handwriting.

E-TU ZEN SUN
*Pennsylvania State University*

Only a few short blocks separate Littauer Center from 1737 Cambridge Street, but the distance between the crowded Regional Studies offices in Littauer in the late 1940s and the present splendid Fairbank Center for East Asian Research represents a great revolution in "Far Eastern" studies in American academe. Starting my apprenticeship with John during the Littauer period (as a kind of gofer but pleased to be given increasingly more interesting chores to perform), I consider myself fortunate to have witnessed the changes that have taken place. As I pursued my own journey along the historian's path, I came to realize with deepening appreciation the many influences I had received from John Fairbank. As historian, academic organizer and entrepreneur, but above all as teacher, colleague and friend to legions of China historians, John lived a life that can indeed be called unparalleled: its effect on intercultural understanding and on the growth of modern scholarship in Chinese history has been unique.

As historian and teacher, John taught by example as well as by instruction. One of the most valuable learning experiences I have had was working as John's research assistant 1949-1950. As a newly minted Radcliffe Ph. D. I was given two assignments: to check the sources and translations for his *Trade and Diplomacy on the China Coast* and to collaborate with John and Ssu-yu Teng in putting together *China's Response to the West.* In our Kirkland House office impressions piled up in my mind that turned into long-term benefits: how to go about revising a dissertation into a book manuscript, the ever-vigilant care with which documentary sources must be treated, the need for meticulously rendering words, phrases and meanings from one language into another and, above all, the lesson that scholarship as a life-long vocation was rigorous and demanding, but delightful. Poring over what Ch'i-ying did with Bonham, and then what he reported to the emperor, and such, also came to exert an unexpected effect on me. Ch'i-ying, for example, did this and said that: what were the factors that guided his actions? These initial peeks into the background of the Ch'ing imperium suddenly lifted me out of a type of *mea culpa* mindset emphasized in a course I had previously taken at Lienta in Kunming: that the history of nineteenth-century China was dominated by the conflict between an aggressive West and a decadent, inept, ignorant, and totally backward China.

The year's work with John taught me that what was needed was to examine the Chinese side more closely, in order to seek out the principles and realities underlying the course of China's historical evolution. Is it, therefore, surprising that many of John's former students have turned to the study of traditional Chinese culture and society? I might add that, in this regard, critics of the "Response" mode of Chinese studies have missed a rather important point: had the "Harvard school" gotten stuck with merely studying modern Chinese history as passive and reactive relations with the West, Fairbank's impact would not have been so profoundly significant in modern scholarship on China.

All his outstanding talents aside, it was John the humanist who wrought the bonds between himself and his friends that endured. When he worked with you, it was never just a job to be gotten over with; he wanted you to become engaged in a project because it was a joy to enter into a new intellectual landscape, be it grand or modest, which would find its place in a larger picture. You had the sense that he was right there with you, and enjoyed viewing what was going on; and don't neglect the details—he was on top of those too. Once

I received back from him a corrected chapter of my draft of *Ch'ing Administrative Terms*, in which a typo had turned "snakes" into "sukes." John had penciled in the margin: "'Sukes' would be even more horrible." It was such spontaneous bestowals that added flavor to a collaboration with John and made his colleagues share in the sense of adventure in academic studies, in which knowledge and humor and good will were all part of the discourse.

Whenever I think of Cambridge, I see John and Wilma and their hospitable household on Winthrop Street, whether it was a Thursday afternoon tea, or a small work session, or an occasion to meet visitors from overseas. John and Wilma knew well many of the Chinese liberal intelligentsia from the 1930s onward, and their sojourn in Chungking clearly was a factor that prompted John to embark on his life-long mission of promoting greater knowledge about China in the U. S. His contact with China over the years had convinced him that an ocean of Chinese history had yet to be explored. In pursuit of that goal he compared (in *Chinabound*) his task to that facing the missionaries in the nineteenth century. The importance he attached to this work, and the dedication with which he pursued it, were an inspiration to many of his students; so many of them have succeeded in establishing East Asian studies, especially China studies, programs in parts of the U. S. where a generation ago people would not have given these subjects a passing thought. As an inspirer toward ever better efforts, John set a fast pace for all of us, and I shall miss crossing Mass. Ave. into Harvard Yard with him—he with just a muffler around his throat against the chill—and hearing him ask, "when is your next book coming out?"

## Olive Holmes
*Damariscotta, Maine*

I worked with and for JKF (as we called him) for thirteen years as an editor, turning out some of the long list of books that he published at the East Asian Research Center, now happily the Fairbank Center.

What I shall remember most about him were his unfailing courtesy and kindness and his positiveness. I do not believe that in all those years, incredible as it may seem, he ever said anything negative to me. He guided me with praise, always a scribbled "Thanx" when any work large or small was done, fulsome praise when a book came through the mill and was published. "Excellent." "You've done a beautiful job on this." "Great!" "Tremendous job on a tough one." He knew, of course, what kind of incentive he was handing me. I redoubled my efforts to turn out what he wanted in order to live up to his comments.

When I made mistakes, and there were plenty of them, he said nothing. The silence was loud and effective. But he paid me the compliment of leaving it up to me to fix whatever it was. He knew that I knew what was wrong and trusted me to have the sense not to repeat it. That, in itself, was a great morale booster. Once, when I really goofed on a manuscript and it was too late to correct it, a situation where I was ready to jump into the Charles, he merely shrugged and said: "You can't win 'em all."

There was always pressure to get the books out, as many as possible in as short a time as possible (often to lend a helping hand to someone up for tenure), but it was invariably a gentle and subtle pressure. He was not always clear about exactly what he wanted (I often had to guess), but he was crystal clear about the overall goal: a lot of well-written, well-edited books about East Asia. He left the details up to the editorial department.

The Grand Historian was also a Grand Editor. I learned a great deal from him: to be meticulous, to scrutinize (one of his favorite words), to leave the things I didn't know (like the Chinese language) up to his scholars, to use whatever knowledge I had of the English language to help those same scholars communicate to the audience he wanted so much to have them reach. He was fond of the editorial department, telling us often that we were the heart of the operations at the Center, and he always backed us up. He gave us his full support whenever author and editor got into a classic adversarial relationship. He taught us respect for the author's words and feelings, but he also told the author to listen to us. He created an atmosphere where good work could be done.

The last time I heard his voice was three or four years ago. I had long since retired and moved to Maine but was still involved in editing as a free-lancer. During my work on the index for his *China Watch*, he phoned me. Even if he had not said "This is John Fairbank" or I had not recognized his voice, I would have known immediately who it was. No unnecessary talk, no chit-chat about irrelevant matters. He opened the conversation in his typical and endearing way with "What page are you on?"

I was right back in the office. The years had dropped away and we were working on a job together again.

FLORENCE TREFETHEN
*Lexington, Massachusetts*

When I was a fledgling editor I used to fantasize about the ideal job—working on prose produced by Bertrand Russell. That would require very little effort. Russell was reputed to write a single near-perfect draft. His editor would, I supposed, coast along on the smooth surface of his precise word choices, cadenced sentences, paragraph structures that appropriately enhanced a superbly logical content. In such a job, one's red pencil would rarely need sharpening.

My real world of work was different; the worn-down red-pencil stubs piled up through the years.

Early in 1974, I joined the East Asian Research Center at Harvard University as an editor. "You'll have to meet JKF," my colleagues told me on my first day. "He more or less runs publications here." I was introduced to an Olympian figure who welcomed me briefly, cordially, then promptly returned to the yellow lined pad on which he was writing in soft pencil—a jagged script, nervous angles, few curves, few truly straight lines, a script with which I was to become so thoroughly familiar that I could recognize it at ten paces.

Many editors worked with John. He typically kept several oranges in the air simultaneously, each for a different publisher, so there was nothing unique in my relationship with him during the 17 years of our collegiality. But he made me feel special by his willingness to answer questions and his absolute and fixed attention to what I needed to know.

And my needs were vast. In the beginning, my information about East Asia was so scant that I wondered whether I could function well enough to be useful. Was the Chin dynasty a typo for the Ch'ing? Was Kwantung the same place as Kwangtung? What was a hoppo, a daimyo, a Taewongun? He would explain carefully and, often thereafter, the "right" reference book would appear on my desk. Bit by bit I learned where to hunt for what I didn't know. One of my life's more amazing growth experiences was this sporadic, subtle, 17-year short course with John King Fairbank. Through his help and the many manuscripts I came to edit (a half dozen for him, most for other authors), facts and ideas about East Asia continuously seeped into my mind by osmosis. I began to feel like an expert (which corroborates Pope's caveat about "a little learning").

John had many professional roles—teacher, mentor, researcher, author, master of written and spoken Chinese. For me he seemed most eminent as the spark that generated hundreds of books. His former students, now all over the map, have among them produced a library of East Asian volumes. Under his aegis the first Harvard East Asian Monograph emerged in 1956. Now, 35 years and 160 titles later, that series is flourishing. I feel privileged to have been intimately involved in the project during the second half of its accumulated history.

John was a prodigious worker. Work was as necessary and natural to him as breathing—and almost as constant. I might wait days for others, even conscientious others, to reply to my queries. From John, I usually had an answer within the hour, always the same day. He was a swift reader, an instant assimilator. Two days before he died, he asked to borrow a set of proof pages from another author's book in progress. I took the packet to his office; we chatted briefly (alas, for the last time). When the office was being cleared after his death, the set of proofs was returned to me. It was full of John's underlinings and a few notations in the margin; he had managed to get through the 363 pages of text. That could have been his final task, but I doubt it. He also delivered the approved edited manuscript for his new history of China to the Harvard University Press during those two days, and there may have been other loops he managed to close.

My big bonus in working with John was the realization of my old fantasy—to deal directly with the prose of a master stylist, a stylist of Bertrand Russell caliber. Everything John wrote was distinctive and distinguished—books, articles, reviews of manuscripts for which he acted as referee, letters. His letter to the Harvard-Yenching Institute requesting that they remove a portrait of the Empress Dowager from the grand staircase at 2 Divinity Avenue stays in my memory as an exquisite piece of hilarious persuasion.

Most editors agree that, the worse the writer, the more wary he/she is of an editor. If an author warns, "Don't ruin my style," one can usually count on there being not one whit of style to ruin. John was from the opposite camp. He typically said, "Change whatever you have to change to make it better." In his graceful, forceful prose there was scarcely anything to change—perhaps a comma to add, the occasional discussion over refining a word choice. At times I suspected that he and I were playing a game when we argued back and forth about a word or a metaphor, the kind of game people addicted to the English language enjoy. John usually won. But he listened. I felt like a contender. I doubt I'll work with a writer of his quality again.

# *Impact on Journalists and Writers*

## Liebe and Tom Winship
*Lincoln, Massachusetts*

John Fairbank was a great scholarly historian, partly because he always updated his history of China. He reached out. He became a follower and admirer of every journalist's adventure into modern China, and made a point of quizzing credible journalists constantly. Consequently, he developed a great coterie of journalistic admirers and collaborators. He taught and counseled at least two generations of journalistic China experts from Teddy White to Fox Butterfield and Richard Bernstein.

## John Hersey
*Vineyard Haven, Massachusetts*

Two occasions, on which I was given lessons, as it seemed to me, in how a great teacher instructs and learns at the same time simply by asking questions:

On the afternoon of May 7, 1946, fresh back in Peiping, as China's capital was then called, from a trip to the Kalgan Communist territory northwest of the city, I dropped in on John Fairbank at the OWI office, hoping he'd help me clear up some questions in my mind before I wrote an article for *The New Yorker* on what I'd seen. He suggested that we take a walk together, and he led me up onto the crest of a section of the city's magnificent wall. There, on uneven footing, stepping around clumps of hardy greenery that had cropped up from between the great stones, pausing once in a while to lean on the outward-facing crenellations, we talked—or, rather, he interrogated me.

Who had arranged for me to go up? How did I travel? Did my having borrowed a U. S. Army Jeep to take the trip make me an object of suspicion? I'd spoken of the jeep's being carried much of the way on a railway flat car—was it easy to get permission to ride that way? Willing help loading the jeep aboard? When I arrived, what sort of persons received me? Party officials? What level? What did they say? Where was I housed? Was I assigned an escort-translator? Did I encounter any Russians? Did they shun me? Could I go wherever I wanted? Did I see any land-redistribution activities? Coercion? Was I able to talk with anyone who was not happy with the way things were going? See any trials of landlords? Cruelty? Hear any harangues? Could I describe the mood of the peasants?

As I answered John's patient questions, he kept looking at me with his characteristically benign, noncommittal squint, like that of a slightly sleepy, very wise, quite contented house cat. He couldn't have helped seeing how hard I worked to answer him clearly; he made no comment at all on what I said, though it did seem to me that he drank in every word I spoke. In any case, immediately after I left him, I realized that my article had suddenly begun to take reasonable shape in my mind: as a dispassionate account of exactly what I had seen and heard, leaving it to the reader to deduce whether the Chinese Communists were much needed "land reformers" or true and ruthless Communists with manifest Russian ties—or both.

The second occasion was at his Winthrop Street house in Cambridge, on July 23, 1979. I was in the early stages of research on a novel that was eventually entitled *The Call*, about an American missionary in China in the first decades of the century. Just as he had in Peiping, John asked me many questions. This time the same thing happened; fragments of the mass of research that I had been struggling with seemed to cluster and shift and arrange themselves in mysterious ways into suggestive patterns. The tendency of his queries brought home to me the differences between missionaries who went to China in the nineteenth century and those who went in the early twentieth; what a great divide the Boxer Rebellion turned out to be; how profoundly the "social Gospel" missionaries affected the course of Chinese history, immediately and in the longer range, with the founding of schools and colleges and hospitals, and with the introduction of ideas about flood control, agronomy, technology, and public health.

I'm not sure that John learned anything, either time, that he hadn't known in a general way beforehand, but he did seem, both times, ravenous for small, telling details. For my part, although he had not "told" me a thing on either occasion, much that had seemed puzzling to me before I talked with him had suddenly begun to come out of the haze into a stronger light.

MARVIN KALB
*Harvard University*

Fidelity and friendship. If there was a single characteristic marking this exceptional man, it was his loyalty to friends, many of whom started out as his students. I had taken his class on China in preparation for a Ph. D. in history, and I admired him from afar, too shy or insecure in those years to offer myself as a conversational companion of a great scholar.

Much to my surprise and pleasure, several years later, in 1960, when I was Moscow correspondent for CBS News, John and Wilma, accompanied by a mutual friend, Mark Mancall, visited us in the Soviet capital. It was John's first visit to Moscow, and he happily shared his impressions of Khrushchev's Russia, and listened intently to our stories about the ebullient Soviet leader, especially his complicated relations with China. In fact, John, always networking on Chinese scholarship, was attending a World Orientalist congress, eager to make contact with both Chinese and Soviet scholars. The Chinese, as I recall, never showed up.

During our many talks in those days, I suddenly became aware of the fact that the distance between us (mostly in my mind) had vanished. We were no longer professor and student, we were friends, scholars, reporters together. And so it was from then to the day he died.

John always had the time to see me. During occasional trips to Cambridge, he was, of course, on my list of people to see. We shared impressions about America, China, Russia, presidents, books, broadcasts. He was always curious about journalism and journalists, family and friends. It wasn't that we saw each other frequently; it was rather that whenever we did see each other, it was as if the last time was yesterday and we were simply picking up the threads of our last conversation.

When I left NBC in 1987 and accepted a professorship at the Kennedy School, John and Wilma were among the first people I called and visited. John seemed so pleased. Yet another one of his students had come home. He provided counsel on the byways of Harvard's bureaucracy, advice on teaching ("listen to your students"), flashes of insight into the faculty ("you'll find many of them are still here") and, in the final analysis, friendship. When I had a problem, I called John. It was that simple.

John Fairbank—every time I pass the yellow house on Winthrop Street, I think of him and wonder why all professors can't be like him. All people, for that matter.

## Richard Bernstein
*New York Times*

In 1979, after a number of years having heard John Fairbank lecture about China, I actually went there with him and saw not only Fairbank react to China but China react to him. The occasion was an official visit by then Vice President Walter Mondale who had invited Fairbank along as a kind of *eminence grise* of the voyage and already on the airplane crossing the Pacific the professor's influence was apparent. About half the press corps and several of the diplomats on the trip had studied with Fairbank at Harvard, either as undergraduates or graduate students. (This aspect of the Sino-American relationship remained conspicuous when American journalists took up residency in Beijing and the correspondents of the *New York Times*, *Time Magazine*, the *Washington Post* and the *Los Angeles Times* were all former Fairbank students.) The other half was brushing up on the country they were about to visit by reading *The United States and China*, which was still then, and perhaps still is today, the best short introduction to China on the market.

A couple of episodes from that trip stand out. One afternoon Mondale gave a speech at Beijing University. The event was much ballyhooed because Sino-American relations, being rather tender and new at the time and much troubled still by the American relationship with Taiwan, ensured that a speech by an American political leader directly to a Chinese audience would be carefully listened to. At one point in the proceedings, Mondale introduced the members of his entourage. He came to Fairbank, and John, who was placed in a rather remote spot on the dais, stood up. The audience heard his Chinese name, Fei Zhengqing, and a ripple of excitement passed through it. The assemblage started to applaud. It applauded long and warmly as Fairbank stood there, a bit surprised, I believe, certainly touched by this unexpected show not just of recognition but of appreciation.

Appreciation of what exactly? How much, after all, could the members of that audience, cut off for so many years from American Sinology, have known about Fairbank, about the McCarthy period, about his creation of scholarly programs, his championship of historical and cultural knowledge? Probably not very much. What the audience seemed to be applauding was a kind of historical past and perhaps the hope of a historical renewal. What moved that university audience was the mere fact of Fairbank's lifelong fascination with them, that after all of those years of isolation, the man most identified with the study of China in America had been able to return, as it were, to his scholarly "home."

If truth must be known, I myself felt just a bit out of synch with Fairbank during other moments of that trip, or, to put things another way, I felt that he was out of touch with the Chinese reality. I believe that I was representative of a point of view that had taken root in the journalistic corps then still based mostly in Hong Kong. It was that many American scholars, including Fairbank, had put something of a gloss on what we felt were the mammoth failures of the Communist regime over the years, failures in both economic development and human rights, failures that it was going to be our duty, once ensconced in Beijing, to reveal to our readerships.

In any case, whether my point of view was closer to the truth or Fairbank's, I found myself sitting on various busses with him as we made our obligatory visits, and we argued about this matter. One day we were rolling through the Shaanxi countryside near Xi'an on our way to a commune visit and I had to admit that it was Fairbank who had more grounds for comparison with the past than I. He had been here before after all and I had not. When he told me that this broad dusty track down which the bus rattled from North Chinese village to North Chinese village represented a great improvement on what had been here before I had no grounds to dispute him. There would have been just a dirt track, no electricity, no motorized traffic at all, Fairbank said. What looked like rural impoverishment to me looked like something close to prosperity to him. This is, he said, a real eye opener, a very heartening sight. The Chinese Communists have effected a tremendous change in the countryside, he said. I didn't want to hear it.

At one point, we passed a power plant, which also impressed Fairbank by its very existence and by its size. He voiced the opinion that, perhaps, it was a nuclear plant. By the time I had verified with an expert along for the ride my belief that there were no nuclear plants in China, John was onto the next observation—maybe it was the improvement in irrigation systems, the regularity and size of the wheat fields.

Fairbank of course was used to a certain degree of dissent from his students. He indulged it with that Olympian calm and large-mindedness for which he was justly famous. Sitting on the bus, even as I argued with him, I remembered how a few years earlier during the protests of the 1960s Fairbank was under pretty relentless assault from some of his graduate students for not being rhapsodic about the Chinese revolution. Now, here I was convinced that he had become too rhapsodic. The debate about China would continue of course. What seems clear and very moving to me now that years have passed is this: Just as he had been before that audience at Beijing University, here too aboard a bouncy bus along a dusty rural road in rural Shaanxi, John K. Fairbank had come home.

# *Participant in Public Debate*

John S. Service
*Oakland, California*

One of the great things about John Fairbank was that he was so much more than just a scholar in an ivory tower. Also, it seemed to me, he was unusual as a historian because history for him reached right up to yesterday. Perhaps it was this that encouraged his immensely broad contacts with people in public life in America and China. It certainly heightened his awareness and concern for the plight of Chinese intellectuals under both the Kuomintang and Communist regimes. And on the American side it meant that he was well acquainted with all the Americans who had been involved in recent China policy and so found their loyalty and integrity attacked in the days of Senators McCarran and McCarthy.

Most American scholars well knew that the huge country of China was not ours for a few American diplomats to lose. But it was not a popular cause to champion and the dangers were real. John Fairbank paid a heavy price (such as denial of a passport, limitation on travel, the ending of invitations to lecture to the National War College and other groups). But he never hesitated or waffled. For those of us who were under fire, his clear testimony, calm example, and steady friendship were an inspiration and great help in difficult times.

William L. Holland
*Amherst, Massachusetts*

In presenting me, in 1982, with a copy of his autobiography, *Chinabound*, John Fairbank wrote on the flyleaf: "For Bill Holland, with warm memories of our parallel and often converging efforts." Cryptic, like many of his remarks, this set me reflecting on how our careers had intersected. Both of us were born in 1907 and both of us had gone to England as graduate students, he to Oxford, I to Cambridge. We both worked in Beijing early in 1932 when he was studying Chinese and I was writing up the Proceedings of the fourth Institute of Pacific Relations (IPR) conference. We each spent brief periods at the North China Language School and both brought our future wives to join us in Beijing.

I believe our paths next crossed when I saw him and Wilma at their house in Beijing about April 1934. By then I had become research director of the IPR and it was in that capacity that I corresponded and talked with John during the next six years. After his return to Harvard he became a trustee of the American Council of the IPR and a contributor to its periodical, *Far Eastern Survey.* Why we never persuaded him to write for *Pacific Affairs* in those years I cannot imagine, but it was not until 1949 and 1963 that he wrote review articles for that journal.

Our careers converged after Pearl Harbor when we found ourselves working in Washington in the Far Eastern Division of the Office of War Information. Early in 1945 I was sent to Chongqing to be director of the China branch of the OWI, and soon after the Japanese surrender John came there as my deputy, and from November of that year as my successor. In mid-October we flew down from Chongqing to Shanghai to collaborate in moving the main operations of the OWI (now called the U. S. Information Service) from the interior to the coast, often against the resistance of the Embassy which remained in Chongqing until about April 1946. I returned to the U. S. late in October and John took over the huge task of expanding the USIS network and programs in eastern, northern and southern China. I was later denied permission to return to the USIS in China. John wrote a strong protest about this to the

State Department but received no reply, perhaps because by that time I had decided to accept an appointment as Secretary-General of the international IPR. (I learned of his protest only in 1988 when it was cited in Paul Evans' book, *John Fairbank and the American Understanding of Modern China.*)

It was during my stay in Chongqing that I came to know Wilma. She had arrrived in May 1945 as Cultural Officer of the Embassy, then under the bizarre reign of the flamboyant ambassador Patrick Hurley. We often compared notes about his antics. For me those months marked the beginning of a warm friendship of 46 years.

My next contact with John and Wilma came in September 1947 at the IPR conference in Stratford, England, where they were members of the U. S. delegation. Then, in 1949, John and I collaborated (with Edwin Reischauer and Harlan Cleveland) in a booklet called *Next Step in Asia*. John edited it and complained that the style was too convoluted.

Nineteen-fifty marked the start of the IPR's time of troubles, with Senator Joseph McCarthy's attacks on Owen Lattimore who had been editor of *Pacific Affairs* (1934-38). They were followed in 1951 by the more devastating investigation of the IPR by the Senate Internal Security Subcommittee under Senator Pat McCarran, in the course of which John was denounced by the ex-communist Louis Budenz. His eloquent and effective defense is well described in his autobiography and in Paul Evans' book. Here it is enough to note that he wrote vigorous letters of support for me and Lattimore and the IPR, and tried to bring about a peaceful settlement of a dispute between me and Richard Walker who had written a hostile article on Lattimore and the IPR in the *New Leader*. One of the after-effects of the McCarthy and McCarran attacks was that John and I were denied renewal of our passports and prevented for a short period from visiting East Asia.

Between 1953 and 1960 I was desperately trying to keep the IPR afloat despite the loss of most of its corporate and foundation support. John and I were often in touch during this period on various research projects. It is characteristic of him that when I once remarked that it was a pity we didn't have fuller accounts in English of how the Chinese themselves in the nineteenth century wrote and felt about foreign pressure and modernization, he promptly organized a project, with the help of Ssu-yu Teng, and eventually produced the valuable study, *China's Response to the West.* In the preface he generously but inaccurately said the book was inspired by me.

As financial support for the IPR dwindled I accepted, in 1960, an invitation to go to the University of British Columbia and start a new department of Asian Studies while also continuing as editor of *Pacific Affairs* under UBC auspices. Though I did not know it at the time, John wrote to the President of UBC urging my appointment although he knew that I had no previous academic experience. Moreover, in my efforts to find staff for the new department (Asian specialists were very scarce in Canada at that time) he helped me to recruit the China scholars Ch'ü T'ung-tsu and Chang Fo-ch'uan who had been working with him at Harvard. But he was most unhappy in later years when my colleagues in the UBC History Department persuaded Alexander Woodside to leave Harvard for UBC, thus depriving John of a key figure in his plans for an expanded program of Vietnamese studies.

When in 1978 I retired from the editorship of *Pacific Affairs*, John contributed an article to a commemorative issue (Vol. 32, No. 4). In his overgenerous tribute to my work I especially relished his remark that I had been "a truly devoted facilitator of international discussion, never grinding an axe himself but getting others on all sides to sharpen their instruments." In June 1984 a small group of IPR "survivors" (former staff members) met in New York to discuss the possibility of a history of the organization. John could not attend but submitted a thoughtful letter on the problems involved in producing such a study. In later talks he encouraged me to compile a review bibliography on source materials about the IPR (published in *Pacific Affairs*, Vol. 58, No. 1) and then urged (more accurately, pestered) me to amplify my memoirs and recollections of the IPR. A set of them was later deposited, along with his own papers, in the Harvard University archives. I sought his advice about a suitable author for an IPR history. We approached Paul Hooper of the Department of American Studies, University of Hawaii, who had previously written an excellent account of the early beginnings of the IPR in Hawaii. With encouragement and useful suggestions from John, Hooper wrote an article, "The IPR and the Origins of Asian and Pacific Studies" (*Pacific Affairs*, Vol. 61, No. 1) in which he cited John's remark that it is necessary "to inform the current and oncoming generation of researchers as to who their great-grandfather was." I think John would have been glad to know that the project is still ongoing and that Hooper has now attracted the support of a group of young Japanese scholars.

I last saw John in 1989 when I walked unannounced into his Widener office and was astonished to find him packing up his collection of IPR documents for transfer to his papers in the Harvard archives. By chance he was holding in his hand the IPR's official reply to the McCarran Committee's report. We talked for a while about those far-off unhappy days and then, true to form, he urged me to expand my earlier recollections of the IPR into a larger oral history. With Paul Hooper as interviewer I was later able to do this.

Though I never saw John again, we talked several times on the telephone. We were never close friends and often for long periods had no contact. I never saw him angry or depressed or afraid. He scolded me at a party in his house for putting too much vermouth in the martinis. He once challenged me to arm wrestle and instantly defeated me. His enigmatic utterances sometimes puzzled or irked me. Yet I often felt a strange affinity for him. Like many others, I found him challenging, quirky, courageous, always a prodigious worker and an inspiring friend. Like the Roman poet, he could say "Non omnis moriar."

ALLEN S. WHITING
*University of Arizona*

Most scholars knew John mainly, if not exclusively, in his role as teacher, mentor, and historian. Initially I knew him in these roles as well. Our first direct contact came in 1956 when I gave a paper at the annual Association for Asian Studies meeting. It drew on my residence and travel in Taiwan, 1953-55, to challenge the public image of "Free China" by focusing on the Taiwanese and their dilemma and proposing changes in U. S. policy. To my astonishment, John introduced himself afterward and invited me up to his room to talk further. His encouragement to persist in my views despite public pressures to the contrary made an important impact on my self-confidence, in addition to demonstrating his lack of self-importance in helping a very junior academic in another discipline.

I came to know John much better during my time in the State Department, 1961-66, in his role as public and private advocate for a change in U. S. China policy. It was not easily undertaken, given the past opprobrium he had suffered from the Institute of Pacific Relations hearings and attacks by academic colleagues as well as Congressmen. Nevertheless he undertook it vigorously, giving generously of his time and energy in various fora, climaxed of course by the famous Fulbright hearings on the Vietnam War in early 1966.

I watched John patiently educating all who would listen—Senators, journalists, and bureaucrats—drawing on wit as well as wisdom to enlarge their understanding of what drove apart and might bring together relations between the United States and China. He was not a political animal. He took a brutal drubbing at the hands of William F. Buckley on "Firing Line" (an engagement I did not have the temerity to accept) without counterattacking. Would that the political trail he blazed could have been as effectively followed earlier by a larger proportion of academia.

I last came to know John as a close friend during his yearly sojourns in Tucson, Arizona. He and Wilma came each February to share the hospitality of a mutual friend. John's never failing interest in what another, far less Sinological, colleague thought enriched many hours. His warmth, his enthusiasm, and his insight will be remembered and treasured.

Ross Terrill
*Boston, Massachusetts*

But for *Trade and Diplomacy on the China Coast* I probably would not be in America, let alone an American. As a student in Melbourne, Australia, I read the book and became fascinated with the clash between Britain and China in the nineteenth century. In 1965 I won two scholarships, one to the London School of Economics and one to Harvard. Because John Fairbank was at Harvard, I accepted the second. To an innocent arrival from the Antipodes, the East Asian Research Center under Fairbank was welcoming, seemingly happy to have one more arrival who wanted to enter the magic cave of China studies. Fairbank was an internationally-minded scholar and his Center, like the Chinese empire, drew in barbarians from time to time and made them part of the enterprise.

It happened that I did most of my Ph. D. work in political philosophy, studying Chinese on the side and listening to Fairbank and others lecture on China whenever I could. Although I was not a China specialist as a graduate student, Fairbank encouraged me and always staunchly supported my plans to ease into the China field. I think back with awe at how much time he gave to apprentices like me.

John Fairbank took a non-moralistic approach to Western power in Asia and during the Vietnam War this bothered me. Soon after my first encounters with him in 1965, I wrote to a Melbourne friend, Bruce Grant, an author who later became Australian ambassador to India, "In these lectures I'm going to, Fairbank says what America is doing in Vietnam etc. is just a phase of the expansion of Europe—and you can't do anything about historical phases." Being still in my 20s, I thought this was rather fatalistic; perhaps it was also rather Chinese.

At the time I felt Fairbank took the Vietnam War too calmly. One day in 1968, after a student-faculty meeting at the Center to discuss the War, I wrote in my diary: "Fairbank puts a lot of stress on cultural malcommunication. Says this is our basic problem with China (implying, I suppose, that the best thing we students should do is to get on with our studies)." Looking back, he was probably correct.

The university has a different function from society at large. Fairbank was trying to hold onto us for the sake of China studies in the midst of the Vietnam War storm. So he was in his way a moralist, in the sense of pursuing an end that he judged the most important, keeping his eye on that end no matter what distractions came up.

At the time of the Vietnam War and China's Cultural Revolution, there was another trait of Fairbank's mind that I found hard to accept. "He seems worried that he might deviate to left or right," I complained in my letter to Grant. "The other day I was talking with him about Vietnam and China. He moved from his desk to pull out from his files a letter from the State Department in the dreadful days when he, even he, was suspect in the McCarthy witch hunt against China Hands, which more or less accuses him of being a Red. Then he took pleasure in telling me how he is attacked on the Mainland [of China]." It was a letter of its time. I did not then understand that Fairbank was teaching me a lesson in taking the long view, and in sticking to a worthy goal despite the change of seasons.

One morning at eight o'clock in the summer of 1972, when he was just back from his first trip through China in decades, John phoned and wondered if I would look over the draft of an article he had done for *Foreign Affairs*. "I want you to check that I have not become too subjective," he said. Actually, objectivity was one of John's virtues. He was detached from small conflicts, took the long view, let the water flow over him when he could, and focused on goals beyond himself. He was a public-spirited man who took China studies as his cause, and he was a happy person, I think, because his own ego was subsumed in that larger cause.

In the early 1970s, both of us had come back from recent China trips wrestling with basic questions of political philosophy. For me the key complaint about Mao's China was the absence of pluralism. John focused on modernization, and wondered if Beijing would permit the freedoms which are essential to modernization.

"Wilma kept asking to see temples and walls," John said to me of his 1972 trip. "I had to keep reminding her that there had been a revolution in China."

"It must have been moving as well as informative," I remarked, "your trip to China after so many years away." John for a moment did not say anything, but nodded his head in the schoolboy's way he sometimes had. "Well, you know," he said at length, "I've been on their side since 1943." I assumed he meant the side of the Chinese Communists. No doubt it was not a purely political remark. Fairbank favored the historic return of a unified China and he felt in 1943 the Communist Party would lead that re-emergent China. The 1990s, as Fairbank knew well, is another era.

Over the years I noticed three traits in Fairbank's approach to China. A pedagogue in every fiber of his being, he believed more knowledge would make for more happiness; understand China better, he thought, and we will get on better with China. Each graduate student he trained filled in a gap, and made the world a little more enlightened, a little safer.

Having spent time in Beijing (then Beiping) in the 1930s and in Chongqing in the 1940s, when Asia was aflame, Fairbank felt cordial American-Chinese relations were vital to peace in Asia. And being a disciplined man who disliked illusions, he admired Chinese culture for its "rational orderly procedures," as he once put it to me. He thought this was the secret of the admirable underlying unity of the Chinese race.

John Fairbank was less stern than his pedagogical image suggested, and I saw a very human side of him in the company of John Carter Vincent and Betty Vincent. It happened that on my arrival from Australia I rented a room in the Vincents' home on Garden Terrace in Cambridge and I soon got to know them well. With John Carter and Betty, Fairbank dropped the guard of being an authority and simply enjoyed himself in the company of equals who shared a passion for China. A short time after John Carter died I was with Fairbank and Betty in the Vincent home and John, on taking his leave, said warmly to Betty, "Well, now, we must all love each other."

At his last lecture at Harvard, John's message was the inseparability of China and the West and the need for history to be studied as world history. Yet what John instilled in me most deeply was the wrongness of assuming the Chinese were just like us. He was criticized for some excesses in this emphasis, but his message was much needed in the 1950s and 1960s by a still-ethnocentric

America. By insisting that the Chinese were different, John effectively counteracted the persistent American tendency to find in China only what one seeks, and his approach was a spur to a curious mind like mine to research the detail of where Americans and Chinese *were* like and unlike each other. How grateful I am for that stimulus!

EDWARD FRIEDMAN
*University of Wisconsin*

John Fairbank meant a lot to me. The older I get, the more I have thought of him and grown in gratitude for his human kindness and extraordinary work, not only in constructing the infrastructure of an entire field of study but for establishing an atmosphere where intellectual merit and scholarly achievement were recognized and rewarded at a time when other institutions were split and weakened by McCarthyite traumas. His goodness was built on iron. John set the standard in integrity and caring.

John Fairbank made a major contribution to a collegial discourse during the Vietnam War era when he involved himself with members of the Committee of Concerned Asian Scholars who organized to stop professional complicity with the useless military intervention and horrendous bloodletting in Indochina. Instead of brushing aside or attacking young, idealistic junior scholars whose arguments were so unfair to John, he engaged the younger generations in an open and generous dialogue. As in the McCarthy era, when John did so much for Owen Lattimore, so in the Vietnam War era, John did so much to preserve a collegial atmosphere free of political vindictiveness. Sadly, not everyone of his senior colleagues elsewhere measured up to his authentic standards of an open marketplace of ideas. John Fairbank was a great liberal, one who actually did defend and protect the right and power of others who disagreed with him vehemently, beyond the bounds of civility. He knew, he cared, he acted.

It is a testament to John's contribution to a free and creative academy that, to the day of his death, rightwing ideologues, in

America and abroad, still saw John as their major adversary. Indeed he was.

And, he was so giving, too. I will never stop appreciating the warm generosity of Wilma and John to my family in their summer home. The memory of my first daughter at the age of one (she is now 21) playing on the knee of John's mother, then 95, makes me feel happy about life's healing continuities.

It is so sad that John Fairbank died so young. He was still contributing so much to all in the profession. He still had so much to give.

# *Later Years*

Paul Evans
*York University, Toronto*

My connection to John Fairbank had some unique features. We met in May 1977, the day after his 70th birthday and in the week he gave his last lecture as a member of the Harvard faculty, when I made the case in his living room for why I wanted to study American scholarship on China by focusing on his life and career. It took more than a decade to finish a biography that developed and expanded in ways not imaginable in that first morning at 41 Winthrop Street.

For me, knowing Fairbank meant a great many conversations, usually the two of us alone, on subjects ranging from Fairbank (we often spoke about him in the third person) to modern China and liquor laws in New Hampshire. Yet I probably knew him best through his written word. My view of him and my book were largely determined by a shelf of his publications and, more importantly, a vast collection of letters, reports, and sporadic diary entries which spanned his life from the age of six.

The living Fairbank had an exceptional memory for events and the characters and personalities of the many people who entered his field and life. But the man in his seventies had little interest in his own emotions, motivations and intentions. The self-conscious, contemplative reflections which emerged so frequently and lucidly in his letters and diaries stopped sometime in the early 1950s. As was evident in *Chinabound*, remembering seemed to be an intellectual exercise in piecing together themes, personalities and events. He strived for edifying generalizations and evocative reconstruction, not self-discovery or even vindication.

Then and later I have wondered about two questions. The first is why he gave me unrestricted and complete access to his papers. The second is whether our personal relationship diminished the value of the biography.

The opening of the papers did not come about through a single decision but was instead a process. It began with some of his professional correspondence and led through the discovery, months apart, of bundles of materials in various locations, all well preserved but much of it not read for many years.

His explicit reasons were that as a Canadian, as a student trained in political science and untouched by Harvard, and as a young man at least two generations removed, I might have something to offer. He was partial to Canadians, affectionately remembering those he knew in Cambridge and elsewhere. Canada, perhaps, was a saner place than America. It at least had the wisdom to produce Frank Scott, give him his first paying job (on the Canadian National Railway) and award him his first honorary doctorate. For twenty-five years, and especially the last ten, he had been the target of various attacks and the recipient of an equal number of hagiographic sobriquets. Not of his circle or the Vietnam War generation, I was nothing if not a fresh face.

There were perhaps other reasons as well. My eagerness to base my study on a documentary foundation must have struck him as reasonable and perhaps ironic. Having founded the first phase of his own career on unearthing Ch'ing and treaty port materials, he clearly believed in documentary research. At one point he contemplated doing a biography on H. B. Morse as his Oxford dissertation. My efforts to put his private papers into chronological order had practical value to him when, after his first heart attack in 1979, he decided to do a volume of memoirs. He was convinced that this would also benefit other researchers who would inevitably use the collection in future. Accessible documentation seemed the best long-term bet that the cause of history, and that of Fairbank, would be properly served. With the exception of a few letters which were removed because they concerned unfortunate events in the lives of others, the collection has been preserved intact.

I have little feel for what Fairbank thought of me or what I wrote. He went over two drafts, but by tacit agreement comments were restricted to matters of factual accuracy. Occasionally he encouraged me to be more critical of his failings. When later he observed that reviews of the book indicated I had indeed been critical, we were both pleased.

One view, the orthodoxy at some universities, argues that biography should be reserved for subjects who are deceased, preferably long so. Just as the passage of time provides an altered perspective on the meaning and proportions of a life, so can personal connections blunt objectivity.

It is impossible for me to tell if I came to see the world through Fairbank's own interpretation of himself and his times. I consciously felt this happening on one or two occasions, particularly concerning his account of the fall of the Nationalist government and, later, his advocacy of expanded US-China relations in the late 1960s. Curiously, however, if I lost balance or independence, the moving force was his written views of the moment rather than those he conveyed in person.

Against this must be balanced what was gained. The papers offered a uniquely detailed portrait of an extraordinary man and an entire professional field. Observing Fairbank, as compared to reading him, meant getting a feel for the man—his exceptional self-assurance and control, his penchant for benign manipulation, his relentless determination, his manner and humor, and his ability to keep friends and foe alike off balance. I regret that I developed very little understanding of the complex and enigmatic nature of his personality and character, but I at least saw them in action.

How these qualities and the living Fairbank affected my book is a puzzle better resolved by its readers than by its author. Their effect, however, on at least two aspects of my professional life are evident. The first is an attitude towards students, seeing them as an opportunity rather than a burden, and treating them with a blend of detachment and intrusive obligation. The second is a conception of academic citizenship and what academic life has to offer. Scholarship and the university should inform public policy, but their value must transcend it. The best academics need not leave the university to serve their community. Here, and probably in other ways as well, he was not just an object of curiosity but an enduring inspiration.

JOAN HILL
*Cambridge, Massachusetts*

In May 1977, just as he was "retiring," I came to work for John Fairbank for two weeks. I stayed for 14 years. It was a period that saw three office moves, his completion of some 17 books, Deng Xiaoping's visit to the U. S., and JKF's (and Mondale's) visit to China (not necessarily in order of importance).

Others can better comment on his place in history and in scholarship. I saw a quieter, less public side of him:

First, there was his caring and concern for people. Whether it was rushing to check out the house of a friend who had had a break-in, taking someone who was "down" to a light movie, lunching with a worried teenager, or phoning a friend who was dying, he was always "there," quietly, inconspicuously, doing what needed to be done.

Then there was his behavior as a boss. He was very appreciative. Notes attached to a manuscript would often include things like "Terrific!" or "Wow!" Partially done mss. would be greeted not with "Where's the rest of it?" but with "Great. We'll have the rest of it tomorrow, right?" Toward the end, with major changes in both our lives, relations became tenser, but the basics remained.

He was not talkative, but over the years we worked out a system. Since I have a broad stubborn streak and strong opinions, our relationship was not always calm. After a stormy session, or during a crisis in manuscript production, oreo cookies would appear on my desk. "I recommend these." When I was feeling guilty or compunctious, a Hershey bar would appear on his desk. "I thought you might like one of these." We each knew that a breach had been healed, an apology offered and accepted.

The joy he experienced with his grandchildren was very special. Seeing him beam at them, be aware of them, pay attention to them, was seeing a whole different side, as was reading the letters he wrote, even to the littlest one. He was attentive, in the best sense of the word.

As a Victorian, much of his caring was shown in very practical ways: "Do you have a warm hat?" "The ski poles are by the door."

(For negotiating snowy Cambridge sidewalks—a bit of esoteric knowledge for which I am profoundly grateful.) A few days before his death, I was telling tales of the eccentric neighbors in my new apartment building. "Do you have a flashlight?" "No." He went to the kitchen and got the family flashlight, a long metal one. "It can also be used like this" (wielding it backhand like a club). He gave it to me. It is on my bookcase now.

This was a gentle, infuriating, wise, caring man. I shall miss him—a lot.

JOSHUA A. FOGEL
*University of California, Santa Barbara*

I hardly knew John Fairbank. I was not an undergraduate at Harvard, nor was I a graduate student there. By the time I arrived as an assistant professor of Chinese history in 1981, JKF had already retired. He was still coming to his office at dawn, but he had ceased to play a role in the bureaucratic or teaching operations of the History Department and the Fairbank Center. In addition, those of us trained at institutions other than Harvard often studied with people who held distinctly different views from JKF; as a result, I for one had not imbibed an especially positive view of the Fairbank School during my years of graduate training at Columbia.

School had not even begun that fall in 1981 when JKF asked, via Paul Cohen, to meet me. Imagine my trepidation—*he* wanted to meet *me*! I did not have the least idea what we would say to each other. He asked me what I was working on, and I told him. He encouraged me strongly to continue working in the area of Japanese views of China. We needed, he said, a better understanding of how others saw into Chinese history, because it might help us understand the myopia of our own views. I remember feeling, for a very brief moment, very special.

Over the next few years, we had probably half a dozen conversations, always geared toward the direction of my present and future research. Although it was not a field of research interest for him, he was always immensely encouraging, and I remember that during low points in my life I often slowed down as I walked by his office en route to the bathroom or wherever in the hope that I might hear him call me in for another pep talk.

I always thought it was extraordinary that JKF would have been that nice to me, especially inasmuch as we had no ordinary academic tie, as teacher-student or colleagues. He was just being kind to a younger scholar in the field. I believe it was in 1987 or early 1988 that I received a phone call in my office from JKF one morning rather early. He was cleaning out his office in Widener Library and was calling to ask if I might help him carry several boxes of books to his car; there were also, he added, some books I might want. I raced over to Widener. And, what do you think he was offering me? A complete set of the *Ajia rekishi jiten* (Dictionary of Asian history) which I had salivated in front of for 18 months in Japan, but could not obtain because it was long out of print and prohibitively expensive in used book stores; an original Couvreur dictionary of classical Chinese; several complete sets of Chinese historical studies in hardback editions published by the Toyo Bunko; a prewar edition of Kenkyusha's *Japanese-English Dictionary*, especially important for someone like myself who works in the prewar period; several basic bibliographic guides; a copy of the *Cihai*; an old Chinese-Russian dictionary; Skachkov's Russian bibliography of works on China; and much more.

I frankly couldn't believe it. It was such a kind gesture, probably worth $800-900 if one could even find such books on sale anywhere. I had never done JKF any particular favors, nor for that matter had I ever done anything for him worthy of remembrance. It still may be the kindest academic gesture I have ever received.

I carried his other boxes of books to his car waiting on Mass. Ave., and I remember thinking as we walked out of his Widener office that our voices were reverberating off the walls and high ceiling. It was both personally joyous and very sad. One era in American Sinology really was coming to a close.

Kwang-Ching Liu
*University of California, Davis*

I shall describe below, as closely as I can, a visit with John Fairbank in April 1987. On April 10-12 of that year, the annual meeting of the Association for Asian Studies was to be held in Boston. As previously arranged by mail, I was to come to 41 Winthrop Street for lunch on April 9.

I arrived promptly at 12. The door opened, and there, towering before me, was John. After chatting with Wilma for a while about families and friends, John and I talked over lunch about a variety of subjects. I remember that he spoke of the Harvard Corporation, wondering whether it was only a corporation or whether it had the attributes of a state—what, after all, was the state in the American context? I was at that juncture still working on a paper to be delivered later in April entitled "Chinese Merchant Guilds." Before coming to Boston, I had scanned the chapter in *The Great Chinese Revolution* on "The Growth of Commerce Before the Treaty Period." I was attracted by John's use of the protean terms structure and substructure. He wrote:

> When we look at China in 1800 the first thing that strikes the eye is a remarkable paradox: the institutional *structure* of the society, especially the government, was showing little capacity for change, but the people and therefore the economy were undergoing rapid and tremendous growth. Until recently this paradox remained largely unnoticed. It may well be called a contradiction between *substructure* and superstructure. [Italics added.]

This masterful analysis has implications for what many of us would regard as a "contradiction" in the PRC in the 1980s. In that decade, as with the China of the early nineteenth century, commercial growth constituted only substructural change. I asked John whence he had derived this theme of substructure versus superstructure. Was it from a social scientist? John said with evident pride, "Well, one is on one's own in such things."

We discussed the theme further. I suggested that some of our colleagues in the historical profession who believed in an "early modern China" erred in mistaking the growth of commerce and urban culture for structural change. Indeed, more rigorous criteria for structural change must be applied to political change as well. John said, as I recall it: "There is indeed the distinction between substructural and structural change. Perhaps we should analyze the Chinese revolution in this way." He jocularly suggested that we should collaborate on a book adopting this approach.

The conversation then turned to the subject of Hong Kong. I said that I had the privilege of knowing a few excellent young scholars from Hong Kong who were promising Sinologists but who knew very little, nor did they greatly care, about such British institutions as common law and the civil service. I ventured the view that both Hong Kong and Taiwan had at different times undergone a structural change that involved the reorganization of the municipal government, resulting in a police force acting professionally and therefore more likely to respect property rights. John smiled and said that in *The Great Chinese Revolution* he had written too briefly about Taiwan and Hong Kong.

After my return to California, I looked over the book and found that John had indeed written little about these subjects. He did point out that by the early Republican period in Hong Kong, as in Shanghai, a new social class had come into being: "A modern Chinese business class was rapidly emerging in the foreign-run parts of the country, beginning in the British crown colony of Hong Kong and the Shanghai International Settlement." A summary of less than two pages was given to the history of Taiwan since the second world war, beginning with an apology for American China policy:

> Only in one small area did the Americans seem to do something right. This was in aiding the development of Taiwan, the island refuge of the defeated Nationalists. Taiwan after 1949 harbored that part of the Chinese Republic's Sino-liberal leadership that chose not to take its chances with the CCP. Although the warlord wing of the Nationalist regime began by slaughtering the Taiwanese Chinese elite in February 1947, the Sino-liberal wing thereafter had its chance.

I wonder whether, in his last book, *China: A New History*, which I haven't read, John takes account of the concept of structural change, discussed in our conversation of 1987? In the perspective of China's long history, from the ancient Shang period to Tiananmen Square in 1989, what place will he give the Shanghai Municipal Council and the institutional history of Hong Kong and of Taiwan? On these and numerous other questions, I look forward to his final insights.

JOHN RAWLINSON
*Hofstra University*

One thing that occurs to me about John King Fairbank is the realization that my acquaintance with this great teacher spans my entire academic career. That 1991 also brought my retirement is of course only coincidental, but to me it brings recollections of contacts starting in Chungking in 1943, running through graduate school, and on through subsequent endeavors to put into practice with my own students his motto, "Pass it on!" One of them, at MIT, after hearing my critical comment in the early 1950s on the alleged "US loss of China," told me that I had persuaded him that the Chinese after all had had something to do with what happened. Pace JKF! And, coming down nearly to today, I was honored by John's agreeing to do the Preface to my biography of my China missionary father. That project was very (too) bulky, but still he read the manuscript while he was "vacationing" in New Hampshire, wryly noting that it took "two men and a boy" to tote it up the hill to him. He made cogent comments, including that I might take a scalpel to it. I had the great pleasure of delivering a copy of said book to him at 41 Winthrop in March of this year, an occasion marked by the easy graciousness of the Fairbanks, and taking place in that living room which I well recall visiting years earlier as a member of John's Regional Studies Program. Like the hundreds of others who know that room, I could go on . . . .

I will go on only long enough to include the dedication I wrote on my title page: "To John King Fairbank, who, from first acquaintance in the purlieus of the Ch'iu-ching Middle School, has been a growing influence on my aspirations. While this prompting has generally been beyond my reach, I am nonetheless—perhaps all the more—indebted. Kan-hsieh [Thank you]." And, remembering his mild admonitions about the length of that two-volume opus, I added, in a stab at pawky humor: "Any excesses perpetrated by me in this attempt to implement said influence are in no way to be imputed to the addressee aforenamed herein." Ever alert, John wondered if I really needed the "a" in "aforenamed." Touché!

PETER RAND
*Harvard University*

John Fairbank and my father, Christopher Rand, were civilians together in wartime Chungking. Later, during the academic year 1948-49, Dad was a Nieman Fellow at Harvard, and for nine months we lived at 21 Kirkland Street in Cambridge, near John and Wilma, whom we saw frequently. In the years that followed, Dad did not see much of John because his professional activities took him away from this country to far-flung parts of the world for long stretches of time, but once you had established a relationship with John and Wilma, the bond was always strong, and I know that Dad held them both in high, affectionate regard.

Some time after Dad's death in 1968, I decided to write about his China years with OWI and the *New York Herald Tribune*. So began my own association with John. I did not visit him often, but over a decade or so he was always cordial and encouraging. Once, at his 41 Winthrop Street home, John made a lunch of deviled ham sandwiches while I asked him all sorts of questions about the wartime years, which he answered while we ate the sandwiches, as I recall, standing up, outside, on the brick patio. He not only encouraged me in my endeavors, he tried to help me professionally by putting me in touch with his publishers and writing to them on my behalf. Then, when my project expanded to include other China hands, he welcomed the enlargement, and in a seamless ten-minute discourse in his Coolidge Hall office fed me the contours of my book. I found him readily accessible when I needed advice, but I also discovered that it helped to have my thoughts and questions articulated before I called him, because the ever forward thrust of his mental processes was like that of the Twentieth-Century Limited at full speed. It could run you down and keep going if you were not on your toes.

I last saw John the Thursday morning before he died. I had not seen him in more than two years, although we had spoken on the phone. In July, however, I had moved to the Boston area and, once settled, was urged, by Muffy Coolidge, to give him a call, which I did, on Wednesday, September 11. To my surprise, when I called his office, he answered the phone himself. "We have pretty hot stuff going on over here," he told me, and explained that he had just that minute finished his latest book, *China: A New History*. He asked me about my book, and I told him that I had finished a first draft. "In fact," I told him, "there is one section you might actually want to read." "I want to read the whole thing," he replied. I sputtered that it was 950 pages long. "Oh we read 950-page manuscripts around here all the time," he said. So we arranged that I would xerox the ms. and get it to him by Friday when he was scheduled to leave for New Hampshire with Wilma.

We had not made an exact appointment, however, and as I sat in Widener Library on Thursday I suddenly thought I ought to go see John, to make sure he would be in his office on Friday morning, when the xerox was due for pickup. I was waiting by the south elevator in the Coolidge Hall lobby when I looked over to see him striding in my direction. He was a pleasure to behold. He looked relaxed and dapper in a hound's tooth jacket, head cocked slightly to one side as he walked. He had just delivered his book to the Harvard University Press. He would not be in his office the next day, he said, and, because the elevator had arrived, and because John was always on the move, I accompanied him to the third floor. On the upward ride we decided that I would bring the ms. to Winthrop Street the next morning before ten o'clock. The door opened, and he stepped from the elevator without a backward glance, and my final impression of John was that of a man facing forward whose mind was already elsewhere.

KARIN LINDT GOLLIN
*Harvard University*

John Fairbank was not a man to waste time. Or mince words. I have been thinking with exasperation and fondness of the man for whom I worked over the final two years of his life. One of the lasting impressions I have is of the extraordinary repercussions which occur when profound confidence is meshed with absolute discipline. John produced essay after essay, book after book—an almost unconscionable prolixity in the cautious, procrastination-ridden world of academe. Quite simply, he believed in himself and in the need for what he did; he was in his 80s when I first met him, and still in his office from breakfast till dinner, with just a brief break for lunch and a nap. He would sit at his desk reading and writing every single day. The routine did not alter, the work did not cease.

That first meeting was a funny thing. I am of a generation who began the study of China when he was already retired. To my college classmates and me, John Fairbank was a name on a rather large textbook we read. We did not know much about him, save perhaps as the gang leader of the notorious "Harvard School" criticized by some visiting professor. Later, when in grad school we delved more deeply into the field, he became recognized by us as one of the famous ones, the old men who founded American Sinology. As good graduate students, my friends and I passionately attacked these men for their biases, their oversights, their hubris and naiveté in attempting to explain an entire civilization (displaying therein not a little of the same ourselves). Then, in my third year of grad school, I actually met the man.

He needed a research assistant for his new history of China, and I needed a job. I'm not quite sure what I expected, but it certainly was not this older gentleman in a red-plaid flannel shirt, who looked like a Maine woodsman lost in the Fairbank Center. A few quick questions later I saw this was no simple woodsman; I was hired, feeling very much out of my depth. That feeling, however, did not last long. Gradually I came to know John as a generous, tough-minded and self-disciplined man who was like a grandfather to me. (My mother's father is as opinionated, as roaringly delighted to get into an argument, and as unreserved in his support of those he cares for.)

Working for him was a mixed blessing, to be sure. My time was not my own when there were things he needed done. There were the phone calls at 8 a.m. (I always knew who it was at that hour). A sample exchange: "Did I wake you?" "Mmph, yes. Went to bed at 3 this morning." "Well, you should get to bed earlier. Now, I've been thinking about X. We need to say something about that. There's a book by P and Q I'd like to see, but I'm afraid it may be out of date by now. Can you find me something more recent?" "I'll see what I can do, boss." Or the calls to bring books and self to New Hampshire—truly a lovely place, but mainly we sat inside and worked. He expected those around him to be as single-minded as he was, and so they became.

Yet I wouldn't have missed the experience for anything, mainly because he was fun to talk and argue with. That is really what hurts most—the knowledge that we won't be joking with each other, munching on the sandwiches he would bring for our lunch, and talking, a conversation that lasted for nearly two years. To be with him was to be with a quick wit and active mind. It didn't matter that we disagreed often (though not as often as I had expected we would); the involvement was what mattered. You never knew where the conversation might lead—from depressing present politics, to speculations on social history, to personal reminiscences about family and life experiences. One evening on the phone a feisty discussion about the economic role of women led him to recall with great clarity a group of bare-chested women pearl-divers in Korea. You just never knew . . . .

I think on what it is to be in this world and leave your mark in it. There are no earth-shattering, world-changing events or people, save perhaps of the disastrous kind. But in passing through we do alter things (and people) in some small but definite way; and John in particular covered a lot of ground in his passage. He has left his mark with me as a model of accomplishment through disciplined work and as a memory of an intellectually challenging and emotionally generous friend and mentor. I loved him. He will be with me always.

PAUL A. COHEN
*Wellesley College*

On the morning of May 20, 1991 John Fairbank phoned me at home. He said he was at the Mount Auburn Hospital, was having a lot of difficulty with his arrhythmia, and that having always been "a prudential fellow" he wanted to make sure there would be someone to oversee the completion and production of his new history of China in the event his health worsened. Since I had already given the manuscript two careful readings and had been supportive, he wondered if I would be willing to take on this role. On at least two occasions in the past I had turned John down. In this instance, with some trepidation, I told him "yes."

In a letter of June 20 to Aida Donald of the Harvard University Press announcing our arrangement, John displayed that rare ability to view himself (including his mortality) with comic detachment that he had earlier demonstrated in a hilarious "circular to friends" following the near-fatal heart attack ("much more interesting," he began, "than the other kind") that he had experienced on Thanksgiving Day, 1979. In the letter to Aida he couldn't resist pointing out some of the promotional advantages of an early Fairbank demise: "With any luck you could get some sales publicity: 'Aged savant exits leaving time bomb.' 'Did Fairbank really say "Confucianism is bunk" or was it slipped into his text by conspirators?'" Clearly, no matter what happened, the book could not lose.

The trepidation I felt over my agreement with John didn't have to do with the work that might be involved. Although I had for many years taken to heart the rule for indebted students he had laid down on the occasion of his sixtieth birthday—"Don't feel you should try to pay it back. Instead, pass it on."—I welcomed the opportunity to express some part of my gratitude to him in this more direct way. What I felt uneasy about was the prospect of having to assume John's voice, so different in style from my own, and drape myself in his interpretive positions, with some of which I was not really in accord. In the event, my worries proved unnecessary. John held on for several more months, during which time, even when hospitalized, he pressed ahead with revisions, the drafting of an epilogue, and the filling in of gaps in the text, in addition to orchestrating the efforts of what seemed (by my standards) a rather large group of individuals involved in one way or another in the book's creation. On the morning of September 12, in an exquisite display of the timing for which John Fairbank was famous, he delivered the completed typescript of *China: A New History* to the Harvard University Press, only hours before suffering the heart attack that two days later would take his life.

During the period of several months between the May phone call and his death in September John and I were in frequent touch concerning the book. Sometimes he would phone because he wanted to talk about what he'd been reading, get my reactions (which, since he was always way ahead of me in his reading schedule, I was usually at a loss to give), and also bounce his off me. At other times I would tell him about something I'd recently read and suggest he have a look at it. When we next talked, he not only had perused the item in question but, if he was persuaded by the author's points, had found a way to shoehorn them into the manuscript.

Sometimes these phone conversations would drift away from the discussion of recent scholarship to less focused talk. For one who at age fifty-seven was much given to thinking about turning sixty as a metaphor for anything other than youth, it was both ironic and amusing to hear John, on one occasion when he was feeling particularly pressed for time, confide that he sometimes had a fantasy about being sixty again!

Several days before John's final heart attack I stopped by his office after lunch to give him my thoughts on the latest version of a chapter in the book that had proved especially troublesome. (As it turned out, he had already drafted a still later version, which effectively addressed the difficulties, and no longer needed my comments. When John was in a hurry, you had to work really fast to keep up.) When I knocked on his door, which was slightly ajar, there was at first no answer. Then I heard John's voice: "Come in." I had, of course, interrupted one of those legendary Fairbankian postprandial naps. But John sat straight up and started talking about the book, as if he'd been lying there thinking (or dreaming?) about it. He said the manuscript was scheduled to go into galleys in a few weeks and he was worried about being unable to incorporate the findings of "the seventeen new books" that were sure to come out between the galley stage and publication. My mind traveled back to all those stories about the stratagems John Fairbank had deployed over the years to pry manuscripts away from sticky-fingered authors, and before I knew it I was Fairbanking Fairbank with a small lecture on how there were always going to be new books, the unreasonableness of expecting to take into account scholarship that hadn't yet appeared, the necessity at a certain point in the life of any manuscript of knowing when to stop, of accepting the finality of being done, and so on. John smiled one of those complex Fairbank smiles. He knew that I was right. But he knew that, in some more fundamental sense, he was right, too, that this was his last book, he probably wouldn't be around to look after it during its passage into the world, and he really wanted to make sure it was safe before finally letting go.

## Holly Fairbank*
*New York, New York*

My mother, my sister Laura and I know John King Fairbank as a devoted, tender and loving husband and father. His ready wit, unflagging support for our endeavors, and consummate belief

* This memoir was delivered at the Fairbank memorial service at Harvard University on October 21, 1991. The poem by Sara Teasdale at the end is reprinted from *The Collected Poems of Sara Teasdale* (New York: The Macmillan Co., 1937), p. 224.

in each of our personalities carried us buoyantly forward together as a family.

Reading the letters that have come in over the last few weeks from students and friends of my father, I have a broader perspective on what kind of a man he was, and how he affected others. So many commented on his "kindness," "patience" and "generosity." Others on his "wisdom," his "humor," his "accessibility," and even how "unusual" he was. As a daughter I particularly responded to these descriptions and especially to remarks about his "persistence and optimistic effort in the face of each goal and every obstacle." In action, more than word, my father exemplified these attributes to his family. I cannot begin to tell you what an extraordinary gift this is to receive. I will miss very much how he literally and figuratively always left the light on for us. One student wrote these words which particularly moved me: "I had the feeling, wherever I was, whatever I was doing, that he was interested and gave his support . . . . He was like the patriarch of a huge family who never lost track of what its members were doing and who let them know that if they ever needed him, he was there."

Poetry and music played an integral part in my father's private life. The following poem by Sara Teasdale was one passed on to him by his mother, Lorena King Fairbank, who lived to be 105. He read this poem, in fact, at her memorial service. She, perhaps more than anyone besides my mother, loved, cherished, and supported him.

*There Will Be Stars*

There will be stars over the place forever;
  Though the house we loved and the street we loved are lost,
Every time the earth circles her orbit
  On the night the autumn equinox is crossed,
Two stars we knew, poised on the peak of midnight
  Will reach their zenith; stillness will be deep;
There will be stars over the place forever,
  There will be stars forever, while we sleep.

# *Author Index*

## S



## T



## V



## W



## Y